Uncovering The Mysteries of Your Hidden Inheritance

by

Robert Alan Balaicius

Sacred Truth Ministries
P.O. Box 18
Mountain City, Tennessee 37683
United States of America

This might be the most important book you will ever read!

To avoid confusion, please start reading at the first page and read on without skipping around. Please follow all footnotes and appendices as they appear.
Truth builds upon truth.

Robert Alan Balaicius
Sacred Truth Ministries
P.O. Box 18
Mountain City, Tennessee 37683

[Uncovering The Mysteries of Your Hidden Inheritance
was formerly titled
Your Inheritance: The Best-Kept Secret In the World,
(by Robert Alan Balaicius, Copyright © 1994)
and has been completely rewritten.]

[The name Balaicius is Lithuanian. Its American pronunciation is băl-ŭh-**KĪ**-ŭhs.]

[Bulk prices available upon request.]

ISBN 1-58840-020-4 Hardback
ISBN 1-58840-021-2 paperback

> **"Everyone has struggled with the question, 'Who am I?' It has been said that, if we could come up with the answer, *everything else would fall in place*."**
> —Dr. Elmer Pendell, Cornell University (Why Civilizations Self-Destruct (1977), Howard Allen Enterprises; p. 1)
>
> **"To Destroy a people, you must first sever their roots."** —Aleksandr Solzhenitsyn

What If You Had A Grand Inheritance?

If you and your family had been left $1,000,000,000 (tax-free) by an unknown relative, would you want to know about it? Further, if you actually descended from *royalty*—if you were the *legitimate heir* to a *factual throne*—would this be of any interest to you? If you were to learn that you *were* the heir to such fortune and prominence, would you continue living as you do now, or would you claim your rightful inheritance and kingdom?

What would be your reaction if a group of people conspired to keep you ignorant of your inheritance so that they could steal it for themselves? What if they hid the original documents that showed *you* to be the heir and replaced them with falsified documents that *did not even mention* you? How would this make you feel? Would you be upset? Would you want to discover the truth, set the record straight for everyone to know, and have what is rightfully yours?

Although this might sound like a crazy episode of some hard-to-believe *soap opera*, the fact is, you might very well have a noble inheritance—one worth far more than $1,000,000,000. Your inheritance might even include royal lineage. Sadly, it is also true that a group of people *has* conspired to keep the knowledge of this inheritance from you. Sadder still, some of your family members *might* even have been *fooled* into joining with these criminals in the attempts to discredit you, your family, and the facts of your family's inheritance.

Bear with me as you read this book. Once you have actually seen the evidence *for yourself*, you will be free to make a knowledgeable decision. You may accept your inheritance, although you will still have the right to reject it. But *please* make your decision based upon the *facts*—not upon the subtle and inconsistent prejudices of modern society, not upon what the state has instructed you to believe is "politically correct," not upon foundationless emotionalism, not upon the modern myths and fables that have replaced the truth. Decide based upon the simple facts! It's *your* inheritance. You have the right to reject it. But only with *informed* consent can you *knowingly* reject it. Without all the facts, however, you cannot fully claim it either.

"So," you might ask, "what is this inheritance, and what powers have conspired to keep it a secret that they might steal it for their own?" Well, before we look into the answer to these questions, allow me to pose another series of questions for you to keep in the back of your mind:

If you and your family had been left an inheritance of $1,000,000,000 by an unknown relative, do you think you might want to do a little family research and learn more about this generous relative of yours? If you were an heir to a monarchy, would you not want to discover the history of your noble ancestors? Would you accept this inheritance and important position that would change your life forever? Finally, since greater responsibility accompanies greater privilege, do you think you would have any desire to live up to the simple, moral expectations set forth in the terms of your inheritance?

(PLEASE, THINK ABOUT THIS BRIEFLY.)

Let's Set The Stage

We will be discussing the Bible and history throughout this book. Since many people have been turned off to the Bible and modern religion, however, let me encourage you to finish reading this book, regardless of what you might feel concerning these subjects. Many people have a bad taste in their mouth for *modern*, *organized* religion—and rightly so. An important part of what has been taught about the Bible within the past 50 years or so has not been true. The mainstream religious establishment, whether it realizes it or not, is part of this conspiracy (Jeremiah 11:9; 50:6; Ezekiel 22:5; Matthew 15:4; Acts 23:13) to hide the truth. In *certain key areas* the establishment has misrepresented God's Word. This is why so many people have been disenchanted with the Bible. God, in the Holy Scriptures, prophesied that many pastors would make the *true* churches of God empty, having alienated the majority of people by their false teaching, either because they are evil or because they are blind and do not know the truth themselves (Isaiah 5:7; 56:10-11; Jeremiah 10:21; 12:10-11; Ezekiel 34; Zechariah 10:1-3). This is one reason that church attendance has dwindled drastically in America. America was founded by *Christians* desiring freedom from persecution—and for many years America was openly, proudly, and by practice a Christian nation.[1] But as America has turned from God and disregarded His Word, crime, evil, sickness, and injustice have skyrocketed, while morality, safety, and prosperity have plummeted, and there is little freedom left. It is the purpose of this book to reestablish *key elements of truth* contained in the Bible and history (which have been carefully kept hidden from you)—truth that many of our ancestors believed before the modern church and state began to dictate what we should believe, turning men's hearts and minds from the truth. This truth has everything to do with a real, physical inheritance on this earth left to you by your actual ancestors. Apart from this truth real, lasting freedom and happiness are impossible.

Actually, most people have not been turned off to the Bible, but they have been turned off to the "bible" that has been incorrectly presented to them. Scripture foretold that some pastors would preach *to the highest bidder*. They would not teach the truth (or at least not the *full* truth), since there is no *money* in the truth. They would teach what is *popular* and that which they *are paid* to teach (Micah 3:10-11; II Timothy 4:3), regardless of whether it is true, and regardless of the harmful consequences. Thus, a clever counterfeit has secretly supplanted the truth.

Would it not be a crime for someone to alter legal documents, changing them

---

[1] For indefatigable, historic proof of this, see America, Christianity, Liberty & Truth: What Famous Men Had To Say by Balaicius/Sacred Truth Ministries.

to record that the *rightful monarch* to a kingdom was merely a *common serf* while maintaining that the most evil person in society was the rightful heir? Well, such a crime *has* been perpetrated against you without your knowledge. This is how the Bible has been misrepresented. This is how secular history has been misrepresented. And thus your true and glorious inheritance and ancestral family history have been hidden from you. This is how you have been wronged and how you have been forced to accept such felonious and immoral treatment. Further, because you and the general public have existed within the myth someone created to keep you in ignorance, your status has been—in your mind, in your daily life, and in the eyes of others—reduced to that of a base and lowly hired hand, a migrant worker with no rights and no respect. You have maliciously been told to be grateful for the little you *are allowed* to have, for you deserve nothing; while in reality you are of noble blood. You were destined to rule, yet you are oppressed and enslaved; and you, therefore, have existed in ignominy and ancestral poverty instead of living within the blessings and prestige of your true, grand inheritance and status. This is how you have been wronged by the shapers and rulers of modern society through their *criminal* misrepresentation of the Bible and history.

("BUT, HOW...?" YOU MIGHT ASK. ALLOW ME TO SET THE STAGE OF THIS CRIME.)

The Importance of History

Few people realize the important correlation between the Bible and history. The Bible is full of the history of God's people and of the prophecies concerning the future and glory of God's people.

NOTE THIS WELL: *IF **HISTORY** IS NOT STUDIED, THERE IS **NO WAY** OF KNOWING **IF** THESE BIBLE PROPHECIES HAVE BEEN FULFILLED, **HOW** THEY HAVE BEEN FULFILLED, AND **BY WHOM** THEY HAVE BEEN FULFILLED—AND THERE IS **NO WAY** OF BEING CERTAIN **WHO** GOD'S PEOPLE ACTUALLY ARE (AND **WHO** THEY HAVE **ALWAYS** BEEN).*

As time passes, political consensus often replaces the understanding of certain elements of the truth; be it in history, morality, or any other area of life that is open to being *redefined* in the minds of the masses. This occurs when people *abdicate their responsibilities*, of being *personally* informed and active in public matters, to *trusted* "professionals" and politicians, so that they have more *free time* for their own *pleasures*. However, a price is always to be paid—and most often a *far-higher* price than imagined. Our forefathers and the greatest minds of the world taught us that very few people can be entrusted with power without becoming despotic—and eventually *all* governments *will* become corrupt and oppressive. Tyranny takes firm root once people take a *back seat*, entrusting the *driving* to someone else so they can *relax*, *snooze*, and *enjoy the ride*. This does not occur overnight but very gradually and methodically. The average person is naïve and trusting and cannot comprehend how evil some people really are. When evil is exposed, many people refuse to believe it, for the admission of such evil is an assault upon their delusional sense of security. However, evil attacks good *continually*—whether or not people see or believe it. And evil breeds rapidly in an apathetic environment. "Professionals" and those entrusted to positions of power are able to subtly make changes and fool the masses into accepting these changes *as if nothing had ever been changed.*

Further, even as tangible realities and concepts are deceptively changed, *words themselves* are often altered. Although the words themselves remain, the *meanings* of those words can change *drastically.*[2] This is also true of names. As a result of the mass migration of third-world peoples to the West, names referring to geographic areas and nationalities no longer have the same meaning.[3]

What makes this confusion of words even more difficult is the language barrier extant in the Bible and history—and further, the educational warfare now perpetrated upon us. People are no longer taught the past and its significance.[4] They are taught only what is currently *considered* relevant.[5] Just as a restaurant might have a sign out front announcing SOUP OF THE DAY or a fish market its sign, CATCH OF THE DAY, it seems our schools, libraries, the media, and the "government" (and even many churches) have an unwritten sign: TRUTH OF THE DAY. Modern "truth" depends upon the current need, whim, or fancy of those who dictate societal norms or political correctness. However, **truth** never *changes*!

> Though Heaven and Earth shall pass away, The Word of the LORD shall endure forever.... Thy Word is Truth.... The truth shall make you free (Luke 21:33; John 17:17; John 8:32).

If one chooses to believe man instead of God, one will easily be confused, misled, and even harmed. Consider a seemingly silly analogy: Imagine a zoo in which the zebra was moved to the tiger cage, and the tiger to the zebra cage—but the name plates of the animals were never put with the proper animal! Now imagine a child growing up in America or a *mentally-challenged* foreigner coming

---

[2] For example, gay no longer connotates being "happy," but *homosexual*; a faggot is no longer a "bundle of sticks or a cigarette," but a *homosexual*; queer is no longer something that is "mysterious or odd," but a *homosexual*. The words fruit and queen are still commonly used with their *original* meanings, but they can also imply a *homosexual*. Such is the degradation of both our society and language. Although these words once had meanings that were innocuous, the average, decent person today would most likely not appreciate any of these words being used in reference to him.

[3] For example, an *American* once meant "a person of European/British extraction," and so did the designation *Englishman*. The word *European* itself once referred exclusively to "Caucasian peoples." But this is no longer the case. The words *Babel* and *Babylon* mean "confusion by mixing." Words, names, labels, and even people themselves are easily confused through mixing. Even the word *Christian* (as it is commonly used by society today) no longer refers to what a *true* Christian is, but what *it has come to mean* as the church has also *adulterated* her true heritage. Nowadays, people who do not even know God or care about His Word, "churchgoers" who do not follow what Christ taught—and further, even *Moonies* (and many other cults)—call themselves *Christians*. However, *God* holds the patent and copyright on the truth, and He has permanently fixed the ***true* definitions (and natures) for all things** He created; whether or not sinful man chooses to acknowledge and utilize these true definitions, does not change reality in the slightest. (See So, You Call Yourself A Christian... by Balaicius/STM.)

[4] Rather, people are urged *to forget* the past and its significance—to all our hurt. George Santayana, the Spanish-American philosopher, succinctly warned, "Those who do not learn from history are doomed to repeat it." Similarly God declared through His prophet: "My people are destroyed for lack of knowledge" (Hosea 4:6).

[5] ...that is, that which is considered "relevant" by the shapers of society who, based upon their personal agenda, determine what *they* think you should know and believe.

to our country and visiting this zoo. Both the animal called a *zebra* and the animal called a *tiger* have four legs, a tail, and stripes. If the child or foreigner were raised thinking the tiger was a zebra and vice versa, they would have a distorted view of reality—but they *would not realize* it. They could also be in grave danger if they had read in a dictionary (one written back when a zebra was still called a zebra) that the "zebra" was "a domesticatable animal that could be ridden like a horse." If the child or foreigner then attempted to ride what *modern society calls* a zebra, not realizing that a switch had been made in terminology, the results would be deadly.

Now, such an example might seem absurd. But the purpose is to give you a vivid picture (which will later become clear as it pertains to our discussion) concerning how the knowledge of things can become drastically changed and how dangerous this change can be.

The only remedy to end such deception and potential hazard would be for a person to do some research on his own, utilizing older, trustworthy books. Such books (as they pertain to our above analogy) would explain in detail how to distinguish each animal by *all* of its characteristics; and such books would show *with pictures* exactly what each of these animals actually looks like. Newer books would be of no use. They would represent only *modern* thoughts and ideas, regardless of fact, based upon the *current way* of doing things (like calling a tiger a zebra).

However, before one can recognize ***the need*** *to do such research, one must come to the realization that he has been being deceived.* This itself is the ***key*** to the door of freedom—and a very hard key to obtain, for *the very nature of being deceived* ***precludes one's awareness of the deception***. The common reply is, "If I was being deceived, I'd know it!" On the contrary, if it was possible for people to always recognize when they were being deceived, no one would ever be deceived. The very meaning of the word "deception" encompasses the fact that a person does not *realize* it. Therefore, it takes either an "*ah-ha experience*," or some outside intervention to bring a person out of the blinding fog.

(It is the goal of this book to bring such deception to your awareness, so you may follow up this evidence with personal study, if the evidence in this book so motivates you. Thomas Carlyl said, "The best effect of any book is that it excites the reader into self-activity." This is the highest degree of self-respect, maturity, and intelligence: to not blindly accept as truth anything anyone tells you, regardless of who the person is—a member of the media, a pastor, a school teacher, college professor, a politician, a lawyer, a friend, a doctor, a relative...or even the author of this book!)

Not all people who teach untruths do so out of malice. We are all human and therefore fallible. For this reason we ought to confirm what we are taught, so we can know *firsthand* that something is true, and so we can defend what we believe. The Bible itself instructs us so: We are told to "prove all things" and to *search* matters out (I Thessalonians 5:21; Acts 17:11). In reality, though, how many "pew sitters" merely live *surrogately through their pastor*? How many churchgoers can actually coherently and convincingly *defend* what they believe? A good percentage of churchgoers do not even know *what* they believe. The average "Christian" when pressed can only say, "Well, my pastor says..." or "Well, my pastor can answer that...." This is simply crude ignorance. If the truth be told, Christianity has a bad reputation in America today because of the *average Christian*, who does not *know* **what** he believes nor ***live*** *what* he *claims* to believe. (Christ had a few choice things to say about hypocrisy and lukewarmness.)

This does not mean you should distrust everyone, but in matters of importance you need to verify the truth. If you were rewiring a kitchen in someone else's house and you needed to know if the electricity had been turned off at the breaker box before you touched the bare wires, would you trust just anyone? Further, even if you knew and trusted the person, would it not be wise to *double-check* by simply flipping the light switch or by using a voltage meter? It is not as much a matter of *distrust* as it is a **vital need to verify the truth**, considering *all* the possible factors. For instance, maybe he flipped the *wrong* breaker, or maybe *someone else* flipped the breaker *back on*, not knowing you were working on the wires in the kitchen. Some matters in life are *so important*, just taking someone else's word for it is not good enough. In matters of life or death, where there is no second chance and no room for error, this is not *distrust*, but **wisdom**.

Shakespeare wrote, "A rose by any other name still smells as sweet." Changing an object's name does not change the thing itself. Things remain what they are, *regardless* of what they are called. Unfortunately, many people are easily fooled. Ironically, those who are quick to ridicule Christians for their "blind faith" in a God they cannot see, are quick to put *even greater blind faith* in people they have never seen and know nothing about. This is foolish since all human beings are potentially untrustworthy, sinful, and prone to error. Dozens of times each day the average person puts his blind faith in a doctor, a lawyer, a teacher, a pastor, a counsellor, a druggist, an airline pilot, a policeman, a food packer, a chef, a mechanic, a factory worker—without asking for any credentials, without knowing where the person went to school (*if* he went to school!), if what his school taught him was true, whether he got good grades or barely passed, if he is emotionally balanced or a mental deviate, whether he is morally principled or unscrupulous, whether he is carrying a communicable disease, and so on. Further, every day people put their blind faith in politicians whom *they know* to be dishonest. This is not just blind faith or ignorance—it is *stupidity*! The average person trusts nearly everyone he meets, not knowing anything about the other person, simply if there is the *illusion* of a "professional environment." Thus the average person blindly believes and does whatever he is told, even if he feels in his heart it is wrong (and he is thus trained to ignore his conscience). This is where tyranny begins. Trust is important. But faith must be firmly grounded upon *facts* and *reality*. Although "a rose by any other name still smells as sweet," if one buys a bottle labeled "rose oil," which is actually oil from *poison ivy*, the effects of using it for perfume will be drastically, even fatally, different.

Consider another analogy: What if, at the grocery store, when the stock-boy restocked the shelves, he placed the new produce on the wrong shelves but never reorganized the shelf labels? A child or foreigner might then grow up thinking an apple was an orange, lettuce was spinach, pretzels were cookies. The dangers of this become clear if one considers that some people are deathly allergic to certain foods. Further, what if this same confusion (whether a result of carelessness or calculated cruelty) was to occur in the drug isle, where the medicines people desperately needed were replaced by other powerful medicines they did not need or to which they were allergic? What if bug spray was placed on the breath spray shelf? What if bleach was placed on the milk shelf and Compound-W was placed in the eye-drops space? What if Ben-Gay was placed where the diaper rash ointment or Preparation-H belonged? If the shelf labels were not changed, children and those who are uneducated, careless, or handicapped by a language barrier or learning deficit would be fooled and grievously wronged.

Even worse would be if the *labels* on the products themselves were switched, so an intelligent person would also be fooled. What if manufacturers chose not to specify on the label *all* the ingredients of a certain product? What if they called certain harmful ingredients by nice-sounding names? There are numerous common food additives that honest research shows to be highly toxic, and informed people read labels as a precautionary measure; but this wise practice is useless if the labels do not identify *all* the ingredients or if the labels do not identify the additives *honestly*.

Worse still, what if the *products themselves* were *contaminated*? Calculated crimes occur occasionally when evil people taint popular products (such as Tylenol, Goodies, Visine) with poison. An AIDS activist once made an anonymous phone call to a supermarket claiming to have injected their meat with AIDS-infected blood. Sadly, there is no limit to the carelessness or evil that is inherent in man's sinful nature. But this is not the only way such evil confusion occurs.

Think of what would happen if such confusion and evil misrepresentation occurred in the *history books*: if one group of people was confused with another. What if one nationality or race was confused with another? What if criminals were confused with law-abiding citizens, or if resident aliens were confused with natural citizens? What if the role of elected officials (who are supposed to be our servants) was switched with the role of dictators, and if the role of the citizens was changed from that of the sovereigns to that of the serfs? This is exactly what *has* happened, but few people realize it.

In all of these areas of confusion, the myth and the bondage, the crime and the danger would all be self-perpetuating once the disinformation had been successfully implemented upon the unsuspecting and forcefully imposed upon the intelligentsia. Any person who had been raised thinking such falsehoods were true would be a helpless victim, unknowingly caught within an unending circle of ignorance—unless that person decided to search out the facts *for himself*. Therefore, if a person was raised not realizing some of what he has been taught is untrue, he will have no reason to suspect otherwise, and there would be no reason for him to investigate the matter further to *stumble upon* the truth. Further, a society that is addicted to leisure and sensual pleasure (video games,

TV, movies, romance novels, science fiction, fantasy, drugs, alcohol, gluttony, sports, adultery, sexual "freedom"—anything but the truth or matters of productive substance) has little desire to search matters out, being drunk on the wine of irresponsible pleasure, forgetting the past and giving no thought to the future.

This is where God comes into the picture. It is God's Spirit that draws men to the truth. The Holy Spirit of God puts it within the hearts and minds of people *to seek* the truth. God is the sole author of truth. The Bible tells us that Christ Jesus Himself (God's Son) is the Truth and the Word (John 1:1). The Greek word *logos* (LAH-gahs), translated as *Word* in English encompasses the concept of "the logical perfection of rational thought originating in God Himself." Only through Christ can one have access to God the Father, and it is the Spirit of truth that draws men unto Christ. One of God's greatest desires is for us to know the truth, so we can be happy and free. But apart from Him this is not possible.

On the other hand, there are those who *hate* the truth and will do *anything* to hide it. Such evil people have turned the hearts of good people away from God (and *true* religion), for they know that ***He*** is the *sole source* of truth and freedom. Those who are slaves to their own additive lifestyles think little about truth or freedom, for they are deceived, and such thoughts are foreign to them. Those who labor to keep the truth hidden and to keep people in bondage have great power and make tremendous profit from this deception. Therefore, know for certain that the originators of such confusion and such lies would not think too kindly of anyone who would attempt to expose their racket. In fact, they will even try to ruin or silence such a person in any way possible. Such evil occurs every day. Self-appointed "masters" do not like for other people to come and set *their* "slaves" free. (See Acts 16:16.)

God reveals in His Word, "My people are destroyed for lack of knowledge" (Hosea 4:6). But Christ Jesus declares that *when you know the truth, the truth will set you free* (John 8:32). Does the person who goes to the average church or school learn the full truth, or is he kept in bondage, to some degree, by being taught only what those institutions want him to know? (Those who think too freely or ask too many questions are usually told to keep their mouths shut and learn what they are taught or they will be asked to leave.) Is the average person taught to live within his God-given freedom, or is he taught how to be part of "the system," whether the system is right or wrong? Nowadays, how often are people taught to oppose what is evil? Rather, are people not taught to be "tolerant" and "understanding" of other people's "lifestyles"? (—regardless of whether such lifestyles are moral or immoral.) Is not evil called *good*, and good called *evil* in today's society? (What else could be expected from a thoroughly corrupt government and liberal clergy?) Are people taught God's Divine Law? (—the only source of morality, true liberty, and happiness.) Or are they taught society's regulations and denominational legalism? (—the Divine Law being cast aside as "obsolete.") Masters are not in the habit of teaching their slaves how to be free; they only teach their slaves how to remain happy and productive slaves.

(It is my hope and prayer that this book will be used to break the cycle, to reveal what has been hidden, to provide truth and knowledge that you may be happy, free, and prosperous, and able to live within the full blessings of your inheritance. Consider now the biblical and historical truths that have been hidden, obscured, twisted, and misrepresented (due either to ignorance or design).

Please note: although I speak of blind pastors and churches that teach things in err, I am ***not*** saying that *all* pastors teach falsely *on purpose* or *maliciously*. Much of the time, they probably do so unknowingly. Further, most likely, they do not teach falsehoods in *every* area, but most likely only in a few important areas. We are all prone to error. However, after one has come into the knowledge of the truth, if he refuses to publicly confess it, it is a far-graver matter. Such a person will be held *doubly* accountable. If a person chooses to remain in error for any reason, he then proves he is not merely blind, but that he is also evil and not of God (Hebrews 10:26). On the other hand, when a person has been liberated by some profound truth, his desire is to share that truth with his family and friends so they too can be free and happy. That is my sole motivation and my goal.)

A Synopsis of True History

Germane to our discussion, the Bible speaks of a Hebrew man named Esau, who was a base individual. He despised his inheritance and rejected it, choosing instead to enter by marriage the vile inheritance of an immoral, impure, and wicked people—the Canaanites (Genesis 25:30-34; 26:34-35; 28:6-9; 36:2, 6, 8, 9; Jeremiah 49:8, 10; Obadiah 1:9, 18; Malachi 1:3; and Hebrews 12:16). The pure Hebrew blood Esau introduced into his Canaanite stepfamily was lost altogether, immediately disappearing without a trace, even as the flame of a match would be snuffed out if dropped into the Atlantic Ocean on a stormy night. Esau's illegitimate descendents came to be known as *Canaanites* (specifically *Edomites* and *Amalekites*)—the very worst enemies of God's people.[6]

Being an evil people and seeing the wondrous inheritance their new son-in-law had forsaken,[7] these Canaanites determined that they would steal this inheritance for *themselves*—through any means possible. The Bible records the conspiracy of these evil people to steal the inheritance of God's people (Psalm 83:2-8; Ezekiel 36:5; Matthew 21:38, 45). These evil people later inhabited the land of Israel and brazenly revealed their intentions to steal the land of Israel itself for *their own* inheritance (Ezekiel 11:15).

"Okay," you ask, "what is this conspiracy and what do you claim my inheritance to be?" I'm glad you asked! Sit back and prepare to learn a few simple but well-hidden facts that could very well change your life.

It should be noted that these facts, although carefully hidden, can be easily uncovered or verified by anyone who simply takes the time to do a little research and study—if a person knows *what* he is looking for and *how* and *where* to look.

---

[6] These people still exist to this day, for there are numerous prophecies against them: the entire book of **Obadiah** is God's promise to judge them once and for all. (See also **Zechariah 14:21**.)

[7] —and which he was unable to reclaim **(Hebrews 12:17)**.

Unfortunately, most people have not been trained to think for themselves, and "free-thinkers" are usually ostracized. The facts have been kept from people as history has been rewritten, while older books have been quietly weeded from libraries; and bookstores no longer carry those books that do not *toe the line* of modern thought. The Bible itself has been "rewritten" by false interpretation. Many people are repulsed by false teaching because God promised to put His discerning Word and Spirit in the inner parts of His people to guide them.

The freedoms of speech, press, and religion exist in America only *in theory*. In practice, they are nearly extinct; even as the right to a fair trial no longer exists. "Fair" trials are reserved only for those who can "afford" them. So it is with the freedoms of speech, press, and religion. Those who have the power and money dictate what we are "free" to speak and print and believe. Those who do not *kowtow* to what is politically correct are blacklisted and black-balled—and even forced out of the marketplace by persecution. In practice, such people are "free" to speak, print, or believe what they want *only if no one else can hear them*. (Even this is threatened by "thought-crime" legislation.) The stranglehold on the media, education, economics, and politics effectively prevents 99 percent of the exercise of these freedoms. When a rare individual succeeds in exercising these rights, he is often persecuted.

(IT SHOULD BE NOTED THAT SO FAR IN THIS BOOK, I HAVE OFTEN SPOKEN IN PARABLES, ANALOGIES, GENERALITIES, OR ALLUSIONS WITH LITTLE EXPLANATION. MANY READERS MOST LIKELY WILL NOT HAVE UNDERSTOOD THEIR *FULL* MEANINGS. AS THE BOOK PROGRESSES, THE HIDDEN WILL BECOME APPARENT.)

Let's Start At The Beginning

The Bible records in its first book that God formed Adam, the first man, and that the Bible is *solely* the history of Adam's people (Genesis 1:26-28; 2:7; 5:1). So, who was this man that God created? The Hebrew word used in reference to *Adam and his descendents*, which is translated as *man* in our English Bibles, is the very word *Adam* itself, and it more properly intimates "Adam-man or Adam-kind." In Hebrew,[8] the words translated as *Adam* and *man* (Adamkind) are numbered in James Strong's, Exhaustive Concordance of the Bible (1890), as #119 (*aw-DAM*) and #120 (*aw-DAWM*) and mean "to show blood in the face, to be fair, rosy-cheeked, to be ruddy, to be able to blush or flush." Unless one holds to the unbiblical and unscientific *theory* of evolution, one must admit that other peoples who do not fit this description do not descend through Adam. God declared that not all flesh is the same. Nature itself has proclaimed this truth from within the very being of decent people for the past 6,000 years. Sadly, the average person is eager to accept, in a limited sense, evil men's *theory* of evolution, because they either cannot understand God's Word and plan or because they *refuse* to accept it. It seems most people have been well indoctrinated by the world's spurious teachings, and they have been controlled by false ideas and

[8] Incidentally, ancient Hebrew (as ancient Greek) was written in characters nearly identical with our alphabet. *Modern* Hebrew is entirely different than Biblical (ancient) Hebrew. It is like comparing *modern Ghetto graffiti* "English" to Victorian English.

misguided emotions that have resulted from such teaching.

It is a genetic *impossibility* for all races to have descended from Adam. Simple biology proves this—and it is an impossibility decreed by God Himself. (Remember, God is a God of order, and He created the physical laws of the universe that govern our lives.) God declared this in His Immutable Law of "Everything After Its Own Kind," which is mentioned *10*[9] times in the *first*[10] chapter of Genesis (the book of *beginnings*). Much Scripture supports this.[11]

Now, God gave man a choice, but man chose to go his own way. Therefore, there comes a time in each person's life when he must choose to follow God's ways (which lead to success and life) or continue on his own ways (which will reap misery, destruction, and death). God declares, "There is a way which seemeth right unto man; but the ends thereof are ways of death" (Proverbs 14:12). Just look at the mess this world is in. It is a result of forsaking God's ways.

LET ME PAUSE HERE TO ENCOURAGE YOU, IF YOU HAVE BEEN SHOCKED BY THE PREVIOUS PARAGRAPHS TO SUSPEND JUDGMENT UNTIL THE EVIDENCE IS IN. ARE YOU WILLING TO WEIGH THE FACTS AND ACCEPT THE TRUTH—REGARDLESS OF WHERE IT LEADS? ARE YOUR STANDARDS HIGHER THAN GOD'S? (SEE PROVERBS 18:13.)

From Adam, there proceeded a *chosen line*: that line which God ordained should follow after His righteousness. The Bible records the descent of this righteous *Adamic* seed-line to whom the promises of Scripture are given. The chosen line of Adam began in Adam's son, Seth (Genesis 5:3). Many generations later, all but one family of even the chosen line had become corrupt. The head of this one Godly *Sethite* family who alone remained faithful to God and pure in his ancestry was Noah (Genesis 6:5-9). God preserved Noah and his family (and representative pairs of each of God's original creation) and destroyed the rest of the world by a flood. **Shem** was the son of Noah, who was then elected by God to constitute the chosen line. Shem's descendents became known as "**Shemites**" or "***Semites***" (a *terribly* misused term). The next major branch of this chosen line was to be found in **Eber**, whose pure descendents became known as "**Hebrews**."[12] Generations later, again, the majority of the chosen line had become corrupt; but God chose one faithful man: **Abram**.[13]

---

[9] In the Bible, God has a purpose and meaning for every name and every number. In Bible Numerics, "10" is the number of *Divine Perfect Order*.

[10] The number "1" is unique. It is indivisible. It stands alone. It represents that which is of primary importance. That which is first mentioned is not only that which is of greatest importance (**Genesis 1:1**; In the beginning **God**), but it is the *establishment* of God's Law and Word by which all that succeeds it is to be interpreted. God cannot change or lie.

[11] Since this departs a bit from our main topic, we shall not go into this any further; however, there are other books available on this topic through Sacred Truth Ministries or the distributor of this book. (See Number in Scripture (1894), Bullinger.)

[12] This word *Hebrew* in the Hebrew language is #5680 *(ib-REE)* and means "colonizer" or, more literally, "one who crosses over."

[13] God later changed Abram's name to *Abraham*. It should be noted here that Abraham was not a "jew"—Abraham was *not even* an *Israelite*. Abraham was the grandfather of Jacob and the great-grandfather of Judah. Jacob himself was *the very first* Israelite, and Judah was the first Judahite (Judean—erroneously referred to as a "jew"). To call Abraham an Israelite or a "jew" is like saying King George was an *American* or a *Virginian*.

The choosing of Abraham marked a special occurrence in the history of God's people (this chosen line). Despite their propensity to wander and live sinfully as other peoples, it was at this time that God ***covenanted*** with His people. Not only did God promise that He would never *utterly* forsake them for any reason and that He would never choose *any other people* (Deuteronomy 4:31,34,37; 7:6-8), God also promised incredible blessings to come upon His people. Some of these blessings were *conditional* upon their moral lifestyle, but many were *unconditional* and inseparable from the very character of God's people: for God designed them and further blessed them to prosper and to glorify Him through not only their worship, but through their inevitable successes resulting from being created in God's very own *creative* image.

The headship of this Covenant was passed on to Abraham's son **Isaac**, "the son of promise" (*after whom the chosen line would one day call itself*, Genesis 21:12; Romans 9:7; Hebrews 11:18). Isaac thus was the promised establisher of the Covenant and the chosen line. Isaac had two sons, Esau and Jacob. As we have already seen, Esau's wickedness and his contempt for and rejection of his inheritance disqualified him from the Covenant. **Jacob** (Esau's younger brother) thus became the patriarchal head of the Covenant of the chosen seed-line. God later changed Jacob's name to *Israel* (#3478, *yis-raw-AYL*), which means "he who reigns successfully as a prince with God over man." Jacob (Israel) sired 12 sons, who founded the 12 Tribes of Israel: (1)Reuben, (2)Simeon, (3)Levi, (4)Judah, (5)Dan, (6)Naphtali, (7)Gad, (8)Asher, (9)Issachar, (10)Zebulun, (11)Joseph (split between his two sons, (a)Ephraim and (b)Manasseh), and (12)Benjamin.

After about 400 years, Israel had multiplied into a large number of people, and God, through Moses, gave these Israel people the *first* ***written*** *copy* of the Laws, which the chosen line had known and followed since creation. At this time, the people of Israel formally, in a national marriage ceremony with God Almighty, accepted their place in the Covenant and vowed to follow these Laws. God also revealed unto His people a special name, a Covenant name, by which *they alone* would know and call upon Him: "YaHWeH."

(Henceforth, we shall use this name that God gave to His people, for it is a name that endears His own unto Him. The consonants appear in full capitals since sometimes in Hebrew vowels were not written but were inserted by the reader. YaHWeH has been loosely translated as "I am that I am," meaning, "I exist." I believe, "I am always as I will," reveals a different angle of understanding the full flavor of this word. It reveals God's *active (not passive)* supreme power, eternal character, and sovereign nature. From here on out, we shall also use the true Name for *Jesus*, as given to us in Scripture. The word *Jesus* is a poor translation from the Greek word *Iesous* (#2424, *ee-ay-SOOCE*), which Strong's Exhaustive Concordance clearly shows is derived from the Hebrew word *YeHoWSHuWaH* (#3091, *ye-hō-SHOO-ah*), meaning "saved by YaHWeH." When the angel told Joseph that Mary was to bring forth a son, who would be conceived of the Holy Ghost (who would actually be the Son of God), he said, "thou shalt call His Name *Iesous* (YeHoWSHuWaH): for He shall save *His* people from *their* sins" (Matthew 1:21).)

Sadly, the Israelites frequently wandered far, deep, and wide from the Covenant of the Law that had been given to them for their good. Many sinful Israelites married foreign peoples, corrupting their holy seed (Ezra 9:2), and disqualifying their descendents through *miscegeny.*[14] True to His promise, however, God *always* forgave His people who *truly* repented of their sins. However, one of the terms of the Covenant was that part of Israel's blessing would be *conditional* upon their obedience to the Law of the Covenant. God warned His people Israel that should their sin become great and prolonged, He would use their enemies to chasten them until they truly repented (Leviticus 26; Deuteronomy 28; II Samuel 7). Sadly, this chastening often resulted in many dead Israelites. It was a refining fire, however, removing much of the dross and leaving the pure strengthened as a result of having passed through judgment, with the price of disobedience leaving a *burning impression* upon their minds.

In time, as prophesied, Israel's sin reached the point where God would no longer withhold His judgment.[15] After the death of King Solomon (c.931 B.C.), civil war erupted within the nation of Israel[16] and the kingdom was split between the North and the South (even as the United States was once divided; even as there have been civil wars and rifts among various factions of the Scottish clans, the Irish, the English, and the Vikings). Ten tribes comprised the *northern* **House of Israel**[17] (Reuben, Simeon, Dan, Naphtali, Gad, Asher, Issachar, Zebulun, and Joseph [Ephraim and Manasseh]), whose capital of Samaria was founded by King Omri. Two tribes comprised the *southern* **House of Judah**[18] (Judah and Benjamin), whose capital remained in Jerusalem.

Later, in a series of invasions spanning nearly 30 years, the 10 Tribes of the northern House of Israel (along with a good portion of the House of Judah) were taken captive to Assyria (c. 721 B.C.). The two Tribes of the southern House of Judah were taken captive to Babylon about 135 years later (c. 586 B.C.). The entire population of Israel at that time was about 13 million people; but of the approximately 11 million people of the House of Israel who were taken captive to Assyria, *none* ever returned to the land of Israel; and of the approximately two million people of the House of Judah who were taken captive (to both Assyria and Babylon), only about 40,000 (or 2 percent) of those taken captive to Babylon

---

[14] —that is, "adulteration, crossbreeding, fornication, out-of-kind reproduction, etc." **Genesis 24:3-4; 26:34-35 Deuteronomy 23:2.** God's Law even forbids cross-breeding animals, plants, etc.

[15] For God is just and true. "Be not deceived, God is not mocked; for whatsoever a man soweth that shall he also reap" (**Galatians 6:7**). (See **Deuteronomy 30:19**; **Galatians 6:8**.)

[16] Do not confuse the **ancient nation of Israel** with the modern *Israeli* state; and do not confuse the ***ancient Israelite and Hebrew peoples*** with the people of modern history who call themselves *Israelis* or "jews." As we will prove, names have been changed, nationalities confused, and therefore, many people have been deceived.

[17] Ephraim became the prominent leader of the *northern 10-Tribed* House of Israel, and thus the entire *northern* House of Israel is at times collectively referred to as *Ephraim*.

[18] Part of the *Tribe* of Judah was referred to as the "House of David," because God promised King David a perpetual throne that would never end. King David, though a sinful man at times, had a heart that pleased God. Although David often sinned, he repented quickly in true shame and remorse. Israel's Golden Age began during the reign of King David.

returned 70 years later to the land of Israel.

So what happened to this huge mass of people who had dominated the world for so long, these people who were the center of biblical attention, who were God's very people (the apple of His eye), the people whom God promised *never* to forsake? What happened to 99.69 percent of all the children of Israel?

The highly acclaimed Judean historian Flavius Josephus (A.D. 37-100?) records the following concerning the children of Israel while in captivity:

> ...The entire body of the people of Israel remained in that country [Assyria]; wherefore, there are but two tribes[19] in Asia and Europe subject to the Romans, while the ten tribes are beyond the Euphrates [River] till now, and are **an immense multitude, and not to be estimated by numbers** (The Complete Works of Flavius Josephus; *Antiquities*, Book XI, Chapter V, Paragraph 2). (Emphasis mine.)

Further, the book of II Esdras (Ezra) of the Apocryphal[20] books of the Bible reveals that these Israelites then left Assyria and migrated into a new country, *where never man had lived*; a land with which Israel's fathers were unfamiliar:

> These are the ten tribes that in the days of King Hoshea were carried away...into captivity, whom Shalmaneser, King of Assyria, made captives, and carried beyond the river [Euphrates]; they were carried off to another country. *But they formed this plan among themselves, to leave the heathen population, and to go to a more distant region, where the human race had never lived,* so that there perhaps they might keep their statutes, which they had not kept in their own country....they went by the narrow passage of the Euphrates River. For the Most High then did wonders for them, for He held back the sources of the river until they had passed over....*it was a long journey* of **a year and a half** to that country, and that country is called Arzareth... (II Esdras 13:40-47). (Emphasis mine.)

Herodotus[21] confirms this account in every detail.

This is a fulfillment of Bible prophesy. God declared that because of Israel's sin, He would drive His people from the land of Israel and scatter them throughout the earth; they would have a new home, a land that their fathers never knew...a land to the north and west...and a land that was previously uninhabited by *man*: a wilderness, a virgin, uncultivated land (Deuteronomy 4:26-27; 28:64; 30:3; Isaiah 34:17; 49:8; 54:3; Jeremiah 9:16; 16:13, 15; 23:3; 30:11; 31:10; Ezekiel 6:8; 11:16-17; 12:15; 20:34, 41; 22:15; 36:33-36).

To determine where the country of Arzareth was, look at a map of the world and calculate where a great mass of people would end up if it left Assyria and made a year's journey by foot in a northwest direction (Isaiah 49:12; Jeremiah 3:18). (See the map on the opposite page.)

It should be taken into consideration that when people migrated with their wives, children, flocks, herds, and all their earthly possessions, travelling with pack animals and wagons, living in tents—not even knowing where they were

---

[19] —a *remnant* of the House of Judah: the Tribe of Judah and the Tribe of Benjamin.

[20] The books of the Apocrypha were originally contained in most all Protestant Bibles, even the King James Version of 1611, but were removed in modern times.

[21] —the Greek historian of the 5th century B.C. who is called the "Father of History."

going—they did not travel very quickly. Travel by foot on poor roads (or ***no*** roads) over mountains and rivers with flocks, herds, and wagon trains is *slow*. They took their time, stopping so that their animals could graze and rest. They often packed up their tents and moved on only when the pasture was depleted. It is reasonable to assume that they covered *less than* 50 miles a week—*when the travelling was* ***easy***!

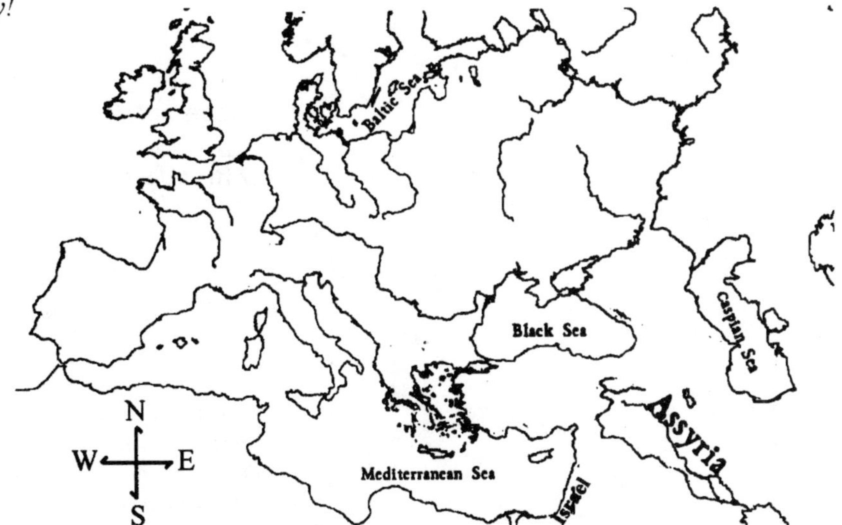

Your Inheritance

Is it just a *coincidence* that at about the same time the Israelites disappeared, leaving Assyria (c. 6th century B.C.) the **Germanic**[22] tribes mysteriously appeared out of *nowhere*? Is it just a coincidence that to this day secular, "scientific" minds that have proposed an elaborate *theory* of evolution, deducing that man came from an ape (and before that, an amoeba that grew out of cosmic dust), have not succeeded in determining where these Germanic peoples[23] originated? Surely, the most significant people the world has ever known, who brought civilization and culture, did not merely evolve out of barbarism. Although "great minds" of "science" can supposedly trace the origins of the earth back *hundreds of billions of years*, using bits and pieces of fossilized weeds and bugs and animals, they claim they cannot trace the origin of the Germanic peoples back a mere 2,500 years, even though a plethora of written records have been com-

22 —also referred to as the Anglo-Saxon, Indo-German, Indo-Aryan or European-descended people; more generically, the white race. The *Germans* (of Germany) are but one of the *many hundred* branches of the *Germanic race*. The ***Germanic peoples*** existed a thousand years before the nation of Germany came to be. Due to the bad publicity the German people have received, those educated in modern schools may not realize that the white race, *in its entirety*, is classified as *Germanic*.

23 *Alans, Albans, Alemannii, Angles, Balts, Belgae, Brits, Burgundians, Cimbrians, Cimmerians, Czechs, Daci, Danes, Dimetae, Eburones, Esuvii, Finns, Fororians (Formorians), Franks, Frisians, Gauls, Gaels, Getae, Goths, Herulii, Iberians, Jutes, Kelts (Celts), Kymry, Letts, Lithuanians, Lombards (Langobards), Marcomanni, Massagatae, Milesians, Normans, Norvegers, Ordovices, Poles, Phenians, Picts, Prus, Quadi, Rus, Ruthenians, Sakae, Saxons, Scots, Scythians, Silurians, Slovaks, Slovenes, Suevians (Swabians), Svear (Suiones), Swedes, Swithoid, Teutons, Ustragoths (Ostrogoths), Vandals, Varangians, Visogoths, Volcae, Walloons, Wends (Venedi), Yatvingians, Žemaičiai, etc.*

ISAIAH 24:5 "ISLES OF THE WEST."
II SAM. 7:10 "THE APPOINTED PLACE."
DAN: 2:34 "THE STONE CUT OUT WITHOUT HANDS."
HOSEA 2:14 "THE WILDERNESS"
MAP PREPARED BY THE REVD FREDK. ASTON, H.H. PAIN & "OXONIAN" (REVD W.M.H. MILNER, M.A.) IN 1900.
(HOSEA IX:17)
ISRAEL'S WANDERINGS.
VIKINGS
NORTH MEN
SWITHOID
SCAN-DIN-AVIA
BALTIC SEA
ROSH
(RUSS)
A.D. 900
PICTS
SCOTS
MILESIANS
DANNANS
SCOTIA
500-100 B.C.
ANGLO-SAXONS
BRIT-AIN
HIBERNIA
DAMNONII
CIMBRI
JUTLAND
DAN-MERK
ANGLI
SUEONES
SAXONS
GERMANIC TRIBES
GOTHS
Lithuanians
VENEDI
SWITHOID
SCYTHIANS
MESHECH
(MOSCOW, MUSCOVY)
Ezekiel 38
TUBAL
(TOBOL-SK BUL-GARIA)
MAGOG
SARMATIA
SCYTHIA
AR-SARETH
DACI
A.D. 100
BELGÆ
NORMANS
NORTHMEN
CELTS
VENETI
GALLIA
VENETIA
LUSITANIA
CELT
IBERIA
BETICA
SAR-DIN-IA
ROME
GREECE
CIMMERIANS
CRIMEA
BLACK SEA
DANITE HERACLIDÆ
DANIEL PASS
KIMMEROII
TROY
GALATIA
ASGARD
R. Araxes
PHOCÆA
the Dispersion
ASSYRIA
(KHUMRI)
HARA
NINEVEH
HABOR
HALAH
MEDIA
BABYLON
R. Euphrates
CASPIAN SEA
ALANS
MASSAGETAE
SAKA
SAKKA
Passage of the Araxes in Herodotus 4.12
Narrow Passages of 2 Esdras 13
ATLANTIC OCEAN
CARTHAGE
MEDITERRANEAN SEA
DANITE PHŒNICIANS
DANITE PHŒNICIANS TO IBERIA & HIBERNIA
CRETE
CYPRUS
TYRE
B.C. 740-721
SAMARIA
• JERUSALEM
ALEXANDRIA
CAIRO
TAPHANES B.C. 588
EGYPT
PHUT
300 B.C.
PERSIA

pletely preserved with incontrovertible proof identifying the Germanic peoples as the *Israelites of antiquity*. Is this silence accidental, or is it *calculated* deception and feigned ignorance?

Given that the huge mass of Israel people (about 13 million) disappeared from history around the same time another huge body of people (the Germanic peoples) appeared, and in roughly the same place, is it not odd that the world's "experts" say they have no clue as to the fate of the one or the origins of the other? Why has no *establishment* "scholar" or "authority" in the education or religious *monopolies **of recent times*** ever officially and publicly connected the disappearance of the Israelites with the emergence of the Germanic tribes?

(The enemies of the truth do not want us to know from where we came or who we are. Aleksandr Solzhenitsyn, the famous Russian author who spent years in Soviet labor camps, said, "To destroy a people, you must first sever their roots." Is it not sad that the vast majority of our people today are ignorant about their own identity? They have no concept of their own heritage, no knowledge of their own ancestors or the values that made those ancestors great.

What is so difficult about putting these simple facts together? What is so difficult about finding something *presumed to be* lost? Is it not interesting that a few hundred years ago, the Anglo-Saxon peoples were nearly obsessed with the fate and identity of the lost 10 Tribes of Israel? It was standard practice to look through the *Bible* for the origins of peoples and to attempt to identify peoples with either lost Israel or pagan peoples mentioned in the Bible. However, such things are never considered by *modern* scholars who godlessly reject the Bible, or by Christian scholars who have been led astray in their thinking. Yet only 75 years ago ***many*** scholars knew we were Israel.)

Looking for something that has been lost is pretty simple. For example, when one loses a book, one will, of course, look for the book *where it was last seen or where it was left*. However, if one is looking for a dog (*or any creature with the ability of locomotion*), one will *start* by looking where it was last seen or left—but one will *not* stop *there*! If the dog is not where it was last known to have been, a person with intelligence will follow its trail. If it is not in its home yard, the searcher will begin checking the neighbors' yards. Further, if the dog's collar alone was found, an intelligent person would deduce that the dog lost the collar and is now unidentified (<u>not</u> *unidentifiable*) and therefore, the dog might have a new home and might possibly even be called by a different name. An intelligent person would never assume that because the dog collar was found empty that the dog no longer exists.

Unfortunately, secular and religious minds of recent date have deduced that because the Israelites are not currently where they were last seen, and since these people are not in their original land, bearing their original name, they no longer exist—*despite the fact* that God's Word, and the very records of these people, indicate that they would <u>not</u> return to their *former land* but would travel to a new land to the north and west, *despite the fact* that records indicate that they were already being called by different names in fulfillment of prophecy. Well, the trail has not yet run cold. And it does not take a bloodhound to pick up the scent.

There exist specific proof, written records, astounding evidence, and unimpeachable artifacts (dating back even to 600 B.C.) which can be pieced together by a child. This is a significant piece of the puzzle which has been kept well hidden from most people. Those who have purposely kept this truth hidden are a part of the conspiracy of evil to keep your heritage and inheritance—*your very identity*—well hidden from you. If the facts truly prove this, do you not want to know it? Do you really want to know the truth about who you are?—or are you content to live within the demeaning myth created to keep you in ignorance while the culprit prances around with your title and glory?

This book presents only a *small fraction* of the evidence. But even this mere fraction of the evidence, which this author has gathered over the past 18 years (and *continues* to gather), is *overwhelming.*

(Most of the books mentioned herein are available from Sacred Truth Ministries (or possibly the distributor of this book), if you wish to verify the facts for yourself. For information concerning Sacred Truth Ministries' catalog of over 3,000 books (including several hundred rare titles, which STM reprints), send SASE.)

- Historical Witnesses -

Ancient Chronicle, Philological, and Archaeological Proofs of True Israel

Abundant evidence appears in secular history that the Assyrians, who conquered and deported the Israelites, called the Israelites by various names—mainly ***Iskuza***, in its various forms. Renowned historians have proven that *Iskuza* was also the Assyrian name for the ***Scythians***. These Scythians later peopled Europe as the Germanic tribes. The evidence reveals that the Assyrians called these people, "Iskuza," because these captive Israelites were then calling themselves "the people of Isaac." This, of course, was in fulfillment of prophecy: God declared that Israel would one day be called after the name of the *son of promise*—Isaac (Genesis 21:12; Hosea 11:1; Romans 9:7; Hebrews 11:18). Yet *nowhere* in the Bible do the people of Israel ever call themselves by this name. However, for the first and only time, just before the Israelites were taken captive, the prophet Amos, in a prophetic announcement, referred to Israel as the *House of Isaac* (Beth-Sak) (Amos 7:16). God declared that the Israelites in their punishment would be driven from the land of Israel and given a new home, and that their identity would be lost to history (Deuteronomy 32:26 [but not lost to God; Hosea 5:3]), *for a time*, because of their sin and since they would have a new name (Isaiah 62:2; 65:15; Hosea 2:17).

Israel, while in captivity and in close contact with many foreign peoples, came to be known by the various names her *captors* gave her and the names by which she would be called in her migrations. Isaac in the various languages became **Iskuza/Isguzai/Sakhi** (Assyrian), **Saka/Sakia** (Roman), **Sacae/Sakae/Saka/Sakka/Sakiya/Scythia/Scythian** (Persian, Median, and Susian), **Saksuna/Sacasene/Sakkas** (Indian), **Skuthes/Skuthae** (Greek), **Scolotoi** (Crimean), **Scolotes** (Scythian), **Skythes** (Welsh), **Sgiathanach** (Scots Gaelic). (The *g* is pronounced like a *k*.) Each of these has been translated into English by modern scholars as **Scythians, Saxons, Sacae, Scots,** etc. (See **Appendix A**.)

Madison Grant
(from bronze bust)

Madison Grant,[24] in The Passing of The Great Race[25] (1916), reveals the *Sacae/Saka* were *the long-headed, blonde peoples who carried the Aryan language into India* (pp. 155, 223-227).

Scripture prophesied that Israel would be scattered north of the river Euphrates (I Kings 14:15). This was fulfilled when Israel was taken captive to Assyria. As the Israelites left Assyria and passed through the Caucasus mountains by way of the Dariel Pass, they became known as "**Caucasians**"—the name by which the white race has ever since been classified. They then passed through the Kerch Straits into the Crimea of southern Russia.

(Note: Many Caucasian people today are afraid to use the word "white" when speaking of race. Let it be known that the mention of the historical description of racial types is *not* latent "white supremacy." These are just the facts. Should we be *ashamed* of who we are?—especially when our identity has been maliciously hidden from us—if that is who God created us to be? 50 to 100 years ago, this would not have been an issue. Then again, that time in history would not have found us drowning in pluralism, humanism, immorality, and godlessness—the hallmarks of today's society.

Please read this prayerfully. If God ordained that our heritage should be an important matter, is God wrong? Or is society wrong? Our forefathers acknowledged the importance of *our* heritage, and they were blessed; the shapers of modern *society* have taught to us reject the importance of our heritage, and we are cursed, being crowded out of, and made second-class citizens in our own country. Our heritage originates in the Scriptural record itself, where heritage was of *utmost* importance. Genealogies and pedigrees are given throughout the Bible for a purpose. It is not "hate" to maintain the purity of the heritage God gave us—the very heritage that He *commanded* us to preserve. It is honor and obedience. If sin has gone on for so many years, to the point that "everything has been turned upside down"—is this any excuse not to return to God's holy standard?)

The Israelites may also have been tagged with the name of Scythian because, in their captivity, the Israelites were forced by their captors to live in tents. In Hebrew, one of the words for tents is *succoth*.[26] The Israelites had lived in tents for so many years (especially in their wanderings in the Sinai desert, due to their sin) that God commanded them to celebrate a memorial festival every year: the *Feast of Succoth*.[27] This festival was to commemorate their ancestors' hardships and to remember God delivering them from their enemies upon their repentance. The Scuths (or more accurately "Scüths") became known as tent-dwellers and, like

[24] —Chairman, New York Zoological Society, Trustee American Museum of Natural History, Councillor American Geographical Society.

[25] First published by Charles Scribner's & Sons.

[26] #5523 (*sook-KOHTH*). In Hebrew, vowels were not written; thus sook-KOHTH would have been written something like "skkhth." The vowels were inserted by the speaker; depending upon his dialect. The vowels themselves, as well as where they were positioned, were subject to variance. Is it just a coincidence that the early Celtic Ogam Script found carved into stone walls throughout North America (as well as Europe), which date between the 6th and 8th centuries A.D., which translate into the ancient Irish language (Erse) is also written *without vowel points*? Is it also a coincidence that many of these early writings contained the Ten Commandments? For more information on the numerous Ogam carvings discovered, see America B.C., Bronze-Age America, Saga America, Barry Fell; In Plain Sight, Gloria Farley; Discovery of Ancient America, David Deal; Christians Before Columbus, Earl Jones; and even *Wonderful West Virginia* Magazine (March 1983).

[27] Coincidentally, the date of this festival/holiday (holy day) occurs around the time of Thanksgiving (which the Pilgrims instituted upon their arrival to the new land (America) to which God led them).

their Israel ancestors, lived in tents and were herders of cattle and sheep.

The name **Saxon** itself is derived from the ancient ***Saka-suni*** and means "son of Saks" or "Isaac's sons." F. Wallace Connon in his Documents of Destiny (1958) records that Dr. Holt Yates revealed,

> "The word *Saxon* comes from *sons of Isaac*," and he gives *Saac, Saak, Saach, Saax, Saach-en* and shows that in many Eastern languages *sons of* is often written *sunnia*, which would give *sons of Isaac* as *saac-sunnia* (p. 102).

(This can be compared to the Germanic languages with similar suffixes: like in Danish *Peterssen*, which means "son of Peters," in Swedish *Anderson*, "son of Anders," etc.)

Austen Henry Layard[28] was a British Assyriologist and archaeologist who collaborated with Sir Henry Creswicke Rawlinson (1810-1895), the foremost Assyriologist cuneiform expert. The Ninevah Marbles, discovered through the efforts of Layard, left a record of a people called *Esak ska*, who rebelled against their conquerors, the Assyrians, in 670 B.C.—*50 years after the Israelites themselves had been taken into captivity by the Assyrians.* There is little doubt that these Esak ska were Isaac's sons—the post-captivity Israelites themselves.

The Babylonians called the Scythians **Gimirra/Gimiri;**[29] the Romans called them **Kimmiri**; and the Greeks called them **Kimmerioi/Kimbroi**. All these names translate into English as **Cimmerian**, **Cimbri**, and **Cymry** (pronounced *Kumri*). The Assyrians and Babylonians also called the Israelites **Sak-Galutha** or **Bit-Khumri**. *Galutha* was the Babylonian word for "captive" (in Hebrew, *Geloth*). *Bit-Khumri* (the Assyrian counterpart of the Hebrew *Beth-Omri*) means "House of Omri." Omri was the famous Israelite king who founded the northern capital of Samaria. The Davis Dictionary of the Bible (1973) records:

> Omri made an impression on history outside of Israel. Not only did the Moabites remember his name; but after his death and the annihilation of his family the Assyrians for a time still attached his name, which they wrote *Humri*, to the reigning monarch of the land of Israel. (See heading "Omri".)

(Some translations render *Humri* as "Khumri." The *kh* indicates that the sound is guttural, similar to the *ch* in Scots "Loch" (lake) or in German "milch" (milk).)

The Rev. W. H. Poole, LL.D. records, in Anglo-Israel or The Saxon Race (1879), that the Septuagint (the Greek version of the Old Testament) clearly revealed the identity of the Israelites: "The Israelites were called *Kymri* soon after they were taken from their own land."

---

[28] Layard was born in Paris in 1817 of Huguenot ancestry, and died in 1894. He became a Member of Parliament in 1852; Undersecretary of foreign affairs from 1861-1866; Ambassador to Madrid in 1869 and Constantinople in 1887. See Discoveries in the Ruins of Nineveh and Babylon (1853).

[29] Gimirra/Gimiri means, "tribes." The Israelites and Germanic peoples were pretty much the only people who were known to have such a multitude of homogeneous subtribes. Strabo, the Greek geographer/historian (63 B.C. to A.D. 21) stated, "Most of the Scythians, beginning from the Caspian Sea, are called *Dahae Scythae* and those situated more towards the east *Massagatae* and *Sacae*; the rest have the common name of *Scythians, but each tribe has its own peculiar name.*"

Incidentally, God declared that His Israel people would be a *peculiar* people (**Titus 2:14**). This word *peculiar* in Greek means "beyond being usual;" that is, a people who stand out from all others. What family of people is more prominent and noticeable in their character and achievements, over all other peoples? This is no coincidence; and certainly not because of any greatness on our own, but solely because of God's predestination.

The Common Origins of The Celts, Cimmerians, Gaels, Goths, Saxons, Scythians, etc.

Evidence proves that the ancient **Cimmerians**, **Sacae**, **Scythians**, etc., were all of the same race as the **Angles**, **Celts**, **Danes**, **Gaels**, **Goths**, **Saxons**, etc. of more recent history, and were the self-same ***Gimiri, Israelites, Khumri***, and ***Saka-sunni***, etc. of Biblical times.

Strabo (c. 64 B.C.-A.D. 23), the Greek geographer and historian in his *Geographica*, recorded that the Sacae were *Scythians*, and that an area in Armenia, *Sakasina*, was named after them.

Pliny the Elder (A.D. 23-79), the Roman historian in his classic *Historia Naturalis*, said that "the ***Sakai*** were among the most distinguished people who lived in Scythia...they had been called ***Sacca-sani***" (Documents of Destiny, p. 102).

Cornelius Tacitus (A.D. 55?-117), the Roman historian, in his classic *Germania*, related:

> I concur in opinion with such as suppose the people of *Germany* never to have mingled by intermarriages with other nations, but to have remained a people *pure*, and *independent*, and resembling none but themselves. Hence, among such a mighty multitude of men, the same make and *form is found in all, eyes stern and blue, yellow hair*, huge bodies...abounding in *flocks and herds*...they rejoice...their only...*most desired riches*...to none else but the *Priests* is it allowed to *exercise correction, or to inflict bonds or stripes*. Nor when the Priests do this, is the same considered as a punishment, or arising from the orders of the general, but *from the immediate command of the Deity*, him whom they believe to *accompany them in war*.... Yet the *laws of matrimony are severely observed* there.... They therefore live in a state of *chastity* well secured; corrupted by *no seducing shows and public diversions, by no irritations from banqueting*.... Amongst a people so numerous, *adultery is extremely rare*.... In *social feasts* and *deeds of hospitality*, no nation on earth was ever more liberal and abounding. *To refuse admitting under your roof any man whatsoever* [of their people], *is held wicked and inhuman.* Every man receives every comer, and treats him with repasts as large as his ability can possibly furnish.... Their food is very simple; *wild fruit, fresh venison, or coagulated milk*.... To the practice of *usury and of increasing money by interest they are strangers*.... (Emphasis and brackets mine.)

(Clearly, these early Germanic peoples were the descendents of the Israelites. Their racial type and racial purity (Genesis 24:3-4, 37, 38; 27:46; 28:1; Lamentations 4:7), their righteous laws (Exodus 21; Leviticus 26; Deuteronomy 28), their diet (Genesis 1:30; 18:8; Exodus 3:8; Leviticus 11:2-3,26; Deuteronomy 14:2-6), their hospitality (Exodus 22:21; 23:9; Leviticus 19:34; I Timothy 5:10; Hebrews 13:2), their prohibition of usury (Exodus 22:25; Leviticus 25:36-37; Deuteronomy 23:19-20; Psalm 15:5; Ezekiel 18:13), their faithfulness in marriage (Exodus 20:14; Leviticus 20:10; Deuteronomy 5:18; Matthew 5:27-28; James 2:10-11), their agrarian lifestyle, the priesthood governing the community as from the mouth of God Himself, rejection of the ways of heathen peoples around them, choosing instead a simple and righteous lifestyle—all these point to not only an *eastern* origin, but an *Israelite* origin.)

Ptolemy (A.D. 100-170) (**Claudius Ptolemaeus**), the Greek astronomer/mathematician/geographer (born in Ptolemais, Egypt) in his *Geographia*, recorded that the ***Saxons*** were a ***Scythian*** people descended from the ***Sakae***, who came from *Media*.

Herodotus of Halicarnassus (485-425 B.C.), the Greek historian known as "the father of history," recorded in his *Histories*:

> The ***Sacae***, or ***Scyths***...bore the bow of their country and the dagger: beside which they carried the *battle-axe*, or *sagaris*. They were in truth ***Amyrgian Scythians***, but the Persians called them ***Sacae***, since that is the name they give to all ***Scythians***. The ***Bactrians*** and ***Sacae*** had for leader Hystaspes, the son of *Darius* and Atossa, the daughter of *Cyrus*. (Emphasis mine.)

(It should be remembered that the Israelites, primarily of the Southern Kingdom, after being conquered by the Babylonians, came under the rule of the Medo-Persians, who overthrew the Babylonian Empire. Darius and Cyrus were the leaders at this time, and Darius was so friendly to the Israelites that he allowed those Israelites who wanted to return to their homeland (roughly 70 years after their deportation) to return home with his blessing. Only 40,000 out of several million Israelites returned home. The remainder stayed in Persia or migrated with their brethren who left Assyrian captivity to the north.)

Flaccus Albinus (also known as Alcuin or Ealhwine) (735-804), the English scholar and ecclesiastic, leader of the Carolignian Renaissance in France (at the request of Charlemagne), and the abbot of St. Martins in Tours, France wrote, "The ***Saxons***...descended from the ancient ***Sacae*** in *Asia*...in process of time they came to be called *Saxons*" (*Patrologica Latina*, Migne). (Emphasis mine.)

Abraham Ortels (Ortelius) (1527-1598), the Flemish-born, German cartographer and geographer (who produced the first modern atlas) and court geographer for Philip II of Spain, recorded "The ***ten tribes of Israel*** took the name ***Gauthei***, which means the people of God. The name Gauthei was later changed to ***Goth***." (Emphasis mine.)

Professor William Camden (1551-1623), the English antiquarian, historian, prebendary of Salisbury Cathedral, headmaster of Westminster, Clarencieux king-at-arms, and founding professor of history at Oxford, stated,

> ...the ***Saxons*** are descended from the ***Saci***, the most powerful people of Asia; that they are so called, as if one should say ***Sacasones***, that is "the Sons of Sacae;" ...out of ***Scythia*** or ***Sarmatae Asiatica***, they poured little by little into Europe, along with the ***Getes***, the ***Swevi***, and the ***Daci***.... And indeed, the opinions of those men who fetch the ***Saxons*** out of *Asia*, where mankind had its rise and growth, does not want some color of reason (The Seed of Isaac, J. D. Granger, p. 168; probably from Camden's Britannica 1586). (Emphasis mine.)

Humphrey Prideaux (1648-1724), the English clergymen and orientalist, canon and dean of Norwich, archdeacon of Suffolk, records, "The ***Cimbrians*** were driven from their country by a people called ***Asaec***, who came from between the Euxine [Black] and Caspian Seas, and from whom came those ***Angli***, who, with the ***Saxons***, afterward took possession of England." (Emphasis and brackets mine.)

The eminent London attorney and historian **Sharon Turner F.A.S., R.A.S.L.** (1768-1847), stated,

> The ***Anglo-Saxons, Lowland Scotch, Normans, Danes, Norwegians, Swedes, Germans, Dutch, Belgians, Lombards,*** and ***Franks*** have all sprung from that great fountain of the human race...distinguished by the terms ***Scythian***, **German,** or ***Gothic***.... The...Scythians crossed the Araxes [Aras River], passed out of Asia, and...suddenly appeared in Europe, in the seventh century before the Christian era (<u>History of the Anglo-Saxons</u>, 184, 6th ed.; Phila., Vol. 1, pp. 79, 81). (Emphasis and brackets mine.)

Sir Francis Palgrave (1788-1861), the English historian, stated, "***Brit[ons]... Anglo-Saxons, Danes***, and ***Normans*** *were all relations*, however hostile...*all kinsmen*, shedding kindred blood" (<u>English Commonwealth</u>). (Emphasis and brackets mine.) Palgrave also stated, "The fundamental rule of science, whether in history or elsewhere, is <u>not</u> *what has been believed*, but what is **true**." (Emphasis mine.)

Professor Thomas H. Huxley (1825-1895), the noted English scientist, surgeon, and educator stated in <u>Racial Origins</u>,

> The invasions of the ***Saxons***, the ***Goths***, the ***Danes***, the ***Normans*** changed the language of Britain, *but added no new physical element*.... ***Celts*** and ***Saxons***...*are all one*. I never lose an opportunity of rooting up the false idea that the Celts and Saxons are different races.... I miss no opportunity of uprooting the notion that the people who form the British nation are descended from various [racially dissimilar] nations. All the detachments who flowed into Britain are *branches of the self-same stock*. (Emphasis and brackets mine.)

Dr. George Moore, M.D., in his <u>The Lost Tribes and The Saxons of East and of The West</u> (1861), records,

> The ***Sacae*** and the ***Getae*** [Geats, Jutes] who formerly invaded *India* sprang from the same source as the ***Saxons*** and ***Goths*** of the ***West*** [Visogoths], and were directly connected with the ***Israelites***... (p. 95). (Emphasis and brackets mine.)

Sir Arthur Keith (MacPherson) (1866-1955), the renowned British anatomist/anthropologist (conservator, and professor at the Royal College of Surgeons, professor of physiology, and secretary and treasurer at the Royal Institution in London, rector of Aberdeen University, who held doctorates in medicine, science, and law), himself attested to the common origin of the Anglo-Saxon peoples. Reverend John Heslip records on page 16 of <u>Who and Where Are The Lost Ten Tribes?</u>, that Keith:

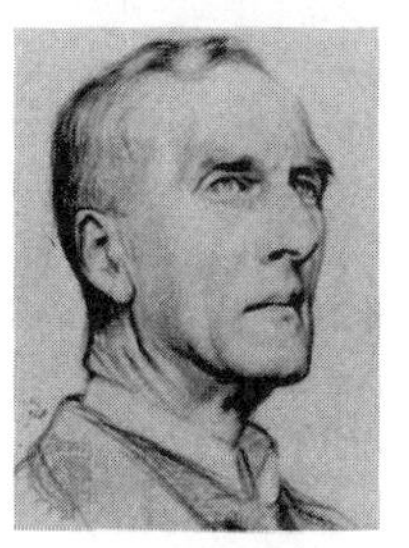

> ...tells us that he had to revise his opinion of the origin of the old ***British people***. *Facts* obliged him to revise his opinion. He tells us that he is satisfied that "the early ***British***, the early ***Scots***, the early ***Ulstermen***, the ***Welsh***, the ***Angles***, ***Saxons***, ***Jutes***, ***Danes***, and ***Normans*** are *all part of one*

common stock which have come from the *east*." (Emphasis mine.)

Professor Max Müller (1823-1900), the eminent German philologist and orientalist, and the historian **John Richard Green** (1837-1883), also independently give us the same testimony.

Dr. Sir Thomas Nicholas (1820-1879), wrote,

> ...modern historians unequivocally favor the opinion that under the name of ***Keltai, Galatai, Gauls, Gaels, Gwyddils, Celts, Cimmerii, Cimbri, Cymry, Brythons, Lloegrians, Scots***, and ***Picts*** *only one race under different tribe or clan divisions*, political organizations, and periods of existence is spoken of; hence, one people (Pedigree of the English People, 1868). (Emphasis mine.)

Professor Dr. Joseph Ehret (1896-?), the prominent Swiss scholar, respected author, and humanitarian, stated ever so eloquently,

> Less blood would flow, if the European inhabitants only knew how closely they are related as brother and sister.... With few exceptions, we constitute a close community of peoples, a true family encompassing the majority of national cultures, stretching from the ***Islandics*** in the north to the ***Italians*** in the south, and from the ***Old-Indians*** in the east to the ***Portuguese*** in the west.

[That is, the ***old world Saka*** who developed the Hindu Empire in India, and the ***original Italians*** and ***Portuguese*** of antiquity.]

> This ***Indo-European*** family, also called by some the ***Indo-Germanic***, encompasses a rich history.... This is especially true when one disregards the more recent peoples and works back toward the oldest who have retained their original primordiality, such as...the ***Greeks*** *of antiquity* or the ***Lithuanians*** and their *stock brothers*, the ***Latvians***. In this case one obtains highly valuable knowledge from which one can draw conclusions about our fore-fathers, about the primordial people from which we stem (Lithuania: The European Adam (1983); pp. 9, 10). (Emphasis and brackets mine.)

Funk and Wagnals Encyclopedia defines *Goths* as

> An ancient Teutonic people who, according to the earliest historical accounts, inhabited a region on the Baltic Sea, between the Elbe and the Vistula rivers.... Tacitus called them "Teutones Gothones" and stated that they possessed great independence of spirit.

Funk and Wagnals... defines *Teutonic stock* as

> ...subdivided into the Scandinavian and the Germanic, the latter including ***Germany*** and ***Switzerland***, and the ***Dutch***, the ***Flemins*** of Belgium, and the descendents of the ***Angles, Saxons***, and ***Jutes***.

Professor George Rawlinson (1812-1902) (brother to Sir Henry Rawlinson), canon of Canterbury and professor of Ancient History at Oxford University, said the ethnic name *Gimiri* in the Babylonian inscription on the *Behistun Rock* (inscribed as *Sakka* in the Old Persian and Elamite portions) was equivalent to the Greek *Cimmeri*, the Danish *Cymbri*, and the Welsh *Khumri* (The Budding Fig Tree (1987), Pat Brooks; p. 29).

It should be clear, even from this brief, oversimplified smattering of quotations from eminent historians, scientists, and scholars, that the majority of European-descended peoples are brothers and sisters and are, in fact, the Israelites of the Bible. Still, we have not even scratched the surface of the evidence. Let us continue.

The Mysterious Origin of The Scythians

The Scythians were first mentioned in history around 681 to 699 B.C. in Assyrian tablets (now in the British Museum) found in the capital of Babylon, Ninevah.[30] Other records in Ninevah and Babylon also prove that the Israelites were the *Sacae* and the *Scythians*.[31] Along an old caravan road that runs between Ninevah and Ecbatana (the ancient capital of Media) is a 1,700-foot high limestone mountain that rises out of the plains near the village of *Behistun* (or, more correctly, "Bīsutūn"—according to Johannes Friedrich in Extinct Languages (1957), p. 58.) in western Iran. About 300 feet from the base of this mountain is a rock face that contains a monument 100 feet wide and 150 feet high that was carved by the decree of Darius the Great[32] (c. 515 B.C.). The record was carved in three different languages, which used cuneiform or wedge-shaped characters: Babylonian (Accadian), Elamite (Susian), and Old Persian. This monument, now referred to as the *Behistun Rock*, was discovered by an Italian traveller in 1621 (about the time the Pilgrims landed on Plymouth Rock). A German scientist, Carsten Niebuhr, published the first accurate reproductions of the inscriptions in 1777 (about the time the U.S. Colonies declared their independence).

Rawlinson

Layard

Although many respected scholars worked on the deciphering of these inscriptions, Sir Henry Creswicke Rawlinson (1810-1895),[33] a young English officer in the Persian army, working independently, is credited with the discovery that held the key to understanding these mysterious languages: *The inscriptions in the three languages were identical.* Rawlinson painstakingly copied the entire inscriptions himself and then undertook the deciphering and translation of these on his own. When Austen Henry Layard (1817-1894) met Rawlinson in December of 1845, Rawlinson had already been working on the project for 10 years. (Layard began his adventures in archaeology on the banks of the Tigris River when he was 23 years old. His fame would eventually distinguish him in several fields.) It seems that both Layard and Rawlinson were led—*driven*—by Divine Providence. Layard discovered the *Nimrod Ivories* shortly before meeting Rawlinson, after having been on the dig site in Nimrud for *only three days*. Rawlinson revealed the amazing discovery that column #5 (a half-column supplement) recorded a "revolt of *Saku'ka* the chief of the *Sacae*, who dwelt upon the Tigris." Rawlinson discovered through the simple act of translation (once

[30] How ironic that Ninevah was spared by God (Book of Jonah) to later record the name of His chosen, Israel, as a future testimony to reveal the identity of His people after the decreed time of their national punishment had expired, leaving them in blindness concerning their racial and historical identity.

[31] For more details see Missing Links Discovered in Assyrian Tablets, by Capt.

[32] Darius I (c. 558-486 B.C.), whose surname was Hystaspis, King of Persia.

[33] Rawlinson entered the military with the East India Company in 1827; helped reorganize the Persian Army; was appointed Political Agent at Kandahar and Consul to Baghdad; became Director of the East India Company and later British Minister in Persia, a Member of Parliament, and member of the Council of India. He authored several scholarly works. He is considered the British father of Assyriology.

he realized the records were identical inscriptions recorded in three different languages) that the ***Gimirra*** *Umurgah* of the Babylonian text corresponded with the ***Saka*** *Humuvaska* of the Old Persian text. J. Bernard Nicklin, in Signposts of History (1956) records that Rawlinson himself stated:

> We have reasonable grounds for regarding the ***Gimiri***, or the ***Cimmerians***, who first appeared in the confines of Assyria and Media in the seventh century B.C., and the **Sacae** of the Behistun Rock nearly two centuries later, *as identical with **Israel*** (p. 178). (Emphasis mine.)

The decipherment of the *Behistun Rock* unlocked the code for understanding the Assyrian languages and did for *Assyriology* what the decipherment of the *Rosetta Stone* did for *Egyptology*—namely, the understanding of ancient Egyptian hieroglyphics.

The Rosetta Stone, a black basalt slab (now in the British Museum), was found by a French officer in Napoleon's engineering corps of French troops in 1799 near the town of Rosetta in Lower Egypt. Unknown at the time of discovery, the stone (inscribed c.196 B.C.), contained a *decree praising the Egyptian king Ptolemy V.* The inscription appeared in 3 different ancient scripts: 1) Egyptian hieroglyphic, 2) Egyptian demotic, and 3) Greek, the first two being languages unknown at the time. Scholars quickly deciphered the Egyptian hieroglyphic and demotic versions by simply comparing them with the Greek version. The deciphering was chiefly the work of the brilliant young French Egyptologist Jean François Champollion (1790-1832) and the eminent British physicist and Egyptologist Dr. Thomas Young (1773-1829).

Champollion

The most striking feature of the *Behistun Rock* monument is the picture of King Darius decked in royal clothes, with 10 captives before him (9 standing, one lying on his back on the ground under Darius' conquering foot), bound at their necks by a rope. The captives of all conquered nations are depicted in 20 panels (5 main panels). Most interesting is the panel marked #10, which describes the 10th captive (who is wearing a Hebrew form of headdress) as Sarocus the "***Sacan***." Most probably these 10 captives represent the 10 Tribes of Israel Darius took captive. The inscriptions also list 23 different peoples whom Darius conquered. One of these peoples is called "***Sakkas***." In both the Persian and the Elamite (Susian) inscriptions, the original word is "***Sakka***." In the Babylonian (Accadian) inscription, however, they are called "***Gimiri***." As a result of this Persian record, as well as other Persian, Babylonian, and Assyrian records, it is beyond dispute that the ***Iskuza***, the ***Sakka***, the ***Scythians***, the ***Cimmerians***, and the ***Gimiri*** were all the selfsame or different tribes of the same peoples—and they were *all **Israelites***.

(Much of the foregoing information on the Behistun Rock was drawn from Missing Links Discovered in Assyrian Tablets (1985) by E. Raymond Capt, M.A., A.I.A., F.S.I., SCOT. (pp. 137-140).)

The Behistun Rock

Sir Henry Rawlinson depicted on ladder copying the transcriptions
(courtesy Missing Links Discovered in Assyrian Tablets, Capt., p. 138)

The Behistun Rock inscription records that the stone memorial had been made to record Darius's quashing of the rebellion of certain rebel chiefs and their subjection by him. It is important to remember that before the 10 Tribes of Israel were conquered and deported by Assyria, *they had been subjugated in their own land* and forced to pay tribute. When they later rebelled against this tribute, they were invaded, conquered, and deported by Assyria. There is no doubt that the same occurred to the two southern Tribes of Judah, as Nebuchadnezzar of Babylon subjugated them. It is also most probable that at times certain of the 12 Tribes rebelled, even while they were in captivity.

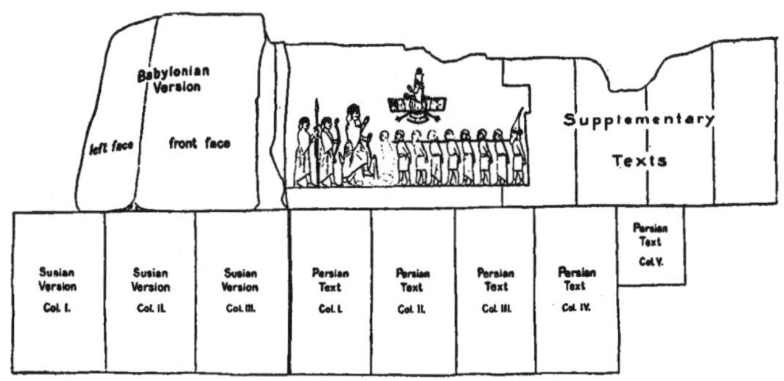

The Mapped-Out Carvings of The Behistun Rock
(courtesy Missing Links Discovered in Assyrian Tablets, Capt., p. 138)

At the time Darius made this monument, the Israelites had been located among the Medes, having been deposited there as captives. This is very significant. It marks the *beginning of the fulfillment of prophecy.* Most likely, the Assyrians called the Israelites *Iskuza,* since the Israelites by now were probably calling themselves "Isaaca," perhaps to remind themselves that they were indeed the *Children of Promise* and that God would not forsake them in their captivity. As generations passed, however, they forgot *why* they had called themselves by this name, and they soon even forgot that *they were Israelites,* although God's Spirit was still upon them. It is very easy for grandchildren and great-grandchildren to forget who their ancestors were, and what those ancestors did, when parents stop teaching their children about their heritage.

(Do you know the names of your great-grandparents? Your great-great-grandparents? Do you know where they lived? Where they came from? What they did? How they lived? What they stood for?)

It should also be noted that when the Assyrians and Babylonians conquered a nation, they deported the inhabitants, broke the families apart; they even gave each of the captives a new name, forced them to speak their captors' tongue and worship their captors' gods. They also forbade them to teach their own history.

(The Soviets practiced much this same strategy in eastern Europe: Lithuanians were forbidden to speak Lithuanian and were forced to speak Russian (which they spoke poorly on purpose). They were forbidden to fly the Lithuanian flag or teach their history. Tradition had to be practiced *underground.* Most of the churches and libraries in eastern Europe were emptied, the books burned, and the buildings used for Soviet purposes.)

This military strategy can be observed while reading the book of Daniel. It then is easy to understand how the Israelites could so quickly forget who they were and how the bits and pieces of the "word of mouth" history and tradition, which they were able to communicate to their succeeding generations, could become corrupted into *mythology* (Greek, Roman, Norse, Druidic, and Eddic).

J. Bernard Nicklin, in his Signposts of History, records,

> On the *Black Obelisk of Shalmaneser*, in the British Museum, *Israel, the Ten Tribes*, are referred to as ***Khumri***. But here in the Babylonian text of the Behistun Rock, a certain rebel is described as the chief of ***Ghimri***, the equivalent of *Khumri.* And the corresponding Persian text on this Rock, *Ghimri* is translated ***Sacae***![34] (p. 178). (Emphasis mine.)

The *Nimrud Obelisk* (now housed in the British Museum) is an ancient Assyrian record that was made 100 years before Israel was taken captive (c. 800 B.C.). The *Covenant Report*[35] (No. 5, 1991) reveals,

> The first archaeological evidence to establish a chronological link in the contacts between Assyria and Israel are

Black Obelisk

[34] For even greater proof on these various names, see The Post-Captivity Names of Israel (1936), by William Pascoe Goard, L.L.D., F.R.G.S., F.R.E.S.

[35] British-Israel World Federation 242 Dominion Rd., Mt. Eden, Auckland, 3 New Zealand.

found on inscriptions on...a limestone stele found at Nimrud known as the Black Obelisk. The stone was inscribed with the records of Shalmaneser III and an illustration of the Israelite king Jehu bringing tribute to the Assyrian king. An inscription above the illustration says, "This is Iaua (Jehu), the son of Khumri (Omri)."

(Brooks records it in her The Budding Fig Tree, "The tribute of Yahua Abil Khumri" or "the tribute of Jehu son of *Khumri*" (p. 28).)

The *Covenant Report* also relates that

Omri in Hebrew begins with the consonant "Agin," formally called "Gayin," which was pronounced [in accordance with the old system] with a guttural *h*, that is *gh* or *kh*. The Israelites would naturally have pronounced ***Omri*** as "***Ghomri***," which became "***Khumri***" in Assyrian (p. 7). (Emphasis and brackets mine.)

(Brooks records in her Budding Fig Tree, (p.28) that this information was the work of the scholar Dr. T. J. Pinches.)

The *Covenant Report* also informs us that cuneiform records on Assyrian clay tablets found in Ninevah and published in The Royal Correspondence of the Assyrian Empire (1930) by Leroy Waterman constitute even more conclusive proof. In tablets dating back to c. 707 B.C., the ***Khumri*** are referred to as ***Gamera*** (***Ghomri***), which is a corruption of ***Gamir***, the inversion of the final syllable being common in Assyrian. Further, in tablets from c. 679 B.C. they are referred to as ***Gimira***. The Greek records refer to the ***Gimira*** as ***Kimmeroii***, which is translated into English as ***Cimmerians***.

(You are reminded again to consult **Appendix A** if there is still any confusion as to the legitimacy of the variations in spelling.)

Proof From More Modern Times

In England around the year 1800,[36] people began to raise questions: "Who are the Anglo-Saxons?" "From where did they come?" "Who were their ancestors?" A distinguished London attorney, Sharon Turner, F.A.S., R.A.S.L., stepped forward to answer these questions. In time, his several volumes of unequalled research, not only answered these questions, but established Turner as the foremost authority on the history of the Anglo-Saxons. To this day, his books remain the last word on the subject. In his work containing nearly 1,200 incredibly researched pages (published in numerous editions containing different numbers of volumes and pages) titled The History of the Anglo-Saxons (written between 1799-1805), Turner revealed that the Anglo-Saxons descended from the *Scythians*, who came to Europe from *the cities of the Medes on the Gozan River*.

(This was the ***exact*** spot where Israel had been placed upon being conquered and deported by Shalmaneser V of Assyria in 720 B.C. (II Kings 18:11) and the exact spot where the Israelites came to be called ***Sacae*** and ***Skuthe***.)

Turner quotes from *The Vetus Chronicon Holsatiœ* which says "The ***Danes*** and ***Jutes*** are *Jews* [sic, Israelites] of the Tribe of *Dan*" (The History of the Anglo-Saxons, Vol. 1. p. 109, fn. "g"). (Emphasis and brackets mine.) Turner also shows the various spellings

[36] —around the exact dates prophesied which would signal the ending of the period of Israel's national punishment. (2,520 years from the date each tribe was taken captive, Daniel 7:25, 12:7.)

of *Jute* as: Geatum, Giotæ, Jutæ, Gutæ, Geatani, Jotuni, Jetæ, Juitæ, and Vitæ.

(Turner records that *The Ancient Chronicles of Holsatia* (*Vetus Chronicon Holsatiœ*) was the record of the peoples (Holtzati) of the ancient region of Holsatia in Old Saxony (Eald Saexen). The name of the region came from the Old Saxon *Holt*, "a wood;" and *saeten*, "to be seated." The region was unique in that it enjoyed firm plains and forests situated a little higher than the other regions of the western and southern coastlines of Old Saxony, which were scattered with quagmires (pp. 90, 91).)

How interesting. It does not take a genius to figure out the simple fact that since all the European peoples are merely different branches of the same family of people, since the ***Danes*** and ***Jutes*** are Israelites, then *so must also **all the other European tribes be Israelites***.

Diodorus Siculus (died after 21 B.C.), a Sicilian historian who wrote his 40 volume *The Library of History* in Greek, noted,

> The Scythians anciently enjoyed but a small tract of ground, but...[through their valour] growing stronger by degrees, they enlarged their dominion far and near, and attained at last to a vast and glorious empire...seated themselves near the River Araxes...prospered more and more, and had kings that were very famous; from whom the ***Sacans*** and ***Massagetae***[37] and the ***Arimaspians*** and many others called by other names derive their origin. Amongst others, there were two remarkable colonies that were drawn out of the conquered nations by those kings; the one they brought out of *Assyria* and settled in the country lying between Paphlagonia and Pontus [in southern Russia around Black Sea], the other out of *Media*, which they placed near the River Tanais [Don] which people are called the ***Sauromatians*** [probably a Lithuanian tribe]. (Emphasis and brackets mine.)

Diodorus also referred to them as "despicable in their mean origin," which is evidence that they were once an enslaved people. F. C. Danvers, K.C.C., F.R.S.S., in his Israel Redivivus (*Israel Second-hand*) (1905), indicates that Diodorus also identified two colonies among the ***Scythians*** who were ***Israelites*** of the Babylonian captivity (p. 97).

Also, map 8 in Aids to the Student of the Holy Bible (1880), which was written by many well-known Bible authorities[38] of the day, shows that the settlement of the Israelite exiles of the second captivity was located in Media, in the very spot where the ***Umman-Manda***[39] revolted in the days of Esarhaddon. At this time the Israelites had been here in captivity for about 40 years.

(How *ironic* that the Scythians, who have all the characteristics of the Israelites, proceeded forth out of the very two places to which Israel was deported in her captivity—and at the exact same time. For those unfamiliar with ancient and biblical history, soon after taking Israel captive, the Babylonian Empire fell to the Medo-Persian Empire.)

William Pascoe Goard, LL.D., F.R.G.S, F.R.E.S., in The Post-Captivity Names

---

[37] The Massagetae were the greater Getae; the Thyssagetae, the lesser Getae. These soon became the Goths: The Ostrogoths (east), and the Visigoths (west).

[38] —including the eminent Professor (Rev.) A. H. Sayce, Professor of Assyriology at Oxford University, who believed the Anglo-Saxon peoples were Israel.

[39] Brigadier-General W. H. Fasken, C.B., in Cimmerians and Scythians, proves that the Umman-Manda, Gimmirra, Saka, Kimmerioi, Scythians, were all identical with the Hebrews.

of Israel (1934), quotes Professor Charles Rollin from Ancient History,[40]

Charles Rollin

> According to...[Justin], the ***Scythians*** lived in great innocence and simplicity...and...were...unacquainted with vice. They did not make any division of their lands among themselves.... Horace, in one of his odes, tells us...**they had no houses nor settled habitation**; but **wandered continually with their cattle and their flocks** from country to country...and made **milk and honey** their principle diet....This contempt of all the conveniences of life, says Justin, was attended with such an **honesty, and uprightness of manners** as hindered them from ever coveting their neighbors' goods (pp. 57-58). (Emphasis mine.)

In his well-researched book, Dan: The Pioneer of Israel (1879), Colonel J. C. Gawler (Keeper of the Crown Jewels in the Tower of London) records other ancient testimonies concerning the Scythians. Gawler writes,

> Strabo likewise quotes several authors who speak of the **excellent laws and habits** of the ***Sakai***, a tribe of ***Scythians*** who are called "***a righteous race***....**The laws, customs, and manners** of the ***Scythians***," says Epiphanius, "**were received by the other nations as the standards of policy, civility, and polite learning**." ...For their [***Scythians***] rapid growth and expansion, **their excellent laws**, their learning, and **abhorrence of swine**, see Diodorus, Herodotus, Strabo, Aeschylus, Epiphanius, &c.... Ephorus quotes Choerilus, who calls the Sakai of Asia "a colony of nomads, **a righteous race**." Herodotus also records that the Scythians "**studiously avoid the use of foreign customs**"[41] (pp. 24, 25). (Emphasis and brackets mine.)

Colonel Gawler continues,

> ...the "*Dacae* [who were also] called ***Polistoe***," who were there in Josephus' time, and whose strict manners of life he compares to the sect of the Essenes among the Jews [sic, Judeans] (Antiq. xviii. i. 5): "And I do verily believe are the same with those which Strabo calleth ***Plistoe*** and were the stock of the "***Abii***" (a ***Scythian*** tribe whom Arrian calls "**the justest people in the world**")... (Ortellius Thesaurus, *Dacia et Moesia* (p. 26). (Emphasis and brackets mine.)

Gawler also relates that the term *Daci* in Latin is *Dacae* in Greek, and following the rules of conversion into Hebrew, the "D" may be corrupted into "Tz" or "S," resulting in *Tsaki* or *Sakai* (p. 26).

W. E. Filmer, in Our Scythian Ancestors, records, "Herodotus tells us that the **Scythians 'never use pigs for sacrifice,' and will not even breed them anywhere in the country**" (*Herodotus*, Bk. IV, para. 63).

Filmer also relates that Herodotus reported that though *some individual* Scythians had a weakness for the pagan customs of other peoples, it was frowned upon by the Scythians at large—and bore severe penalties. He relates one specific incident: A man by the name of Anacharsis, while travelling in Greece, saw some

[40] —(written between 1730-1738) taken from Book VI, Chapter I, Section III; (pp. 18-19 in the 1828, New York edition). Charles Rollin (1661-1741) was a distinguished French historian, and the Principal of the University of Paris in 1694, Professor of Eloquence, and Member of the Royal Academy of Inscriptions and Belles Lettres.

[41] —even those of kindred nations, especially the Greeks; *The Histories of Herodotus of Halicarnassus* (written c. 450 B.C.), Book IV, paragraph 76.

people worshipping and sacrificing to one of their mother gods. When he got home, he himself offered sacrifices to this goddess, for which the Scythians punished him by death. Herodotus records, "and now, if anyone asks about Anacharsis, the Scythians say they do not know him" (IV, p. 76). Herodotus records that the same death penalty was enforced upon Scyles, when his people found out that he was worshipping the Greek god Bacchic Dionysus—*even though he was their **king*** (IV, pp. 78-80). Herodotus recorded that the Scythians also put *false prophets* to death (IV, pp. 68-69).

These historical records perfectly describe the Israelites. After coming out of Egypt they ***wandered as nomads without any permanent land divisions***; they were ***herders of cattle and flocks***; they entered the Promised Land—a land of ***milk and honey***. (The Israelites traditionally ate honey (Genesis 43:11; II Chronicles 31:5; Isaiah 7:15; Ezekiel 13:16; Matthew 3:4; Luke 24:42) and were even *instructed by God* to eat honey (Deuteronomy 32:30; Proverbs 24:13; 25:16).) Although the Israelites were not sinless, even in their punishment, ***they did stand out recognizably from other peoples in their overall morality***. They were given the Law of God under Moses, which ***forbade coveting their neighbor's possessions and which forbade other vices***. Further, God declared that ***other peoples would learn from Israel*** and that Israel ***would teach the nations*** (Micah 4:2); and here we see that the Scythians' manner of life and morality became the standard; ***so it was also with ancient Israel***. It is recorded in the Bible that when other nations refused to accept Israel's moral ways, these other peoples attempted to seduce Israel into immorality. (See the numerous accounts in the books of Exodus and Numbers.) Further, in their punishment, although at times they were rebellious, it seems likely the Israelites were *more careful to follow God's Law* and "*not learn the ways of the heathen*," as they wanted the punishment lifted, not increased. Finally, we see that the Scythian who worshipped a pagan god was put to death. *NonIsrael* people pretty much tolerated the worshipping of foreign gods, *providing that the national god was also recognized*; further, many nations were continually "trying" *new gods*, since their current gods could not provide for their needs. However, the ***Israelites were commanded by God to put to death any of their own people who worshipped any god other than the true God YaHWeH*** (Exodus 20:4,5; Deuteronomy 13:4-10; II Chronicles 15:12-13). Further, ***those who turned from the truth were either put to death or cut off*** (executed or excommunicated) and ***their names were forgotten and rendered a curse*** (Numbers 5:27; Jeremiah 22:30; Isaiah 65:15; Matthew 18:17; I Corinthians 16:22; Galatians 1:9). Even ***Israel's kings, princes, and priests were held to the same standard***. Although the people often failed to carry out the sentences on their leaders who sinned, God frequently administered the punishment Himself. God further commanded Israel to ***put to death any of their prophets whose prophesies did not come to pass*** or any prophets who would ***try to lead the people to serve other gods*** (Deuteronomy 13:1-5; 18:20-22).

(Liberal minds might think that such capital punishments are barbaric. If the penalty of the crime is not great enough to deter the criminal, however, all of society is in danger and *society itself* becomes barbaric.)

It should also be noted that in the above descriptions, the Scythians are described as **extremely peaceful and yet fierce in battle**. ***This describes Israel's character***, as ordained by God. When Israel met another people (other than

God's worst enemies) in war, they were to first offer peace; if peace was rejected they were *to utterly destroy them* (Deuteronomy 20:10-12). This was the deeper meaning of the *olive branch* and *arrow*, two symbols of Israel.

Concerning the beginnings of the Scythian nation, Frederick Haberman, in his classic, Tracing Our Ancestors (1934), states,

> The ***Scythians*** told Herodotus [Bk. IV, par. 5, pp. 93-94]...their nation had been in existence for a thousand years previous to the invasion of Darius. If we date, therefore, a thousand years back from the time of Darius (515 B.C.), we arrive at 1485 B.C., the date of the Exodus [from Egypt], when ***Israel*** was founded.... These lived on the Gerrhus, a tributary of the present *Dneister*. Herodotus includes among the ***Scythian*** tribes the ***Getae***, who lived on the shores of the *Danube*, i.e., the *Arsareth* of Esdras.... Those ***Getae***, as Herodotus tells us, believed in their immortality, going after their death to *Zal**moxis***, which means...the "God of Moses." So also was the country where the ***Getae*** lived named ***Moesia***, for in it lived the "people of Moses" (p. 129). (Emphasis and brackets mine.)

Herodotus also records that the ***Greeks*** living on the *Hellespont* (*Dardanelle Straits*) and the Pontus (shore of the Black Sea in Cappadocia) said that *Sal**moxis*** was **a man** who was once **a slave** living in Samos (Greek Island in the Aegean off the western coast of Turkey), who *after gaining his freedom made a great fortune* and *went back to his own country*. The Thracians at that day were primitive and simpleminded, yet Salmoxis was ***well-educated*** and ***refined***. He built a hall where he assembled his chief men and taught them that neither they (who were in good standing at his table) nor their descendents would ever die, but would pass on to a place where they would live forever and have all manner of good things (IV, p. 95).

This clearly is the story of Moses: Moses was well reared in Egypt and raised with one of the finest educations of the day. He became a slave, however, when he refused to live in luxury while his fellow-Israelites in Egypt were being abused as slaves. When Moses saw a fellow Israelite being beaten, he killed the assailant and had to flee Egypt (Exodus 2:14-15). The Book of Jasher confirms this (LXXI, 8-11; LXXII, 22). The Book of Jasher also indicates that Moses, after leaving Egypt, went to Cush (Ethiopia[42]) and became king there. From thence, Moses went to Midian, as Scripture records. When God ***raised up Moses*** to lead the children of Israel out of Egypt, the Israelites were told to borrow everything they could from their Egyptian neighbors. Thus, upon leaving ***they came out a wealthy people*** (Exodus 11:2; 12:35-36). Upon leaving Egypt, they set out ***for their former home***. Moses, at YaHWeH's command, ***built a Tabernacle around which the people gathered***. Scripture clearly teaches that the Israelites were instructed ***that if they followed God's ways, "they and their seed after them" would live forever in God's Presence, in the New Kingdom***.

Now, you might wonder what connection *Egypt* has with our discussion of the *Grecian* legend. As we shall see, all evidence of secular history and tradition records that the nation of Greece itself was founded by "a group of slaves" who left Egypt and who were considered a *holy people*. The main portion of these

[42] —which, as Egypt, was originally a white nation. This would seem to explain why Ethiopia has some symbol fragments of Israel origin.

slaves *returned to their original home in Canaan.* Legends and obscure histories, passed down by word of mouth, are easily corrupted, with details being oversimplified or left out; and they are a bit imprecise in certain details, although the overall story draws a clear parallel.

(It should be understood that any nation will record the history of its neighbors (or enemies) in a much different light than those neighboring nations would record their *own* histories. Even in the drawing of maps, most nations place *their own* country in the center. People of one nation, when viewing the maps made by another nation, usually think the maps look odd, since they are accustomed to seeing *their own* country in the middle of the map. So it is also with histories. Further, secular histories are usually written only in a manner that *complements* the nation writing it rather than recording the history frankly,[43] as unflattering as it might be. The Bible is pretty much the *only* historical record that presents "warts and all."[44] To the other extreme, the enemies of the truth in America are continually "rewriting" history, even as the Soviets customarily have rewritten their history every decade or so to cover up the truth.)

Since Greece was founded by slaves from Egypt, one branch of their descendents, the ***Getae***, most likely only remembered the more recent facts of their history. (We shall soon cover much more detailed information concerning the Greeks of antiquity.)

Finally, concerning the similarities between the Scythians and Israelites, Herodotus records that there was a special tribe among the Scythians who **lived separately** from the rest of the Scythians. They were called the ***Argippaei***. They lived in a dwelling made of white felt. Herodotus recorded, "**No man harms these people, for they are regarded as holy, and they own no weapons of war. They judge their neighbors' quarrels, and the fugitives who go to them for protection are left unharmed**" (IV, p. 23). These are clearly the Priests and Levites of Israel, ***who were considered holy, wore white linen, and separated themselves from the rest of the Israelites*** and ***did not even fight in battle***. They also ***often acted as judges*** (Numbers 27:2; I Chronicles 23:2-4; 26:20, and 28-29; II Chronicles 19:5-11). Further, ***cities of refuge existed*** and were ***headed by a High Priest***. Men guilty of causing an accidental death, who fled to these cities, ***were not allowed to be harmed*** (Numbers 35:6-32).

There was a branch of Scythians known as ***Royal Scythians***, who were **very valiant** and **looked upon all other Scythians as their slaves**. There were also

---

[43] Is it not interesting, that the Germanic people have been so well known for their honesty, that even a word meaning "blunt honesty" was fashioned after the very name of one of the Germanic tribes: the *Franks*.

[44] It should be pointed out that the Bible is *completely* reliable, regardless what the liberal, God-hating "experts" say. No archaeological discovery has *ever* proved the Bible wrong—archaeology has only "proved" the Biblical record to be true. The book The Signature of God by Grant Jeffrey is highly recommended to the discerning reader. Though I believe Jeffrey to be in err concerning prophecy and who true Israel is, I believe he has done a marvellous job showing that the Bible is completely trustworthy. He convincingly proves that the Bible could not have been written by mere humans, but could only have been written by *God Himself*. Archaeology has proved that the information contained in the Bible is true (although "experts" denied it for years). Much of the information contained in the Bible could not have been devised by men, since much of the scientific information in the Bible was a thousand years ahead of even the most advanced knowledge of the times. Jeffrey proves from about a dozen different angles, that the Bible could only have been written by God Himself, and the Bible has never been proved wrong in history or science.

various Scythian tribes who revolted against the Royal Scythians and moved to different regions so they would not be subject to their rule (IV, pp. 20-21).

The ***Tribe of Judah*** was the *royal* tribe of Israel. *The founder of the Tribe of Judah, Judah himself, was reported to be very valiant and fierce in battle.* (Although Judah was not the firstborn, he prevailed over his brethren (I Chronicles 5:2). See also Book of Jasher XXXIX, LIV.) Prominence and power often breed arrogance and contempt. ***Many kings abused their power*.** **When *the kingdom of Israel split, the northern 10 Tribes of Israel splintered away from Judah after Solomon's son increased the tax burden upon Israel*.** There were other times in which ***portions of various Israelite tribes split apart and went their own ways from the rest of their brethren*.**

In his Israel's Racial Origins and Migrations (1934), Brigadier-General W. H. Fasken, C.B., relates,

> It must be realized, as Dr. Goard has reminded us, that the history of Israel as given in the Bible is the history of Israel *in Palestine*. If any section [remnant] of Israel, during Israel's national sojourn in "the Land," left the geographical boundaries of that land, they [then] ceased to find a place in its [biblical] history. [However,] they are not forgotten in covenant or prophecy, but having marched out of the land they have, for that very reason, marched out of the [biblical] historical record (p. 67). (Italics and brackets mine.)

Let us consider a very important piece of evidence that links the Israelites with the Scythians. Colonel Gawler states, "Arsareth...[is] the city or country of the River *Sereth*, which flows into the Danube...." Brigadier-General Sir Standish G. Crawfurd, Bart., C.B., C.M.G., C.I.E., D.S.O., in his book Our Celtic Heritage, attests to this and indicates the River Sereth is a tributary of the Danube in Moldavia and that Arsareth simply means "another land" (p. 1). In context then, when the Israelites spoke of Arsareth, "another land," they were referring to "another land of Israel"—the new home that God had promised them.

Colonel Gawler further indicates that,

> M. Sailman, a Jewish[45] writer in 1818, in Researches in The East, quotes Ortellius, "who notes that the kingdom of Arsareth (see II Esdras xiii. 45), [was] where the Ten Tribes...[finally settled and]...took the name of ***Gauthei***...." John Wilson has pointed out [presumably in his Our Israelitish Origin (1870)] that the country of the ***Getae*** was on the borders of the Danubian principalities, on the River Sereth, where is a town of the same name, which in the Hebrew tongue would be *Ar-sereth* (p. 28). (Boldface and brackets mine.)

The name ***Gauthei*** is important, for this distinguishes the Israelites as the Germanic tribes of Europe. Colonel Gawler states, "The Scythians were later known as ***Goths***, or ***Gothi***, possibly because the ***Getae***...were most in contact with the Romans, with whom, therefore, all Scythians were [called] ***Gothi***" (pp. 27-28). (Boldface and brackets mine.)

Dr. George Moore, in regard to this, stated,

---

[45] It should be noted that it has not only been non-"jewish" people who have made the claim that the Anglo-Saxon peoples are in fact the Israelites of the Bible; there have also been various "jewish" authorities who have confessed this. See **Appendix B**.

The name ***Goth***, as already surmised, was probably transferred from Palestine to the neighborhood of the Caspian Sea, where the ***Gatae*** and the ***Sacae***, the ***Goths***, and the ***Saxons*** are historically found together (p. 13, British History Traced From Egypt To Palestine (1927), Commander and Rev. L. G. A. Roberts, R.N.).

The Roman historian Pliny the Elder (A.D. 23-79) indicated,

The name ***Scythian*** has extended in every direction, even to the ***Sarmatae*** and the ***Germans***.... Beyond the Danube are the peoples of Scythia. The Persians have called them by the general name of ***Sacae***.... The more ancient writers give them the name of ***Aramii*** [Arameans]. The multitude of these ***Scythians*** is quite innumerable;[46] in their life and habits they much resemble the people of ***Parthia***. The tribes among them that are better known are the ***Sacae***, the ***Massagetae***, the ***Dahae***... (*Historia Naturalis*). (Emphasis and brackets mine.)

It should be noted that the land of Israel in the days of the Bible was part of *Syria*, and the language Christ spoke was ***Aramean***. The Israelites themselves are described in Scripture as Syrians, and Abraham's family was Syrian.

(See Deuteronomy 26:5 and Genesis 25:20. The word *Syrian* (#761) means "an Aramaean; a highlander." The people known *today* as "Syrians" are as different from the ***original*** Syrians, as the Greeks of today are different from the ***ancient*** Greeks; even as the ***original*** Italians,[47] Spaniards, Portuguese, and French, etc., were ***entirely*** different peoples from those people who now predominate in the lands that carry the names of their founders. So it is in America today.)

Greater evidence that the Scythians who sired the Germanic peoples are in fact the Israelites of the Bible is found in the Scythian tombs (*tumuli*) themselves, which have been found in southeastern Russia (Scythia and Crimea). These tombs date from 580 B.C. to the 1st century and contain many of the symbols of the Israelites, as well as fine animal drawings of near-eastern derivation.[48] In several of these tombs, Hebrew manuscripts were found, some of which are translated by Professor Herbert Bruce Hannay as follows:

I am Jehudi, the son of Moses, the son of Jehudi the Mighty, a man of the Tribe of Naphtili, which was carried captive with the other tribes of Israel, by Prince Shalmaneser, from Samaria during the reign of Hoshea, King of Israel. They were carried to Halah, to Habor—which is Cabul—to Gozan and to the Cheronesus—which is the Crimea (Haberman, p. 129).

Thousands of tombstones have been found in the Crimea in Scythian grave-

---

[46] "...I will make thy seed as the dust of the earth...if a man can number the dust of the earth, then shall thy seed also be numbered.... Look now toward...the stars, if thou be able to number them...so shall thy seed be.... thou shalt be a father of many nations.... I will make nations of thee, and kings shall come out of thee..." (**Genesis 13:16; 15:5; 17:4,6**).

[47] The highly esteemed Major Robert H. Williams (Military Intelligence) reveals in The Ultimate World Order (c. 1947) that the original Italians were light skinned, blond-haired and blue-eyed, and descended from the north. Alfred P. Schultz in Race or Mongrel (1908), gives a very detailed and enlightening early history of Italy, and the racial composition of that nation from its earliest days.

[48] These can be seen in the *American Journal of Archaeology* (1914), Vol. 18, and the *Illustrated London News*, January 3 and February 14, 1914.

yards with Hebrew-Phoenician inscriptions, 700 of which have been translated by Professor Chwolsen of Petrograd. Some of these read:

> This is the tombstone of Buki, the son of Itchak the priest; may his rest be in Eden, at the time of the salvation of Israel. In the year 702 of the years of our exile.

Another tombstone reads,

> To one of the faithful in Israel, Abraham ben Mar-Sinchah of Kertch, in the year of our exile 1682, when the envoys of the Rosh Meschek came from Kiou to our master...Prince David, Halmah, Habor, and Gozan, to which place Tigleth Pileser had exiled the sons of Reuben and Gad, and the half have been scattered through the entire coast...as far as China (Haberman; p. 130).

E. P. Ingersoll in Lost Israel Found, In The Anglo-Saxon Race (1886), states that many of these tombstones (some of which are housed in the St. Petersburg Museum), contain records that are clearly Israelitish; such as, "Moses Levi [a priest] died in the year 726 of our exile" and "Zadok the Levite, son of Moses died 4,000 years after the creation, 785 of our exile" (p. 34).

Herodotus also reported (c. 450 B.C.) that the Scythians used this area as their burial ground. He stated, "The tombs of their kings are in the land of the Gerrhi, where the Borythenes [Dneiper River] ceases to be navigable" (IV, p. 71).

The Original Greeks

The original Greeks of antiquity—the Greeks who were renowned for law and order, art, philosophy, and science, from whom we all have benefitted—were Israelites, mostly of the Tribe of Dan: the *Achaeans, Argosians (Argonauts), Athenians, Bithenians, Cappadocians, Carthaginians, Colchinas, Corinthians, Cilicians, Dalmatians, Dorians, Danaans, Hellens, Illyrians, Ionians, Lacedaemonians, Laodacians, Lyconians, Macedonians, Milesians, Mycenians, Pelasgians, Pelopannesians, Philippians, Phryggians, Thessalians, Thessalonians, Thracians,* and *Spartans*.

Ingersoll relates that according to Oxonian,[49] Herodotus himself was an Israelite of the Tribe of Dan (p. 50, footnote). The Apocryphal book of I Maccabees reveals that the Greek Lacedaemonian Spartans were of Israel ancestry (12:1-21). Josephus, the renowned Judean historian, confirms this (Josephus; *Antiquities*, XII, IV, 10; and XIII, V, 8).

Brigadier-General Fasken writes that "it was Israel, and principally the Tribe of Dan, which furnished the human element of classic Greece" (p. 64). In his scholarly book, Dan: The Pioneer of Israel, Colonel Gawler quotes the monumental Ethnology of Europe (1852; p. 137) by the esteemed Professor Robert Gordon Latham M.D., F.R.S., as follows:

> I think that the eponymous[50] of the ***Argive Danai***[51] was no other than that of the ***Israelite Tribe of Dan***, only we are so used to confine ourselves to the soil

---

[49] Rev. W. H. M. Milner, M.A., F.R.G.S., A.V.I. (c. 1883). See Israel's Wanderings (1900).

[50] Eponym = "the name of a real or mythological person which is presumed to have been the origin of the name of a particular region or people."

[51] Argive = "a region of ancient Greece."

of Palestine in our consideration of the Israelites, that we treat them as if they were *adscripti gleboe* [*bound to the land*] and ignore the share they may have taken in the ordinary history of the world. The sea ports between Tyre and Ascalon, or Dan, Ephraim, and Ashur, must have followed the history of sea ports in general, and not have stood on the coast for nothing. What a light would be thrown on the name of Peloponnesus and the history of the *Pelop*-id family, if a *bona fide* nation of *Pelopes*, with unequivocal affinities and contemporary annals, had existed on the coast of Asia! Who would have hesitated to connect the two? Yet with the ***Danai*** and the ***Tribe of Dan*** this *is* the case, and no one connects them! (pp. 11-12). (Emphasis and brackets mine.)

What a statement! The only explanation is either *profound ignorance* or a *conspiracy* to hide the truth. The fact that God declared that His people Israel would be the sole agent through which all the nations of the earth would be blessed and that Israel would be the light of the world demands that true Israel (regardless of what name by which Israel is known), in every century of every age from Abraham until now, must be fulfilling this role of distinction—a people who fulfill this role in such a manner that one does not need a microscope to discover or notice them: a people whose role is so extraordinary, outstanding, and in the forefront that it cannot be missed. *Only **one** group of people* has ever been able to fill the shoes of this distinct, prophesied character of true Israel. Yet for some reason, modern "scholars" seem to think that it is impossible for historical Israel to be anyone but the modern "jews" (or they know they are not, but want to keep everyone else from learning the truth)—even though all evidence proves otherwise. (Although modern "jewish" rabbis themselves claim they don't know what happened to the *lost* 10 Tribes of Israel, a few have confessed the Anglo-Saxon peoples are Israel.)

Ingersoll reveals,

From historic evidences that have come to light recently, it seems that Dan had been long familiar with the then Western world; that he had been accustomed to the performance of voyages with the ***Phoenicians***[52] all over the Mediterranean Sea, and beyond outside the Straits of Hercules; and that alone, unaccompanied by any of his neighbors, he had sailed to Egypt, and thence into ***Greece***, taking with him a colony of his own people; and that these ***Danai*** are said to have been among the *first settlers of Greece*. It is further stated that ***Dan*** was engaged in the sacking of Troy; that afterwards he conquered Macedonia, and that Alexander [the Great] seems to have descended from this very tribe of Israel.... Dan settled, after the sacking of Troy, in that very region, where he built *twelve* cities (p. 14). (Emphasis and brackets mine.)

Colonel Gawler states that Allatius indicated that,

...the ***Israelites***...peopled...***Iberia*** [Spain] and ***Colchis*** [Greece]; and he adduces the authority of Constantine Porphyrogenetes in support of the Israelitish origin of the inhabitants of Iberia. The name ***Iberia***, as well as ***Bithynia***—also on the South of the Black Sea—certainly strike one as *of Hebrew origin* (p. 18). (Emphasis and brackets mine.)

Legend has it that Greece was founded by Egyptians. The Israelites themselves were, at times, referred to as *Egyptians* (Exodus 2:19). (It is well docu-

---

[52] See **Appendix C-1**.

mented that the *original* Egyptians were white.[53]) God Himself declares, "...out of Egypt have I called my Son" (Hosea 11:1). Eldad, a Hebrew writer from the 9th century, writing to Spanish Hebrews, indicated that the *Tribe of* ***Dan***, in Jeroboam's time (c. 975 B.C.), was unwilling to shed his brethren's blood; and rather than shed Judah's blood, left the land of Israel and migrated to ***Greece*** and ***Denmark***. (See both Ingersoll (footnote. p. 16) and Gawler (p. 6), quoting Researches in the East (1818), Sailman.)

(This corresponds with the story we just saw concerning the *common* Scythians breaking away from the *Royal* Scythians.)

It is interesting to note that when Greece became independent in 1832, the Bavarian prince, Otto I, was chosen king. He was deposed in 1862. In his place, Greece chose a ***Danish*** prince, who became King George I. Greece adopted a democratic constitution and the coat of arms of ***Denmark***.

Jeoffrey Keating, in his General History of Ireland (1620), records,

> The ***Dan-ans*** were a people of great learning and wealth. They left ***Greece*** *after a battle with the Assyrians* and went to ***Ireland***, and also to **Denmark**, and called it ***Dan-mares***, ***Dan's country***. (Emphasis mine.)

Herodotus recorded,

> The most distinguished of expelled foreigners [from Egypt] followed ***Danaus*** [Dan] and [later] ***Cadmus***[54] into Greece, but the greater number of them was led by Moses into Judah [Canaan]. (Emphasis and brackets mine.)

The Greek poet Aeschylus (525-456 B.C.), in his *Suppliants*, similarly records, "***Danaus*** and his daughters are represented as a 'divine seed,' and 'exiles from Egypt.'" (Emphasis mine.)

Dr. William Smith (1813-1893), in History of Greece (1855), says, "Of all the heroic families of Greece, none was more heroic than that of ***Danans*** of *Argos*"[55] (p. 18). (Emphasis mine.) Grotius records the ***Danites*** disappeared from Canaan at a very early date. The French historian Dude stated that ***Dan*** came from Greece.

The German statesman, naturalist, explorer, and scientist Alexander von Humboldt (1769-1859) believed the original Greeks to be Israelites.

The Tribe of Dan was known to be a seafaring tribe, constantly travelling

---

[53] This is easily proved when one realizes that Moses (the famous Israelite leader) was raised from infancy by an Egyptian princess, and neither the Egyptians nor the Israelites had any reason to believe that he was *not an Egyptian*. Speech, education, customs, and dress/hairstyle were the main characteristics that differentiated the two; not the color of the skin, hair or eyes, shape of the face, or other genetic characteristics. See **Appendix C-2.** Further, around the first century A.D., a large contingent of Israelites of the southern kingdom (Judah) moved to Alexandria, Egypt, where they formed an Israelite community in the attempts to live outside Rome's tyranny. Israelite settlement there was encouraged by Egypt, and Israelites were admitted to the highest class of citizenship (as were the Greeks, who were fellow-brethren). Many nations in South America (even in our modern era), have encouraged white, European immigration, hoping to revive their dying nations.

[54] Cadmus was the great-grandson of Chacol (**I Kings 4:31**; **I Chronicles 3:6**), who was the great-great-grandson of Judah. Cadmus and his group entered Greece after the children of Israel had already entered the Promised Land, and had been allotted land according to their tribe. The ancient region of Greece, *Colchia*, gets its name from Chalcol,* even as the ancient region of *Argive* (*Argos*) Danai got its name from Dan. *See **Appendix C-3.**

[55] See footnote # 54.

about and colonizing. In his book, The Assyrian Invasions and Deportations of Israel (1937), J. Llewellyn Thomas, F.R.C.S., states,

> It is noteworthy that the Tribe of ***Dan*** is not mentioned in these accounts [of Assyrian deportations] whilst the other tribes are named. The northern ***Danites*** should have been the first to feel the Assyrian impact. They were not there and are believed to have migrated by sea to avoid the Assyrian menace (p. 15). (Emphasis and brackets mine.)

Further, in To Heal The Nation (1977), Dr. J. Franklin Snook reveals that the Tribe of Dan was not the only tribe of Israelites that left the area before the foreign invasions. Snook states,

> During the 38 years between the two censuses taken in the wilderness, the five tribes of Reuben, Gad, Ephraim, Naphtali, and Simeon decreased in numbers by 61,080 men. During the same period the other seven tribes increased by 62,260 men [See Numbers 1:18-46; 3:39; 26:4-62.]. These figures can only be a result of the beginning of the fulfillment of God's promise in Genesis 28:14 wherein He told Jacob that he should spread abroad to the west, east, north, and south (p. 10). (Brackets mine.)

It should be noted that in the censuses Israel took, only the *men* who were of military age (above the age of 20) were counted. The entire number given was barely over 600,000. Thus the numbers recorded are most likely only about one fifth of the entire population of Israel. The One Volume Bible Commentary (1954), edited by Rev. J. R. Dummelow, M.A. (Queen's College, Cambridge), indicates the entire population of Israel at the time was most likely 3,000,000 (p. 103).

It is also odd that in the records the Kings of Assyria made detailing their exploits and victories, certain tribes of Israel are conspicuously missing, while others are named specifically. Obviously, many escaped in early migrations—and by ship, with crews that had already proven themselves in journeys to Britain and back. In fact, the navy that King Solomon developed was reported to have made it even to China.[56] Further, Frederick A. Kent, in his book I Believe God (1942), indicates that members of the "...family of Zarah [one of the sons of Judah, twin brother to Pharez] were the earliest of the Hebrew colonists into Europe, eventually arriving in Ireland and Britain" (p. 129). (Brackets mine.)

The Racial Type of The Ancient Greeks, Scythians, Phoenicians

These original Israelite-Greek peoples were described as follows:

> The "**pure**" Greek is [according to Polemo[57]] ...**of a fair face with light complection mixed with red**...**soft reddish hair, not only curly, but combed and straight**, **with a square countenance, thin lips, and a moderate straight nose, moist, shining eyes, which move quickly and contain much light**.... The man devoted to literature and philosophy...**of fair complection mixed with red, his hair verging on yellow, neither curly or shaggy**, his build compact...and **with moist and shining eyes, filled with joy**.[58]

[56] See **Appendix C-4.**

[57] —considered the foremost ancient physiognomist.

[58] Elizabeth C. Evans, Physiognomics in the Ancient World, *Transactions of the American Philosophical Society*, I, 1969.

...Wherever the ***Hellenic*** and ***Ionic*** race has been kept **pure** [according to Adamantios[59]], we see proper **tall men of fairly broad and straight build**...**of fairly light skin and blond**; the flesh is rather firm, the limbs straight, the extremities well made...*the eyes bright, piercing, and full of light; for of all nations, the* ***Greek has the fairest eyes*** (Hans F. K. Günther, The Racial Elements of European History (first English edition (1927), translated from second German edition; p. 157). (Emphasis mine.)

And further,

...A golden-haired race called the ***Greeks*** began to settle in the big midway island of Crete and on the north side of the Mediterranean Sea around the straits connecting with the Black Sea.... much like the Aryans who were invading India.... They were a delightful people, indeed, who contributed so much to poetry, art, sports, trade, and liberty that their memory has been kept fresh by all people since, in gratitude and admiration.... **These nomads from the north were not the *swarthy* people of today's Greece, but a tall, muscular, blue-eyed race**.... They never numbered more than a few millions, and they flourished for about 500 years only.... But to us **they are the most important people of ancient times, for they became the teachers of all European and all Americans of European origin** (The Ladder of History (1945); MacMillan & Co., a high-school textbook).[60]

The Scythians were also referred to as *ruddy, fair*, and *beautiful*. Dr. Hans F. K. Günther, professor of physical anthropology at Berlin University, in his book Racial Elements of European History, stated,

...Ancient writers (such as Polemon of Ilium, Galienos, Clement of Alexandria, and Adamantios) state that the ***Sacae*** [***Scythians***] were like the ***Kelts*** and ***Germans*** and describe them as *fair* or *ruddy-fair*. The Scythian (Sacae) tribe of the ***Alans*** are also described as having a ***Nordic*** appearance. Ammianus (about A.D. 330-400) calls them "almost all tall and handsome, with hair almost yellow, and a fierce look" (p. 131). (Emphasis and bracket mine.)

The English church historian the Venerable Bede (672-735 A.D.) records that Pope Gregory I, while in Rome, upon seeing young Anglo-Saxon children taken captive in war and being sold in the marketplace, remarked upon their *beauty* and *charm*, declaring it was like looking into *the face of an angel* (Ecclesiastical History of the English People (c.732), Book II Chapter I). (Emphasis mine.) An Arab diplomat, Ibn Fadlan (presumably in the Middle Ages) met the ***Rus***[61] on the Volga River and declared, "Never had I seen people of more perfect physique; they are tall as date palms, blond and ruddy" (The Vikings (1972), Howard La Fay; National Geographic, p.38).

The above correspond with the descriptions the Bible gives of the Adamic Israelites. The Hebrew words translated as *fair* and *beautiful* (#3303, yaw-FEH;

[59] —4th-century A.D. Hebrew sophist and physician.

[60] Do you think a book like this would be allowed in the public schools today? Is it any wonder that the Grecian Israelites were the most significant people of the ancient world? The Nordic Israelites of every age have been the most significant race the world has known. This is so, only because God decreed that Israel would be so great and eminent.

[61] The ***Rus*** were ***Swedish*** Vikings who settled in Russia. The ***Scythians*** passed through Europe in three major waves: the first into the *Baltic*; the second across *Western Europe* and into *Britain*; and the last into *Scandinavia*.

#3302, yaw-FAW), used in Scripture in reference to Adamite/Israelite people, mean "to be bright (white or shining)"; and the words translated as *ruddy* (#132, *ad-mon-EE*; #122, *aw-DOME*; #119, *aw-DAM*) mean "to show blood in the face; to be rosy-cheeked" and even "red-haired." (See Genesis 12:11-13; 29:17; I Samuel 16:12; 17:42; 25:3; I Kings 1:3; Song of Solomon 1:15-16; 6:10.) Further, the name *Laban*[62] even means "to be white." King David is recorded as being *ruddy*.[63] The Israelites of the Bible (including Christ YeHoWSHuWaH) were a *white, fair-skinned, light-haired, and blue-eyed people*.[64] Sarah, the wife of Abraham through whom Isaac (the Son of Promise) came, is described in Scripture and other literature as being *very fair* (#3303; Genesis 12:11,14).

Is it just a coincidence that the physiognomy of the *Germanic peoples* is identical with that of the *ancient Israelites, Greeks, Scythians, and Phoenicians*, as the historical record shows?

It seems odd that the great minds of the European-descended peoples, who invented nearly everything we enjoy today, who discovered most everything we know today, and who advanced all civilization to the level it now enjoys, are completely ignorant when it comes to their own racial origin—*as if the Germanic tribes that sired Europe just appeared out of nowhere in the 6th century B.C., as if they had not existed before that time*. Surely their migrations and origins would be recorded in their own *meticulous* histories and in records of other peoples with whom they came into contact throughout their numerous worldwide migrations.

The bilinear edition of The Saxon Chronicle (translated by Rev. J. Ingram and first published in London in 1823), recording events from A.D. 1 to A.D. 1154, gives a brief introduction gleaned from the histories of Pliny, Solinus, Orosius, Gildas, and the Venerable Bede. It records:

BRYTENE ıᵹlanꝺ.... heꞃ ꞅẏnꝺon on þam ıᵹlanꝺe ꝼıꝼ ᵹeðeoꝺu. Ænᵹlıꞅc. ⁊ Bꞃẏt-ƿẏlıꞅc. ⁊ Scẏttıꞅc. ⁊ Pẏhtıꞅc. ⁊ Boclæꝺen. Æꞃoꞅt ƿæꞃon buᵹenꝺ þẏꞅeꞅ lanꝺeꞅ Bꞃẏttaꞅ. þa comon oꝼ Aꞃmenıa. ... Pẏhtaꞅ comon ꞅuþan oꝼ Scıtthıan.

The English translation reads:

> In the island [Britain] there are five nations: The Anglish, British/Welsh, Scottish, Pictish, and Latin. The first inhabitants were the Britons, who came from Armenia.... The Picts came south from Scythia (p. 1).

This is highly significant. *Armenia* was right where the captive 10 Tribes of Israel were deposited; and as we have already seen, Scythia was just north of this area in Asia Minor. As we shall soon see, even the ancient *Scottish* documents declare that the Scots themselves descended from the Israelites. Other histories,

---

[62] (#3837/3836) Laban, Abraham's grandnephew, was father of Jacob's wives, Leah and Rachel; Jacob's father Isaac got his wife Rebekah from ***Laban's*** father, Bethuel.

[63] —red hair, fair skin, rosy cheeks; **I Samuel 16:12; 17:42**.

[64] —in stark contrast with the dark, swarthy, mongol people who now occupy the land of Israel, who "claim" to be the *Israelites* of the Bible. See **Appendices C-5 and C-6**.

artifacts, and information prove the other European nations also are descended from the ancient Israelites.

Well, as you have briefly seen, such records do exist—and they form a broad spectrum of hard evidence from secular history, church history, the biblical record, literature, philology (language), archaeology, physiognomy, and legend/mythology. We shall offer enormous evidence from each of these areas; however, first we will turn to the Bible itself for undeniable proof written more than 2,000 years ago. The prophecies of Scripture regarding God's people are too numerous (many hundreds) and too spectacular to be merely *coincidental.* In a moment, we shall discuss a few of these prophecies. But first we must deal with a small area of confusion that most likely has crossed your mind already.

A Bit of Confusion

There are a people today who *call* themselves "jews" and who *claim* to be the Israelites of the Bible, yet they reject Christ YeHoWSHuWaH and constitute the greatest enemy of Christianity. Further, we have demonstrated that the ancient Israelites of the Bible are not the "jews" but rather the Anglo-Saxon and related peoples. How can these things be? Intriguingly, God, in His Word, ***warned*** His people about *those who would one day lie, claiming to be Israelites, when in fact, they are of Satan, and not of God* (Revelation 2:9; 3:9). Certainly God would not so warn us *if it was impossible* for us to be fooled or if the danger did not exist. What can this warning possibly mean? God also enlightens us to the fact that not *all* those who may have *partially* descended from Jacob (Israel) are *legitimate* Israelites (Romans 9:6). *Even as Esau*, many Israelites sinned and intermarried with *non-Israelites.* Their illegitimate children always themselves became (and further sired) the very worst enemies of God's true Israel people. *We reap what we sow.*

God declared that He would cast Israel out of her land, and she would have a new home, mainly to the north and west, but also to every corner of the earth; she would have numerous kings and a perpetual monarchy (Genesis 17:16). She would constitute an immense multitude, and she would be a great nation and a company of nations and a people who would bless all the peoples of the earth. God declared that He would give Israel a new name (a name *other than* the name "Israel") and that the true Israelites would be lost to the world scene—*for a time.*

When Assyria conquered and deported Israel, the king of Assyria imported Canaanite tribes to people the vacant land. It was *these peoples* who fought against the remnant of the House of Judah when they returned from their deportation and captivity in Babylon; it was these peoples who eventually outnumbered the true Israelites in the land of Israel; it was these peoples who tried to steal the inheritance of true Israel by claiming the land had been given to them (by the king of Assyria—*not* by God) (Ezekiel 11:15); and it was these peoples who later claimed to be Israelites in order to steal this inheritance. Scripture records,

> And the King of Assyria [Shalmaneser (Pul)] brought men from Babylon and

from Cuthah... from Ava... from Hamath, and from Sepharvaim[65] and placed them in the cities of Samaria instead of the children of Israel (II Kings 17:24).

J. Llewellyn Thomas, F.R.C.S., in his book, The Assyrian Invasions and Deportations of Israel, also quotes an Assyrian inscription in which the succeeding king of Assyria (Sargon), in a later invasion, deported Israelites and also imported various alien peoples. Thomas quotes,

> In the beginning of my reign, the city of Samaria I besieged, I captured.... 27,280 of its inhabitants I carried away.... The conqueror of the Thamudites, the Ibadidites, the Marsiminites, and the Khapaijans, the remainder of whom was carried away, **and whom he transported to the midst of the land of Beth-Omri** (p. 23). (Emphasis mine.)

More intriguing still is the fact that God declared that because of the sins of His people, they would, in their captivity, become *blind or ignorant as to **their own** factual and historical identity* (Deuteronomy 29:28-29; 32:26; Isaiah 42:16-23; 56:10; Jeremiah 50:6-7; Hosea 1:9-10; 2:6; 8:8; 9:17; Romans 10:1-3; 11:5-11, 25; II Corinthians 3:14-15). And as we have seen, the *world* at large would also be blind to Israel's identity (Deuteronomy 32:26; Hosea 5:3).

Note This Well: The Bible does not state that God's Israel people would be blind to *the Messiah, Christ YeHoWSHuWaH,* but that they would be blind to ***their own identity*** due to their sin. On the other hand, Scripture tells us that whoever does not confess that YeHoWSHuWaH is the Messiah, the Son of God, that person is *anti-Christ* (I John 2:18-22; 4:3; II John 7). Which people, more than all other people combined, deny that YeHoWSHuWaH (Jesus) is the Messiah? Which people attack Christ YeHoWSHuWaH and Christians—even though Christians (in their ignorance) are the ones who help them the most? Who is it that has gotten prayer, Bible reading, and the 10 Commandments stricken from the halls of our schools and most public places in our land? Christ forbade *His* people to call their priests by the title of "rabbi" (Matthew 23:7-8); yet those who spuriously claim to be God's Israel people use this very title.

In Scripture, the word "jew" is most often used to great confusion. The word "jew" (as many other *seemingly* racially indicative words) is not always as clearly understood as one would think. In fact, it is not a *legitimate* word. The word "jew" never appeared in the 1611 King James Bible, nor the Geneva Bible of 1599, nor any of Shakespeare's plays, nor in any English Bible or any English literature before or during the Victorian Era. In fact, the word "jew," according to many sources, did not appear in the English language until 1620. The word used before this time was "Iewe" (pronounced *hew-ee*). The reason is that the word "jew" is not to be found in the original Hebrew or Greek Scriptures.

[The word "Iewe" should not have been used either. This shall be explained shortly.]

According to the esteemed Colonel Curtis B. Dall (Franklin D. Roosevelt's

---

[65] Interestingly, one of Esau's descendents (a Canaanite) was named Kenaz **(Genesis 36:11)**. Is it just a coincidence that the "jews" refer to themselves as either ***Sephar**dic* "jews" (II Kings 17:24) or *Ash**kenaz**i* "jews"? The "jews" are neither Israelites nor Hebrew: they are Edomite Canaanites; they are not even pure Semites. The "jews" are no more descended from Israel than *Martin Luther **King*** was descended from Martin Luther.

son-in-law), in his Israel's Five Trillion Dollar Secret (1977), the word "jew" did not exist until 1775. The word itself was a corruption from the Latin *Iudaeus*, which meant "Judean." It underwent numerous forms, from "Giwis, Gyues, Geus, Iuys, Iows, Iews," and finally "jews." It appeared for the first time in an English Bible, when a mass-printing was made of a new 18th-century edition that "updated" the 14th-century translation. This special edition was then distributed throughout the English-speaking world to people who had never before owned a Bible. Dall also asserts that the word "Iewe," or "jew," when first translated in the Scriptures, referred only to the ancient Judeans of the Bible and not the *modern* "jew" (pp. 28-31).

In the Hebrew Old Testament, the word *mistranslated* "jew" in Scripture is **Judahite** [#3064 (*yeh-hoo-DEE*)]; in the Greek New Testament the word used is ***Judean*** [#2453 (*ee-oo-DAH-yos*)]. These two words can refer to someone who was:

(1) *racially* of the Tribe of Judah,

(2) a *resident* in the geographic land mass of Judah, or

(3) a *political subject* of the later Roman-controlled district of Judea.

(Even as we saw earlier, no longer can a person's race be discerned by the words "American," "Briton," or "European," so it is with the word "jew.")

Christ warned us that tares (non-Israelites) had been sown among the wheat (Israel) and that goats (non-Israelites) had slipped in among the sheep (Israel), which would one day be separated (Matthew 13:25-30; 25:32-33). Christ told us, *by their fruit you shall know them* (Luke 6:43-44). Therefore, to be able to discern when the word "jew" in Scripture refers to a ***true Israelite*** or a *Canaanite imposter*, each passage must be studied *in context.*[66]

In the Apocryphal book *The Story of Susanna*, this point was powerfully proved when young Daniel exposed two immoral *Canaanites* who were *masquerading as true Judeans*, who lied attempting to condemn an innocent Israelite woman to death because she would not consent to their sexual advances.

A Bit More Confusion

We run into the same problem with the word "Gentile," which seems to be the *illegitimate stepchild* of the word "jew." Strictly speaking, the words "jew" and "Gentile" are not *mistranslations*, because they are *not even translations*; they are ***transliterations*** or ***Anglicizations***[67] (and worse still, they are ***second-hand*** *Anglicizations*).

One of the problems with the word *misrendered* "Gentile" is that it is not a proper noun but a generic, collective noun. It should *not* be translated "Gentile" (a misleading word), and should never be used in reference to a *single indi-*

---

[66] The Mystery of the Law and Grace Solved!, So, You Call Yourself A Christian, and Apologetic Expositions Refuting Universalist Interpretations of Isolated Passages of Scripture: Isaiah 56 by Balaicius/STM clear up many passages of Scripture which confuse most people; these books clearly show the Covenants and Promises God made to Israel have not failed; and that true to His Promise, they have not been given to any other people.

[67] —that is, making a foreign word appear in English form, as is done with most all proper nouns (names, places, etc).

vidual—because the word exists only as a *collective* noun.[68]

In Hebrew, the word mistranslated "Gentile" is *gowy* (singular) [#1471 (*GŌ-ee*)] or *goyim* (plural). In Greek the word is *ethnos* (singular) [#1484 (*ETH-nŏs*)] or *ethne* (plural). The problem appears to have arisen with the Latin Vulgate[69] in which these Hebrew and Greek words were rendered into Latin as *gentilis*, from which we were unfortunate enough to be given the new and inaccurate English word "Gentile." A similar *miscarriage* of "translation" occurred with the word "jew."

Most people erroneously think the word "Gentile" means, *anyone who is not a "jew."* To the contrary, the words "goy" and "ethne" (improperly rendered "Gentile") are *generic* nouns with **no *distinct racial connotation whatsoever*.** These words simply mean ***"nation"*** or ***"people."*** Further, these words should **never** be translated as *heathen*: that meaning can only be implied through context. Further, "goy" and "ethne" are ***collective* nouns**: *One **individual*** cannot constitute a "Gentile";[70]—there can only be a *group* of people (who are Gentile), or different *groups* of people (who constitute Gentiles); that is, if "Gentile" is to be used to convey the *true* meaning of "goy" and "ethnos." Since the word "Gentile" is misleading and inaccurate, it should be discarded.

Even as the words "goy" and "ethnos" cannot refer to *a single individual* but only to a ***group***, so also these words cannot *categorically* refer to any single race of people *exclusively* (i.e., only "non-jews"). For example, if you and I were Germans visiting China, the Chinese could refer to *us* as *goy/ethnos* (if they were speaking ancient Hebrew or Greek). If two Frenchmen also accompanied us, the Chinese could refer to us *all* as *goyim/ethne*. Likewise, if a few Chinamen visited us in our native Germany, we also would refer to *them* as goy/ethnos; if two Japanese accompanied these Chinamen, *we* would refer to them *all* as *goyim/ethne*. *Goy* and *ethnos* are generic terms meaning simply "people" or "nation." Whether these words refer to natives (of one's own race or of another race) or foreigners (of one's own race, or of another race) must be determined from *the context* of any given biblical passage.

It should be understood by all that the word "flock" *cannot* refer to ***one** sheep*, but only to a ***group** of sheep*. Further, it should be understood by all that the word *flock* cannot be used ***exclusively*** in reference to *sheep* ***alone, to the exclusion** of all other forms of animal life*: for it can also be used in reference to goats, ducks, geese, etc. In fact, in Scripture, the main Hebrew words used for *cattle* [#4735 (*mik-NEH*); #6629 (*tsone*); #7716 (*seh*)] themselves do *not* mean "cows" ***exclusively*** but can be used of ***any form of livestock:*** *cows, sheep, goats, rams,*

---

[68] This difference can be understood by realizing the distinction between the words ***person*** and ***people***. Clearly the word *person* is an individual noun; while *people* is a collective noun (which itself can also exist in the plural; for example, many *people**s***).

[69] —the *Latin translation* of the Bible, by St. Jerome c. 370 A.D., made from the *Septuagint* (the *Greek version* of the *Hebrew Old Testament)* with the Greek New Testament.

[70] —even as *one single individual* man or woman could not be referred to as "a tall or mean ***people***;" each could only be referred to as "a tall or mean ***person***." When the colloquial phrase (slang) "he's good *people*" is used, the person is being considered *as belonging to* an entire group of people who fit this "good" description.

etc. Interestingly enough, the Hebrew word "goy" *can also* refer to ***a troop of animals*** or ***a flight of locusts***; although to my knowledge it is not used this way anywhere in Scripture.

The "jews" have taught us that *goyim* ("Gentiles") means "non-jews." Whether they have lied to us or actually believe this[71] is simply *more proof* that the modern "jews" are not the Biblical Israelites, for God promised Abraham (Israel's grandfather), "I will make of thee a great and mighty ***goy*** [nation]...a father of many ***goyim*** [nations] have I made thee" (Genesis 12:2; 17:4,5; 35:11; 48:19).

These Hebrew and Greek words clearly ***can*** refer to a ***specific homogeneous*** group of ***Israelite*** nations or people (Isaiah 1:4; Jeremiah 31:36; Luke 7:5; John 11:48-52; 18:35; Acts 10:22); however, these words ***can also*** refer to any groups of *non-Israelite* nations or people—homogeneous or not (Genesis 14:9; 21:13; 21:18; Exodus 9:24; 34:24; Isaiah 37:12; Matthew 10:5; Acts 7:7). Further, these words can also *generally* refer to a heterogeneous group composed of *both Israelite and non-Israelite nations or people* ***in the very same sentence*** (Genesis 22:18; 25:23; I Chronicles 16:23-24; Psalm 9:19-20).

Therefore, we see that the words "goy" and "ethnos" are no clearer in their meaning than is the word "jew" and that the word "Gentile" (which, like the word "jew," should not even be used) also *can **only** be understood **in the context** of the passage in which it is used.*

A QUICK WORD ABOUT CONTEXT: TO UNDERSTAND SCRIPTURE, ONE MUST APPLY ***BIBLICAL*** **RULES OF INTERPRETATION (HERMENEUTICS)**. THE **FOUNDATIONAL RULE** IN INTERPRETING SCRIPTURE IS THAT OF ***CONSTANCY***: GOD ***CANNOT*** LIE; HE ***CANNOT*** CONTRADICT HIMSELF; GOD DOES ***NOT*** CHANGE, AND THEREFORE HIS WORD ***CANNOT*** *CHANGE* OR *CONTRADICT* ITSELF (PSALM 15:4; 89:34; MALACHI 3:6; MATTHEW 5:18; MARK 13:30; ROMANS 3:4; TITUS 1:2; HEBREWS 13:8; JAMES 1:17). SCRIPTURE CAN BE INTERPRETED ONLY IN LIGHT OF **PREVIOUS** SCRIPTURE (WHICH SETS THE PRECEDENT BY WHICH ALL SUBSEQUENT SCRIPTURE IS TO BE INTERPRETED). THE LATTER IS ALWAYS TO BE INTERPRETED **BY THE FORMER**. GOD DOES NOT NEED TO "AMEND" HIS RULINGS, AS MAN DOES. GOD IS PERFECT. SADLY, MODERNISTS "MAKE THE WORD OF GOD OF NONE EFFECT," (MATTHEW 15:6; MARK 7:13; GALATIANS 3:17) WHEN THEY EITHER CANNOT UNDERSTAND THE RECONCILIATION OF TWO SEEMINGLY CONTRADICTORY PASSAGES OR WHEN THEY SIMPLY REFUSE TO ACCEPT WHAT GOD HAS SAID.

Resolving of One Final Confusing Word

Let us clear up one final bit of confusion due to another miscarriage of translation. Seven places in the New Testament in the King James Version of the Bible, the Greek word *Hellen* [#1672 (*HEL-lane*)], which means "Greek," is erroneously translated as "Gentile." One example is John 7:35: "Will He [Christ] go unto the dispersed [of Israel] among the ***Gentiles*** and teach the ***Gentiles***?" In this verse, the word translated "Gentiles" is the Greek word *Hellenes*. The verse

---

[71] If they actually believe this themselves, then it is clear that they do not even understand the true Hebrew tongue, the original language of God's Israel people. Modern Hebrew is not the same as ancient Hebrew—the alphabets are even entirely different (as different as the English alphabet is from the Arabs' alphabet).

should read, "Will He [Christ] go unto the dispersed [of Israel] among the ***Greeks*** and teach the ***Greeks***?" As we have already seen, the Greeks were *dispersed Israelites*—and those in Jerusalem knew this. E. W. Bullinger, who was considered one of the greatest Hebrew and Greek scholars, in his Critical Lexicon and Concordance (1877), under the heading "Hebrew" stated,

> [ʽΕλληνιστη΄s, is a Hellenist, i.e., a Hebrew who has unlearned his own tongue and speaks Greek....]

One final mistranslation we shall mention that has led to confusion with the word "Greeks" can be found in Ezekiel 27:17-19, which is a pronouncement against the people of Tyre at a time when Israel was in captivity. The verse reads, "Judah, and the land of Israel, they were thy merchants...***Dan*** also and ***Javan*** going to and fro occupied in thy fairs." Colonel Gawler in Dan: The Pioneer of Israel, states,

> ...In three places in Daniel, where Alexander the Great is distinctly indicated, and one in Zechariah, **Javan** is translated "*Greece*"; Josephus (i, vi, 1) also mentions ***Javan*** as being *Greece* (p. 7). (Emphasis mine.)

There is a distinct connection between ***the Tribe of Dan*** and ***Greece***. The Davis Dictionary of The Bible (1973) of "***Javan***" states: "The name corresponds etymologically with Iona, and denotes Greeks." The New Unger's Bible Dictionary (1988) also confirms this, stating that ***Javan*** refers not only to the Greeks, but more specifically to the Ionians, who inhabited the coasts of Lydia and Caria, two important commercial centers which existed about 200 years before the Peloponnesus. Unger's... also indicates that Sargon II of Assyria mentioned ***Javan*** (c. 721-705, around the time Assyria was conquering *northern Israel*) after having had a naval battle with Greece. This is significant, since Keating has shown us that the Greeks migrated to Ireland and Denmark *after a battle with the Assyrians*. As we have seen, the Greeks were Israelites of the Tribe of Dan.

- Biblical Witnesses -

Scriptural Proofs of True Israel

When seeking the truth, unless we are firsthand witnesses to events, we must rely on the records and testimonies of others. *Second- or third-hand information*, by its very nature, is subject to err. The further one stands from a given event, the odds become greater that inaccuracies will occur. Some people might *innocently* pass on erroneous information, but today, when politics govern nearly every aspect of our lives, we must sadly acknowledge that evil people *knowingly* engage in dishonesty, as they pursue their own agenda. When even *the meanings of words* are changed, we must be wary as we attempt to discern the truth.

Word of mouth is by its very nature unreliable and inaccurate. A parlor game called *Telephone* illustrates the point. In this game, everyone participating sits in a circle. (Each person can represent a period of time, to represent the inaccuracy of the transmission of oral testimony. The greater the number of individuals, the more significant the result becomes.) One person starts the game by whispering a brief story into the ear of the person on his right. This person is supposed to whisper exactly what *he* heard into the ear of the person on *his* right, and so on, until it is once again whispered into the ear of the person who started it. The story the originator hears at the end of the game is usually *far* different from the story he told at the beginning of the game. Why? Simply because most people do not remember *what was said* but they "remember" *what they* ***think*** *they heard.* To make matters worse, there will often be one immature individual who will *purposely* change the story as a joke, or out of malice.

How fortunate we are that we do not have to rely upon the word of *fallible man*. We have the Word of God. Let us look to that *ultimate authority in all matters of faith and conscience*—**the Holy Bible**. Let us use it as a *template* or *pictorial encyclopedia* to identify God's true, Israel people.

God ordained that every matter be established in the mouth of at least two or three witnesses (Deuteronomy 19:15; Matthew 18:16; II Corinthians 13:1) and that He would do nothing without first revealing it to His prophets (Amos 3:7). Let us establish the matter through the *second and third witnesses* of history and current events as they bear testimony to the fulfillment of prophecy.

Israel's Great Numbers

God declared that His people Israel would become a **great** nation, a **mighty** nation, a **company** and **multitude** of nations ruled by **kings** and **princes** and led by **priests**, a people *as numerous as the stars of the sky and the sand of the sea* (Genesis 12:2-3;13:16;17:4,6,16,19,21; 18:18-19; 21:12; 22:17-18; 24:60; 26:4; 35:11; Psalm 89:29, 36; Isaiah 65:15).

God declared through the blessing Jacob bestowed upon his two grandchildren, *Ephraim* and *Manasseh*, that they would grow into a multitude in the midst of the earth (Genesis 48:16). This Hebrew word *grow* [#1711 (*daw-GAW*)] is used only once in the Bible, and it means "to move rapidly or spawn in great numbers as fish." Is it just a coincidence that the early Christians (who were all Israelites) used the *fish* as their symbol, even as do Christians in America and Britain? Further, Jacob said, this was to occur "in the *midst* of the earth." This Hebrew word *midst* [#7130 (*KEH-reb*)] means "in the center" (literally or figuratively). *Which people* have been more *in the center of world attention*, and *which nations* are more *in the center of the Earth* than the ***United States of America***, ***Britain and her colonies***, and ***Europe***? The United States, Britain, and the other Germanic nations have traversed the earth throughout their migrations and colonization. Clearly America has become that "**great** nation"; **Great** Britain (the United Kingdom), with colonies all over the world, has become the "**great** *company* of nations"; and the other white nations of Europe (Germany, Denmark, Sweden, etc.) have become a "**great** *multitude* of nations." Has *any* other family of people fulfilled these prophecies?

I call your attention again to the testimony of Josephus. He recorded that the Israelites, in their captivity, had grown into "*an immense body of people, not to be estimated by numbers*." This was the beginning of the fulfillment of the prophecies and promises that God made to Abraham, Isaac, and Jacob. Nowhere in Scripture is the population of Israel ever described in this manner. God has always blessed the true Israel people with the ability to reproduce in great numbers—especially under difficult circumstances.

One of the characteristics of a *strong people* is the measure of their performance during *intense trials*. In the early days of our nation, even throughout the great depressions, it was not uncommon for families to have 10 or 12 children. It should be remembered that the children of Israel moved to Egypt to escape famine while the House of Jacob was still in its infancy—only 70 souls. After the good pharaoh died and a wicked pharaoh ascended the throne, Egypt held the Israelites prisoners and became cruel taskmasters, using them as slave labor. The Egyptians became distraught, alarmed, and infuriated that even when they increased the burdens cruelly upon the Israelites, abusing them without mercy, the Israelites continued to multiply greatly. Israel went into Egypt as only 70 persons but came out about 440 years later as a multitude of 3 million. When the Israelites were deported to Assyria and Babylon, about 750 years later, they were 13 million strong. While in captivity they grew into an "immense multitude." Is it not easy to see how, in the next 2,500 years, the Israelites could then grow to nearly three-quarters of a billion, as the *Germanic peoples*?

It is difficult to believe that secular scholars do not know what happened to the 11 million Israelites of the House of Israel who were taken captive to Assyria and the roughly two million Israelites of the House of Judah who never returned from captivity in either Assyria or Babylon, but it is even *harder* to believe that they cannot explain what happened to the possibly 20 to 100 million Israelites, the immense multitude into which they grew while in captivity, as recorded by Josephus—and as ordained by God (Jeremiah 29:4-6).

Interestingly, the "jews" have never numbered over 20 million people—*ever*. It is reported that the "jews" have what is called a *regressive birth rate*. Their natural death rate surpasses their natural birth rate. This is a sign of a curse: barrenness. Actually, because of this regressive birth rate, the "jews" would long ago have ceased to exist *if* they had not continually intermarried with other peoples. This itself is in violation of the law God gave to His *true* Israel people—to keep their race pure.[72] The "jews" of today are not a pure race. In fact, they are not truly a *race* but a hybrid ethnic group: a crossbreeding of racial

---

[72] Most white people today shy away from the idea of *purity of race*, having been told that racial pride (if you are *white*) is wrong. They have been told the *lie* that it is *diversity* that makes America strong. Rather, it is the few remaining remnants of God's Word & Law that make our nation strong—and the waning remnant of pure Israel blood, and the even fewer *righteous* Israelites left. It is sad that most intelligent people today take more care in preserving the pure bloodlines of the horses, dogs and cats they breed than they take in preserving their own bloodlines which they pass on to their children. Are we worth less than animals? God commanded His people to maintain the purity of their bloodlines—and not only their own, but that of their livestock, their crops, etc.: it is a matter of *holiness*: preserving what God created and *ordained to remain* as He created it. Modern society rejects God's Word and all "antiquated" concepts—and this is why our nation has degenerated into a crime-ridden, immoral, government-oppressed, pluralistic, nearly-totalitarianistic state. Positive correlations exist between the downfall of the world's greatest nations, to the degree their people mongrelized: Greece, Rome, Byzantia, Parthia, Spain, Italy, Portugal, Brazil (and now Canada, Britain, America, etc.). Can we not learn from history?

elements from the Canaanite and other Oriental people, Africans, and more recently the Germanic peoples into which they have intermarried in the attempt to camouflage themselves. Many even change their names, and undergo cosmetic surgeries to hide the mark God placed on their forefather Cain, to hide this witness of their countenance which does testify against them (Genesis 4:5-6, 11, 12, 15; Isaiah 3:9).

Israel's Great Power

God declared that His *true* Israel people would *possess the gates* of their enemies. They would overpower the peoples of the earth. They would rule over but not be reigned over *by* others. They would lend to other peoples but borrow from none. They would comprise the greatest military powers the world would ever know. They would be wealthy in agriculture and livestock. They would harvest the wealth of the planet and tame the powers of the universe with great discoveries (Genesis 22:17; 27:28-29; 32:24-28; 49:25-26; Deuteronomy 8:7-9; 15:6; 28:2-12; 33:13-28; Isaiah 60:5-11; 61:6; Ezekiel 36:29-30; 38:12; Joel 2:19; Micah 5:8; Luke 10:19-20).

Do America, Britain, Germany, etc., borrow money from other nations or, rather, do they loan money to all other nations (which loans are rarely repaid) and also freely give to those in need? Does the State of *Israeli* loan money to all other nations and *freely give* to those in need? Or does it demand financial assistance from other nations to the tune of many billions each year? Is it not true that the State of *Israeli* owes its very existence (since 1948) to the financial and military aid of the white Christian nations? Do the verses above describe the "jews," or do they describe America, Great Britain, Germany, and the European and European-descended peoples?

God said that Israel would be his *battle-ax,* with which He would conquer the nations (Jeremiah 51:20; Numbers 24:8-9; Psalm 2:8-9; Isaiah 41:10-16; Jeremiah 51:19-24; Micah 5:8; Malachi 4:3). The battle-ax was a weapon of the Israelites and was the famed weapon of the Scythians, Vikings, Celts, and Saxons. No other people have been renown for this weapon. Scripture prophesied that Israel would destroy Rome (Daniel 2:34-35; 2:44-45). It was the ***Vandals*** and ***Goths*** who conquered Rome. Trouble for Rome began in the mid-250's A.D., when Emperor Decius (one of the most violent persecutors of Christians) was killed in battle against the ***Goths***, who were the first of the *Germanic tribes* to overwhelm the Roman Empire. Alaric I, the ***Visogothic*** king, conquered Rome in 410; Gaiseric, the ***Vandal*** king in 455; and in the end, Odoacer, the ***Gothic*** king, in 476.

Can the "jews" claim to have fulfilled this prophecy? Certainly not. In a queer twist, it was the "jews" who so infuriated Rome that Rome sent General Titus, who destroyed Jerusalem and burned the Temple to the ground in 70 A.D. It seems this was planned, for the *genealogical records* were kept in the Temple. You see, when the small remnant from Babylon returned, the genealogical records were consulted, and those Canaanites and illegitimates who claimed to be true Judeans were proven to be impostors and were rejected. (See the books of Ezra and Nehemiah.) By this clever plan of stirring up trouble with Rome, they got Rome to do their dirty work for them. By having *true Israel's genealogical records* destroyed, they prevented their being exposed as the imposters they are. Thereafter, *Edomite Canaanites* (Idumeans) set themselves up *not only* as *kings* of Israel, but also as *High Priests*. The *Herods* were the most infamous, bloodthirsty family of Edomites (Idumeans) to ever spuriously rule over Palestine.

It was the *Germanic tribes* that crushed the invasion of the Muslim Saracens in Tours, France, under command of the ***Frankish*** king Charles Martel (grandfather of Charlemagne) in 732. It was the ***Lithuanians***, who, for more than 500 years, kept the Muslim Mongols, Tatars, Saracens, and Huns from pouring into eastern Europe; and it was the *early, old-world* ***Spaniards*** who checked the Moors for many centuries in southwest Europe. It was the ***British*** forces under General Allenby who delivered Jerusalem from the Turks in 1917 (which also was a fulfillment of prophecy).

How do the "jews" fulfill *any* of these prophecies? Are the "jews" a great military power? Certainly not, they rely on America and Britain to give them weapons as gifts, to protect them, and to fight their wars for them—while they also secretly rely on the Soviet Union for the same. No, these verses can describe no people other than the white Christian nations of the world.

Israel's New Name

God declared His people, Israel, would no longer be called by the name of *Israel* but that they would be called by *another name* and that they would specifically be *named after* ***Isaac*** (Genesis 21:12; Isaiah 62:2; 65:15; Hosea 2:17; 11:1; Romans 9:7; Hebrews 11:18). The *Germanic peoples* are called ***Saxons*** after *Isaac's sons*; and further, they are called the *Nations of Christendom*. ("If My people, who are called by My Name..." II Chronicles 7:14.) Many Anglo-Saxons peoples are also classified as *Gaels*, *Gauls*, and *Goths*. All three of these terms mean, "the people of God." Yet the Edomite "jews," who falsely claim to be the descendents of Biblical Israel, have stolen the name of Israel in fulfillment of prophecy. (Isaiah 65:15; Jeremiah 24:8-9; Revelation 2:9; 3:9. Only negative prophecies or other Scriptures apply to them. See Matthew 23:31-33 and Romans 9:14-23.) In many of their own writings, they admit that they are not the Israelites but invented this myth to fool us.[73]

Israel's New Home

God declared *true Israel* would *not* be in the land of Israel: but because of their sin, God would drive them from the land of Israel to a *new land*; they would be rooted up and driven out of Palestine; they would be scattered throughout the earth; they would have a *new home*, to the *north and to the west*; they would migrate into all the world, in all directions, and *occupy islands in the sea, coastlines*, desolate *wildernesses*, and *previously uninhabited lands*, lands that were *previously untilled and uncultivated, lands their fathers never knew*; and God would eventually sift them among the nations, regather them, and give them the land of Israel once again to possess in the Kingdom Age. (Thus, *true Israel* is *not* in the land of Israel at this time.) (See Genesis 28:14; 49:22; Leviticus 26:18, 21,

[73] *This* and more will be revealed and documented in Vol. 2: The Imposters Exposed.

24, 28, 33; Deuteronomy 28:36, 63-64; 29:25-29; 32:8; 33:17; Judges 5:17; II Samuel 7:10; I Chronicles 17:9; Psalm 2:8; 65:5; 80:11; 89:25; 97:1; 106:27; Isaiah 3:18; 11:11; 18:1; 24:15; 26:15; 27:6; 35:1; 41:1-10, 19; 42:4-6, 10, 12, 24; 43:10, 19-20; 48:18-23; 49:1-9, 12, 19, 20; 51:5; 54:2-3; 58:11-12; 66:19-20; Jeremiah 1:10; 2:2; 3:18; 6:8; 15:14; 16:13-16; 17:4-6; 18:17; 29:14; Ezekiel 11:16,17; 17; 36:17-29, 33-34; 36:17-29; 38:12; Hosea 2:14; 12:1; Amos 3:12; 9:9; Zechariah 10:8-9; Acts 2:5-11). Is it just a coincidence that when the first colonists came to America, the first settlement they formed they named *Virginia*—which means "virgin land"?

As we saw (in footnote 12), the name *Hebrew* means "colonizer"; and the true Hebrew-Israelites must certainly be fulfilling their name, since God declared they would colonize the coastlines, islands, and once desolate (untamed or barren) lands. These prophecies can point to *only one people*—the *Germanic peoples* who have colonized the world. It was the ***Dutch***, ***English***, ***Spaniards***, ***Germans***, ***Portuguese***, ***Normans*** (and other ***Vikings***), ***French***, ***Belgians***, and ***Italians*** (as well as the ***Phoenicians)*** who colonized the early world.

(Many of these colonies came to be the homelands of some of the Germanic tribes. However, as in more recent times, many of the colonies were simply extensions of their homelands, and the local people were governed beneficently. Sadly, however, most of these latter colonies (which were once prosperous and safe lands) have been "surrendered" to the locals (after many years of having been financed and developed into prosperous colonies by the white Christian nations). As we have turned from the ways of God and allowed the flood of third-world immigration to inundate our lands, and as we have allowed God's enemies to take the reins of our government, we have lost our favor in God's eyes, and everything we have developed has been taken from us and will fall into ruin. The other nations will suffer because they cannot govern themselves. (Consider Somalia, Haiti, etc.) When true Israel is punished by God for her sin, all those under her will suffer. Most of the colonies that have been surrendered are now plagued with famine, pestilence, tyranny, war, and poverty—and they expect us to periodically go in to restore order, give them monetary relief and supplies, and save them from themselves, after which they demand that we leave. Further still, they continue to leave their "liberated" homelands and come to *our* country. (Even now, whites are being tortured and murdered *en masse* in many African countries and all that they developed razed.) When we sin against God, everything goes wrong—not just for us, but for the whole world. The name *Israel* means "he who rules with God successfully over man." If God is not with us due to our sin, however, we cannot properly rule over ourselves or anyone else.)

This certainly cannot be fulfilled in the "jews." They historically moved into a new country only after it had been developed, so they could live off what other people developed by their own hard work, ingenuity, and expense. The "jews" also often entered *established nations* after they *had been expelled* by the nation in which they formerly resided, once it had fallen into some degree of degeneracy under their influence. Now they enter the U.S. demanding welfare benefits.

Israel, a Perpetual Nation

Scripture prophesies that Israel would *never* cease to be **a nation** (II Samuel 7:16,24,29; I Chronicles 17:22-27; Jeremiah 31:35-37; 33:20-26; 46:28; Hosea 1:10; Amos 9:8). Yet the "jews" of today were not a nation before World War II; the State of *Israeli* did not exist until Britain and America betrayed the Arabs and gave the land to the "jews." The State of *Israeli* exists today only as a welfare state supported by the United States, Britain, Germany, and other white nations. The "jews" do not *bless* other nations, they *demand a blessing*. In contrast, as far back as they can be traced, the Germanic peoples have been a multitude of prosperous, generous, self-supporting family of nations.

Israel's Perpetual Throne

God declared that His true Israel people would be blind to their own identity, and for a time they would be without a king or a prince or an *ephod* or *teraphim*—that is, without a *sign* or a *vision* from God, without direct communication with Him, without ordained priests to lead them to God (Hosea 3:4). (Israel would be blind to her own identity: Deuteronomy 29:28-29; 32:26; Isaiah 42:16-23; 56:10; Jeremiah 50:6-7; Hosea 1:9, 10; 2:6; 8:8; 9:17; Romans 10:1-3; 11:5-11, 25; II Corinthians 3:14-15. The world at large would be blind to Israel's factual identity (Deuteronomy 32:26; Hosea 5:3).)

God ***swore*** that the people of Israel would ***forever*** have a *king of the Tribe of Judah* (Genesis 49:8-10); that there would **never** be a time in which an *heir of King David was not ruling on the throne over Israel*, and that there would also be priests of the Tribe of Levi to minister to the people—for as long as the sun and moon were in the sky, as long as there was day and night. God made this ***solemn promise*** to David—a vow that could not be broken (Numbers 23:21b; II Samuel 7:13-16; I Chronicles 22:10; II Chronicles 13:5; Psalm 89:1-6, 20, 27-29, 35-37; 132:10-14, 17; Jeremiah 33:17-26; Ezekiel 37:24). God cannot lie. Yet He *swore* this promise by an *oath* making this promise even more significant.

This promise has never been broken. Now, God also stated that Israel *would* be *without* a king for a *short time* (Hosea 3:4). This might seem confusing to some people, in light of God's promise to the Tribe of Judah and to King David. These two passages are easily resolved, however. When God said *Israel* would be *without* a king, this was in reference to the *House of **Israel***, since Hosea prophesied against ***northern*** **Israel** in her sin. Hosea prophesied around 760 B.C. This prophecy came to pass roughly 40 years later, when Assyria conquered and deported the *northern* Israelites. During their captivity, the *northern 10 Tribes of the House of **Israel***—not *all* of Israel—were without a king. However, God's promise to *all* of Israel, and specifically to the *Tribe* of **Judah** and to King David held true, for the *southern* Kingdom, the *House of **Judah*** was still in existence, with King Jotham ruling on the throne during the time of the conquering and deportation of the *northern* Kingdom of Israel (c. 722 B.C.). By the time Nebuchadnezzar, king of Babylon, conquered the remaining remnant of the *House of **Judah*** (a good portion of which had already been taken captive into Assyria with the *House of **Israel***) in 584 B.C., those of the *House of **Israel*** had already left their captivity in Assyria and spread across Europe, setting up little kingdoms, with their kings being chosen from those who descended from the *Tribe* of Judah (to which their heraldries attest). Further, even before the reign of King David, the Israelites had already begun migrating into other parts of the world, establishing great empires (such as the Grecian Empire) with kings of the *Tribe* of Judah ruling over them.

Further still, even after the *House of **Judah*** had been conquered and deported by Babylon, God, being faithful to His Word, had prepared for the transfer and transplanting of the seed of David from the land of Judah. Mattaniah was the last king of Judah before it was conquered by Babylon. King Nebuchadnezzar killed all of Mattaniah's sons and all the nobility before his very eyes. Mattaniah's eyes were then put out and he was taken captive in chains to Babylon. Nebuchadnezzar then changed Mattaniah's name to Zedekiah. Now, it would *seem* that the entire line of this Israelite king had been wiped out. But Scripture reveals that King Zedekiah also had *daughters* (Jeremiah 41:10; 43:6). These daughters were taken under the protective custody of the Prophet Jeremiah in his divine mission to transplant the throne of David in the British Isles (Jeremiah 1:10; 18:7-9; 31:31-37; Ezekiel 17:1-6). In uncharacteristic behavior for a conquering pagan king, the king of Babylon gave Jeremiah *complete freedom* to go wherever and to do whatever he wished—even giving his own general to Jeremiah as a servant and a grant of money to provide for whatever he needed (Jeremiah 39:11-14). What pagan king does such a thing for a lowly prophet of a conquered nation—*unless* it had been divinely appointed to pave the way for Jeremiah's important mission of transplanting the throne?

However, a small group of Judeans refused to repent and obey God. They rebelled and took Jeremiah and the king's daughters into Egypt (Jeremiah 43). It was from here that Jeremiah and his scribe, Baruch (Jeremiah 36:4), split apart from this sinful group and travelled to *Spain* with the daughters of Zedekiah, after which they journeyed to the British Isles, from where God would eventually call His people (Isaiah 42:4; 49:1; 51:5; Jeremiah 31:10; Hosea 1:10; 2:23). As we saw, the original Grecian dynasties were founded by Israelites. After founding the city of Troy, many of these Greek Israelites migrated to the *British Isles*. There they met up with many of their Israelite brethren *who had already been there for some time*, including descendents of King David's son, Nathan. Nathan himself had migrated to the British Isles and had already established a monarchy by the time Jeremiah arrived with King Zedekiah's daughters, who then married back into the line of King David. Hence, there has *always* been an heir of David ruling on the throne somewhere over God's true Israel people as they spread across the globe.

Modern preachers try to "spiritualize" away the Word of God, claiming these prophecies are fulfilled in Christ. This only *makes the Word of God of none effect* (Mark 7:13; Romans 9:6; Galatians 3:17). Ultimately, all prophecies are fulfilled through Christ; however, those *physical* prophecies and promises God made *specifically of and to His people* are fulfilled ***physically in His people***, as God *promised*.[74]

However, the "jews" have had no king in this millennium—and they were *not even a nation* before 1948. More importantly, when Pilate tried to spare the life of Christ, the Edomite (Canaanite) "jews" boldly declared (c. A.D. 33), "We have no king but Caesar" (John 19:15). Since they are God's enemies they oppose God's plan of legitimate, righteous governmental order.

God declared that Israel's throne would be overturned *three* times (Ezekiel 21:25-27). This was fulfilled as the throne (Jacob's Pillar Stone, called the *Lia-*

---

[74] For more along these lines see, The Mystery of the Law and Grace Solved!, So, You Call Yourself A Christian..., and Apologetic Expositions (on the Exclusive Promises God Gave to Israel: Refuting Universalist Interpretations of Isolated Passages of Scripture): Isaiah 56, by Balaicius/STM.

fail[75] by the Irish) was taken by Jeremiah to Ireland (c. 584 B.C.), where it resided in the royal hall of Tara for 1,000 years, until it was overturned to the Abbey of Scone in Scotland by Fergus Mor McErc (the Great), (c. 498 A.D.). The Scots call it the *Stone of Scone*. In 1296 it was finally overturned to England by Edward I. It has since resided in Westminster Abbey under the Coronation Throne and thus is called the *Coronation Stone*. (On November, 15, 1996 it was given *on loan* to Scotland.) History indicates that this stone came to Ireland (Hibernia) from Spain (Iberia) and that it originated in the Holy Land. Geologists indicate that it is comprised of rock similar to that found near the Dead Sea. It has metal rings in it for carrying with staves, even as did the Ark of the Covenant. It is also no mere coincidence that the national symbol of Ireland is the *Harp of David*. A plethora of ancient documents support this. (See Jacob's Pillar (1977), by Capt.)

Haberman, in Tracing Our Ancestors, records:

> Irish historians are unanimous in agreement that about 580 B.C. there arrived in Ulster a notable man, a patriarch or saint, accompanied by an Eastern princess, and a lesser person by the name of Simon Brach or Barech.[76] This party brought with them several remarkable things about which Ireland's songs and legends cluster; those things were a harp (David's harp), and a wonderful stone—the Stone of Destiny—the Lia-Phail. According to many traditions, Jeremiah took the princesses to Spain, where one of them married a prince of Zaragossa.[77] With the other princess he arrived in Ulster sometime later. Irish tradition tells us that Jeremiah married princess Tamar Tephi to Eochaidh, the Heremon, or head king of Ireland, after the latter had embraced the worship of the true Jehovah (p. 153).

As you see, this claim that the Coronation Stone was taken to Ireland by the Israelites from their homeland is no modern fancy. Further, Nicklin, in Sign-posts of History, details an account of this drawn from Dean Stanley's Memorials of Westminster Abbey (1868). Nicklin records:

> In the capital of the Scottish kingdom was a venerable piece of rock, to which, at least as early as the 14th century, the following legend was attached. The stony pillar on which Jacob slept at Bethel was by his countrymen transported to Egypt. Thither...to Spain...from Spain to Ireland. On the sacred hill of Tara it became "Lia Fail," "the Stone of Destiny." On it the kings of Ireland were placed.... Fergus, the founder of the Scottish monarchy (brother of the then-reigning king of Ireland, having conquered the Scots and become their king, needing it for his coronation) bears it across the sea from Ireland to Dunstaffnage.... The Stone was moved by Kenneth II (840 A.D.) and placed on a raised plot of ground at Scone... In 1296, Edward I carried the Stone off to London and placed it in Westminster Abbey, where, ever since, it has been

[75] —one of the most sacred relics of the United Kingdom. All Kings and Queens of Ireland, Scotland, Wales, and England have been coronated upon this since recorded history. It is recorded to have been in Tara Island, Ireland some 5 centuries before Christ.

[76] —Jeremiah's scribe, Baruch. Ancient Irish records also refer to this as the arrival of a wise, holy man who came from the East (c. 525 B.C.) to Dan, bringing with him his scribe, Brugsch, also a beautiful princess, daughter of a king (Lost Israel Found in the Anglo-Saxon Race (1886), E.P. Ingersoll; p. 20).

[77] —meaning "Stronghold of Zarah," a descendent of the Zarah line of the Tribe of Judah.

the Coronation Stone of English sovereigns" (pp. 100, 111).

Jeremiah himself is reported to be buried in Ireland. It is interesting to note that Jeremiah was of the Tribe of *Levi*. The High Priest of Israel wore a breastplate that contained 12 precious stones, each one symbolizing one of the tribes of Israel. The stone of Levi was the *emerald*. Is it just another coincidence that Jeremiah, who was of the Tribe of Levi, is the Patron Saint of Ireland (who was the *original* Saint Patrick) and that Ireland is referred to as the **Emerald Isle**?

The kingly Tribe of Judah was divided between Judah's two sons, *Zarah* and *Pharez*[78] (Genesis 38:27-30), and the Tribe of Zarah itself was divided between Zarah's two sons *Darda* and *Calcol* (I Chronicles 2:6). Tea Tephi herself was of the Pharez line. She married King Eochaidh,[79] who was of the Calcol-Zarah-Judah line, thus reuniting *half* of Zarah with Pharez. It was not until Queen Victoria[80] married Prince Albert that the whole royal Tribe of Judah was once again fully united with the Darda-Zarah-Judah line. When all the kings and queens of Europe through Prince Albert (Darda-Judah line) united with the kings and queens of Scotland and Ireland through Victoria (Calcol-Judah line), all of Israel was finally reunited to form the current **United Kingdom**.

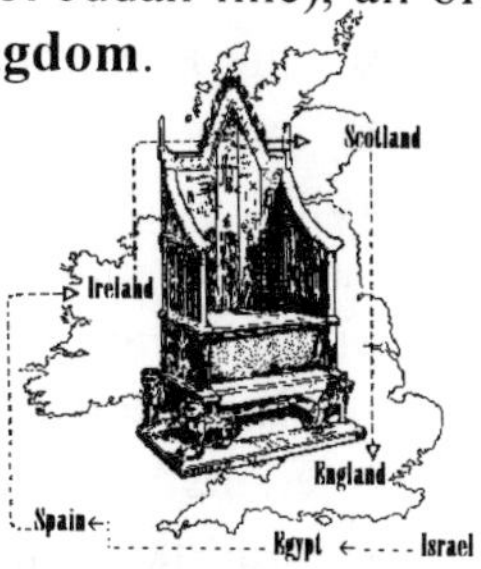

Bishop J. H. Allen, in his ground-breaking Judah's Scepter and Joseph's Birthright (1902), records:

> On...Queen Victoria's coronation, June 28th, 1837, an article appeared in the London *Sun*, which gives a description of the coronation chair as follows: (Illustration at right courtesy of Symbols Of Our Celto-Saxon Heritage (1976), W. H. Bennett, F.R.G.S..)
>
> This chair...St. Edward's chair, is an ancient seat...in which the kings of Scotland were...constantly crowned, but, having been brought out of the kingdom by Edward I, in...1296...it has ever since remained in the Abbey of Westminster, and has been the chair in which the succeeding kings and queens of this realm have been inaugurated.... At nine inches from the ground is a board, supported at the four quarters by as many lions. Between the seat and this board is enclosed a stone, commonly called Jacob's.... History relates...it is the stone whereon the patriarch Jacob laid his head in the plains of Luz. (pp. 251-252).

Allen further records,

> The possible descent of Queen Victoria from King David was first entered upon in the present day by the late Rev. F. R. A. Glover, M.A.... Rev. A. B. Grimaldi says, "The descent of our Royal Family from the royal line of Judah is, however, no new discovery. The Saxon kings traced themselves back to Odin, who traced his descent back to David, as may be seen in a very ancient MS. in the Herald's College, London, and in Sharon Turner" (pp. 370-371).

Allen also lists the complete genealogy from Adam to King George VI, which occupies six pages. His Royal Highness Prince Michael of Albany, head of the

[78] Is this from where the *Faeroes* Islands (off the coast of Scotland) receive their name?

[79] —from whom all the kings and queens of Ireland and Scotland descended.

[80] —who had her ancestry traced back to King David.

Royal House of Stewart, in his recent book The Forgotten Monarchy of Scotland (1998), concurs and traces his own royal ancestry back to David through the daughters of Zedekiah.

After Israel and Judah split as a nation (c. 945 B.C.) they had separate kings. Further, the monarchy had also been established in the British Isles. *Those Israelites* ***who were later deported*** *from the land of Israel* (as opposed to those *who had left on their own* centuries earlier) were without an *official* king or priests from 781 to 712 B.C., when Israel was deported by Assyria. As they began migrating throughout Europe, however, they met up with their brethren who had already established myriads of fiefdoms and kingdoms.

Finally, between 850 and 900 A.D., Alfred the Great united all of England under his rule, thus reuniting the northern and southern houses of Israel. This was the beginning of the fulfillment of prophecy in which Israel and Judah (who were once estranged) would be reunited and appoint themselves one head and that they would walk together in the land of the north (Jeremiah 3:18; Hosea 1:11).

Alfred was a brilliant, godly king who founded the laws of England upon the laws of the Bible.[81] Alfred himself translated the Scriptures into Anglo-Saxon. Alfred knew that the Anglo-Saxon peoples were the Israelites of the Bible. Before the descendents of those Israelites who were deported migrated throughout Europe, rejoining her brethren, they were without a king and without God's direction *because they were under judgment.* Is there any better reason for this to have been called the ***Dark Ages***? Haberman maintains that the Latin word "Cimmerians" means "darkness" (p. 121). The Scythians were called both Scythians and Cimmerians; under these two race-names all the sub-tribes (Goths, Celts, etc.) were grouped. Is it just a coincidence that the Israelites, in their punishment and blindness, were also called *Cimmerians/Cymri*, which means "those in darkness"? (There is a Hebrew word, #3650, kim-REER, which means "blackness.")

As we saw, God swore that the people of Israel would *forever* have a king of the Tribe of Judah, and specifically an heir of David, ruling on the throne over Israel. Yet the "jews" have no king or queen, while the European nations have *always* had interrelated monarchies. Is it just a coincidence that Queen Victoria had traced her descent back to King David? Is it just a coincidence that the current queen's name (*Elizabeth*) itself means "**oath of God**"—since God swore by an *oath* never to leave David without an heir on the throne?

Israel, A Blessing To The Whole World

God declared that all the nations of the earth would be blessed through His people Israel (Genesis 12:3; 28:14). What people have blessed every other people on earth? What people are responsible for the world's major inventions and discoveries—*and* for spreading this wealth and blessing across the globe, especially to those in need, to friend and foe alike? *Only one family of people* fulfills Biblical prophecy: the Germanic peoples.

---

[81] See The Dooms (Laws) of King Alfred the Great.

The "jews" have not blessed all nations but have *demanded* blessing *from* them. Further, they have been instrumental in the demoralization, de-Christianization, and destruction of other nations. (See **Appendix D**.)

Israel, a Righteous Missionary People

Israel was to be a missionary people who honored God's Word, a nation of priests, and a holy people whose laws would be based on the Bible (Genesis 28:14; Exodus 19:6; Psalm 78:5-7; 147:19-20; Isaiah 26; 43:1, 10-12, 21; 48:10-12; 49:3, 6, 8, 9; 59:21; 61:6; Jeremiah 33:21-22; Micah 5:7; Acts 1:8; I Peter 2:5, 9). Yet it is the "jews" who have succeeded in getting prayer, Bible reading, and the 10 Commandments *out of* our high schools and other public places. It is the "jews" who have subverted the Godly laws of our land. The Germanic peoples, in contrast, have had God's Word *since their earliest recorded histories*.[82] They have translated the Bible into more than 2,000 languages.[83] They have been responsible for 99.9 percent of the world's missionary endeavors. Do the "jews" send out God's Word to other peoples? Do the Chinese? Do the Arabs? the Africans? Indians? Hispanics? No. It has always and only been the white nations. Why?...?

Israel, A Hospitable People

God commanded Israel to be kind to strangers *of their own people* who sojourned in their land (Leviticus 19:33-34; Matthew 25:31-46) and to be kind also to *certain* non-Israel peoples in their land if they would obey Israel's laws (Deuteronomy 20:10-18). The Germanic peoples are renowned for their hospitality, and America especially is a shining beacon to this. Yet the Soviet "jews" who leave the U.S.S.R. to go to Palestine are treated worse than second-class citizens, and most of them end up coming to America or returning to the Soviet Union.[84]

(Blind Christians think the migration of Soviet "jews" to Palestine is the regathering of Israel prophesied in Scripture. This is untrue. The vast majority of "jews" who leave the former Soviet Union use Palestine as a stepping stone to America or other Christian lands. They know there can be no safety unless they live within the borders of the white Christian nations. More "jews" leave Palestine every year than enter it. There are more "jews" in New York City or South Florida than there are in *all* of Palestine. The regathering of true Israel (the Germanic peoples) will not occur until Christ has returned for His people—and He will return *only* after they have repented of their sins and returned to His ways. Sadly, the "jews" have fooled Christians into thinking that they are God's people. In truth, 95 percent of the "jews" in Palestine are atheists (as are most "jews" in other countries). Since the "jews" have fooled mainstream Christians into thinking that they are God's chosen people, when in fact they are the Canaanites of the Bible, they have secured preferential treatment. They, more than any other people, receive special privi-

---

[82] The Gothic tribes are *recorded* to have had God's Word in their own language as early as c. 350 A.D.. Wulfila (Ulfilas) the Bishop of the Goths, was consecrated by Bishop Eusebius of Nicodemia in 341 A.D. and translated the Scriptures into Gothic. Wulfila is also credited with having invented the Gothic alphabet for this translation.

[83] —often having had to *first develop the languages* of other peoples and *create a written form for them*, before the Scriptures could be translated—and then teach them *how to read* it.

[84] The same is reported to occur to American "jews," and is documented by "jewish" testimony. See The Life of An American Jew in Racist, Marxist Israel and My Farewell To Israel: The Thorn in the Middle East, by Jack Bernstein. Other testimonies are prolific in "jewish" periodicals.

leges and benefits (automatic dual citizenship, welfare, government housing, Social Security they never paid into, etc.). Further, they can perpetrate all sorts of criminal acts (from war crimes and subversion of governments to white-collar crimes) and not be prosecuted for them because they cry "anti-Semitism!" if someone accuses them.)

Not only are the white races hospitable to their own kin, but they are hospitable to all those not of their race—even their very enemies. No other race allows every type of alien people to enter its lands *en masse*, gives them citizenship and rights equal to or better than its own, and pays for their education, health care, cost of living, etc. On the other hand, in Palestine, *no one* but the "jew" has any rights. All other peoples are forbidden to enter—except white Christian tourists, who are allowed to enter *briefly* to spend their money[85]—and they are welcome only as long as their money lasts.

Israel, A Teaching Nation

God declared that His true Israel people would teach the nations (Isaiah 2:2-3; Micah 4:2). Truly, it has been the white race alone that has taught culture, civilization, modernization, education, health, cleanliness, and morality to other peoples. Germanic missionaries have gone into all the world and developed the languages and even written the histories of these other peoples; taught them medicine, agriculture, religion, animal husbandry, construction, industry, technology, morality, diplomacy, law, and so on. It is the white nations that allow all other kinds of people to come to our lands to study medicine and technology. Yet sadly, after learning so many wonderful things from the white race, hardly any of these people ever return to their own lands to help their own people. No, they would rather live in comfort, luxury, and safety in the white nations. Do the "jews" or any other people practice such philanthropic, humanitarian self-sacrifice? No. Again, this is a phenomenon peculiar to one race of people.

Israel, a Merciful and Protective Nation

Scripture declares that God's true Israel people would be a merciful people. They would be a blessing to others in need, and even set slaves free (Deuteronomy 15:7, 11; Psalm 72:4; Isaiah 42:7; 49:9; 58:6). No other race is so compassionate that it delivers foreign and unfriendly people from their famines, plagues, epidemics, internal wars, external invasions, and disasters—spending untold billions of dollars of their own money.

In <u>Faith & Freedom</u> (1988), Benjamin Hart records,

> [Thomas] Hooker warned that "mercy will never save you until it rules you too." This idea became the underlying principle of Connecticut's government. It also established a tradition of American generosity and mercy unparalleled in history. German soldiers at the end of Word War II, for example, threw their rifles down and eagerly surrendered to the American side rather than risk capture by the Russians [sic, Soviets]. And, after defeating them in war, America rebuilt Japan and West Germany's industrial base at enormous expense. Nc

---

[85] Tourism is the number-*two* source of Palestine's "income." The number-one source is *welfar* handouts from the white, Christian nations.

other people have been as magnanimous toward its enemies as has the American people, though we have often paid dearly for what most of the world would consider hopeless naiveté. Mercy, forgiveness, and almost limitless charity are distinctly American characteristics that can be traced to the heart of Puritan society in 17th-century New England (pp. 102-103). (Brackets mine.)

The other nations of Christendom (United Kingdom, Holland, etc.), including Germany, are also well known for these very virtues. Lithuanians, Latvians, and other peoples preferred occupation by the Germans (who were civil, kind, and humane—despite the false propaganda) over the Soviets.

(Although many Russian peoples are Israelite, the Soviet Union had successfully mongrelized the peoples under its tyrannical power far sooner than in other countries, and communism turned many otherwise good people into animals.)

It was the nations of Christendom that abolished slavery,[86] but few people realize that it was the "jews" who bought the African slaves *from their very own black African chieftains* and then sailed them into the white world to be sold.[87] (Albert Schweitzer himself recorded his internal conflict between the "exploitation" of the Africans under European rule and the fact that European rule, if nothing else, kept the Africans from exploiting, oppressing, and exterminating one another. See Out of My Life and Thought, 1933.)

Further, it is the "jews" (by their own numerously recorded confessions) who have been the cause of all wars, chiefly through communism, which (again by their confession) is purely "jewish." It is indisputable that no nation is safe, free, or prosperous without the aid of the white Christian nations. Yet apparently, in the "jewish" mind, mercy, compassion, monetary aid, disaster and famine relief, military protection, and medical assistance are only a *one-way street*—and the "jews" are *always* on the *receiving end* of charity, *never* on the giving end (even though they control the majority of the world's wealth).

No doubt, many people will feel uncomfortable reading the numerous statements regarding the virtues and accomplishments of the white race. If it is true, why should we be ashamed to be proud and teach the truth to our children? Good, decent white people have been programmed to feel ashamed of their

---

[86] —which might or might not have been a good thing. Most blacks lived a lot more prosperously, peacefully, and happily as slaves than they do today. Some might say, "But they were not free!" Free to do what? Free to live in poverty and squalor? Free to kill and enslave each other wantonly? Free to kill, rape, and rob the people of their host nation? Free to be devoid of self-respect? As slaves, they were well cared for in return for their service—but they were required to be lawful and obedient. The stories of the whites abusing their slaves is nothing but propaganda, created to cause the blacks to hate the whites and to cause the whites to feel guilty. Slaves were not all abused. Certainly, no doubt, there were a few *base individuals* who abused their slaves (even as some *base individuals* beat their children, wives, horses, dogs, etc.). This was the *exception*, however, not the rule. Tell me, would any intelligent person have beaten a slave (that cost *thousands* of dollars; maybe $20,000 in today's money), who produced for him, and who oversaw his livelihood? Would anyone be foolish enough to terribly mistreat the slaves, who cared for his infants and children, who cooked his food (which could be poisoned), who oversaw the master's wealth, who could easily sneak into the house some night and cut his master's throat and those of his family? Certainly not. Many slaves *took the last name of their masters* (out of admiration), and some continued to work for their former masters as hired hands. This is unimpeachable evidence that, as a rule, the slaves were not abused. Stories to the contrary have been concocted to create racial tension.

[87] See Who Brought The Slaves To America by Walter White; The Secret Relationship Between Blacks and Jews by Nation of Islam.

wonderful heritage. They have been brainwashed with all sorts of vile, baseless propaganda. They have been conditioned to exhibit the modern neurosis of "white guilt." Through propaganda, ***false guilt*** is induced and the glorious truth of our heritage is kept *from us*, while we are forced to "celebrate" *other peoples'* heritage, being sensitive of *their* cultural persona while shunning our own.[88]

Likewise, no doubt, many people will feel uncomfortable reading the numerous statements regarding the vices and crimes of the "jews." (Even though all these facts are documentable from the "jews'" very own testimony.) Unless sin is pointed out, the sinner will continue to sin. If criminals are not exposed and punished, they will continue in their crime. (In fact, they are banking on the hopes that you and most other people *will feel uncomfortable* and *refuse to entertain such thoughts*—so they can continue on unopposed with their evil plans.) One day it will be too late, if more honest people do not wake up and confront evil—*regardless of* ***who*** is to blame. The truth can only set you free *if you know it* and *incorporate it into your life*. *Please* consider the evidence which proves—*beyond a shadow of a doubt*—that all the statements made herein are true. It is not a matter of having someone to blame. It is a matter of discovering who has been killing and robbing our family, *so it can be stopped*—and so we can *truly* be *free* and *safe* and *happy*. It is a matter of recognizing crime and identifying the criminals so that we can put an end to it, which will once again enable us to be a prosperous and godly nation (family).

(Please send SASE to learn shocking, documented facts the media suppresses.)

The Symbols of Israel

The following are just *some* of the symbols that Scripture prophesied would be symbols of true Israel. It is no coincidence that they are all to be found in the coat of arms of the European and European-descended peoples. These symbols are by no means new; many have been in use for over 2,000 years by the ancient Germanic peoples, the Scythians, and their ancestors—the Israelites.

The **Eagle**, **Hawk**, or **Falcon**: Exodus 19:4; Deuteronomy 32:11; II Samuel 1:23; Job 39:26-30; Psalm 103:5; Isaiah 40:27-31; Ezekiel 1:10; 17:3-5; Micah 1:16; Revelation 4:7; 12:14; Luke 17:37.

* * * * * * * * * * * * * *

---

[88] See Stop Apologizing! by Jud Cyllorn.

The **Lion**: Numbers 23:24; 24:8-9; Deuteronomy 33:20-22 (49:9; **Judah: 3 Lions**); Proverbs 28:1b; Isaiah 11:6; 65:25; Ezekiel 19:1-9; Hosea 5:14 (13:7; **Leopard**); Micah 5:8; Zechariah 11:3; Revelation 4:7; 5:5.

* * * * * * * * * * * * * *

The **Bull (Bullock, Ox, Heifer)** and **Unicorn** (which can be the **Mythological Creature**, a **Bison**, or a **Wild Ox**) and a **Horn** or **Horns**: Numbers 23:22; 24:8-9; Deuteronomy 33:16-17; Job 39:9-12; Psalm 22:21; 29:6; 92:10; 149:1; Isaiah 11:6; 34:7; 65:25; Jeremiah 50:11; Ezekiel 34:17, 20, 22; Hosea 4:16; 10:11; Malachi 4:2; Hebrews 3:17; Revelation 4:7.

* * * * * * * * * * * * * *

The **Deer** (**Hart**, **Hind**, and possibly **Elk** or **Moose**): Genesis 49:21; Job 39:1b; Proverbs 5:19; 6:5; Habakkuk 3:19.

* * * * * * * * * * * * * *

The **Lily** and **Rose** (of Sharon): Song of Solomon 2:1, 16; 5:13; Isaiah 35:1; Hosea 14:5; Matthew 6:28; Luke 12:27. An **Olive Branch** or **Olive Tree**: Genesis 8:11; Deuteronomy 8:8; Judges 9:8,9; Psalm 52:8; 128:3; Jeremiah 11:16; Hosea 14:6; Zechariah 4:3,12-14; Romans 11:17-24; Revelation 11:3,4. **Wheat, Sheaves** or **Bread**: Genesis 37:7; 49:20; Matthew 13:24-43; John 12:24; I Corinthians 10:17.

* * * * * * * * * * * * * *

Sheep, Ram, Wild Mountain Goat: Job 31:9; Psalm 71:4; 74:1; 77:20; 78:52, 70-71; 79:13-15; 80:1; 95:7; 100:3; 107:41-42; Isaiah 11:6; 40:11; 65:25; Ezekiel 34:11-12, 17, 31; 36:37-38; Hosea 4:16; Micah 7:14; Habakuk 3:17; Zechariah 9:16; 10:3; Matthew 5:6; 15:24; 18:11-14; 26:31; Mark 6:34; Luke 10:3; 12:32; Romans 8:36; Hebrews 13:20; I Peter 2:25; 5:2.

* * * * * * * * * * * * * *

The **Wolf**: Genesis 49:27; Isaiah 11:6; 65:25; Ezekiel 22:27; Zephaniah 3:3.

* * * * * * * * * * * * * *

   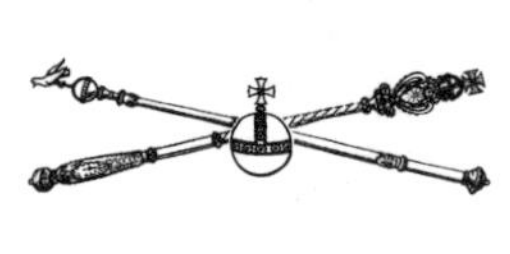

Symbols of the divinely appointed monarchy: a **Throne**, a **Crown**, (**Jewels**), a **Scepter** (or **Rod)**, an **Orb**: Genesis 49:10; Exodus 19:5; Numbers 24:7; Deuteronomy 4:10; II Samuel 3:10; 7:13, 16; Psalm 2:9; 8:5; 74:2; 89:3-4, 28-29, 36; 132:18; 135:4; Isaiah 10:15; 11:1; 28:5; 62:3; Jeremiah 1:11; 10:16; 51:19; Ezekiel 7:10, 20; 16:11-12; 19:11,14; 21:10,13; Zechariah 9:16; Malachi 3:17; Luke 6:45; II Corinthians 4:7; Revelation 21:21.

* * * * * * * * * * * * * *

A **Serpent** or **Dragon** (in *limited* use and *special* meaning): Genesis 49:16,17; Exodus 4:3; Numbers 21:8,9; II Kings 18:4; Matthew 10:16; John 3:14.

* * * * * * * * * * * * * *

A **Harp:** I Samuel 16:16; I Chronicles 25:1,3; Psalm 33:2; 98:5; 137:2; 147:7; 150:3; Revelation 15:2.

* * * * * * * * * * * * *

A **Shield** (or **Buckler**): Genesis 15:1; Deuteronomy 33:29; II Samuel 22:3, 6; Psalm 3:3; 4:13, 16; 5:12-13; 18:2, 35; 28:7; 33:20; 47:9; 59:11; 84:9; 91:4; 115:9-11; 119:114; 144:2; Proverbs 30:5; Nahum 2:3; Ephesians 6:16.

[The shields above are: (left) the arms of Canute (Knute) the Great (1016-1035); (middle) William III and Mary II (1689-1702); and (right) arms of William the Conquerer (William I) (1066-1087).]

* * * * * * * * * * * * * *

  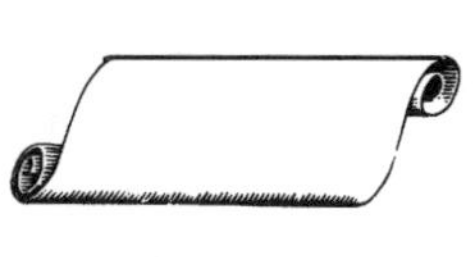 

Banners Standards, **Ensigns** or **Flags** (of Heritage), and **Scrolls** (Geneology or Law): Numbers 1:52;2:2-34;10:14-25; Judges 5:14; Ezra 2:62; Nehemiah 7:5, 64; Psalm 20:5;60:4;61:5;74:9; Isaiah 10:18;18:3;49:22; 59:19;62:10; 66:19; Jeremiah 4:6,21;50:2;51:27; Zechariah 9:16.

* * * * * * * * * * * * * *

A **Ship**: (Zebulun; Genesis 49:13; Deuteronomy 33:18); Numbers 24:7; (Dan; Judges 5:17); I Kings 9:26;10:22;22:48; II Chronicles 9:21; Psalm 80:11;89:25; 107:3,23-30; Isaiah 18:2;60:5,9; Ezekiel 27:9,25,29;30:9; Daniel 11:30,40.

* * * * * * * * * * * * * *

The **Horse** (especially *white*), **Horse and Rider**, an **Armed Rider**, and a **Troop** or **Regiment of Soldiers** (Gad): Genesis 49:17,19; Judges 5:15; Job 39:18,19; Jeremiah 8:6,16; Zechariah 9:10;10:3;12:4.

* * * * * * * * * * * * *

Arrows, Bow and Arrows: Genesis 49:22-24; Numbers 24:8b; Deuteronomy 32:23b,42; II Kings 13:15-17; Psalm 7:12,13; 78:9; 97:11; 127:4; Isaiah 49:2; Habakkuk 3:11; Zechariah 9:13,14; Romans 11:24. **Battleaxe, Sword, Spear, God's Weapon:** Genesis 49:5;34:25,26; Numbers 24:8,9; Deuteronomy 33:29; Joshua 8:18,26; Judges 7:18; I Samuel 13:19-21; Psalm 2:8,9; 7:12; Isaiah 41:10-16;49:2; Jeremiah 51:19-24; Ezekiel 21:9; Micah 5:6,8; Habakuk 3:11; Zechariah 9:13; Malachi 4:3.

* * * * * * * * * * * * *

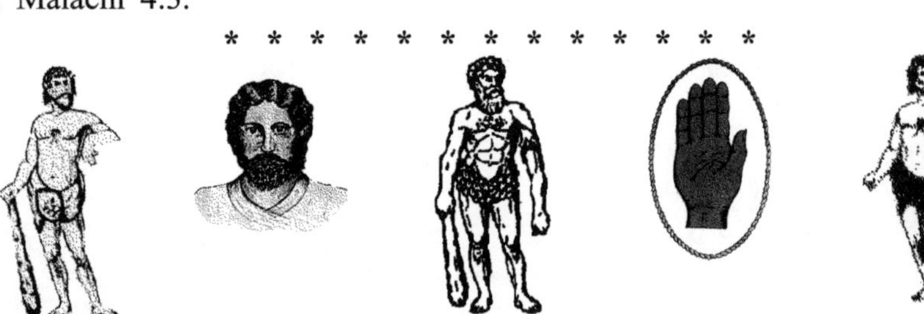

A **Man** (God's *son* and *firstborn*): Genesis 29:32 (*Reuben* means, "look at my son the builder of man"); Exodus 4:22,23; Deuteronomy 14:1; 32:5,6,19; Psalm 65:4; 80:17; 89:27; 92:6; 95:2; Isaiah 43:6,7; Jeremiah 31:9,20; Hosea 1:1;11:1; Zecharaiah 9:13; 10:7; Luke 3:38 (Adam, the son of God)); I John 1:12; Romans 8:19; II Corinthians 6:18. **Uplifted Red Hand** (in some cases with a **Red Thread, Cord, or Rope** around it): Deuteronomy 33:2,3; Genesis 38:27-30; Joshua 2:18,21.

* * * * * * * * * * * *

(It should be noted that some nonwhite nations may have ***some*** of these same symbols, but it must be remembered that the vast majority of these symbols came about *during the time Britain or other nations (Belgium, France, Netherlands, etc.) ruled these countries*. There are very few, cases in which nonwhite nations have any of these symbols (and no cases in which they have all of them) where it is not a result of European colonization—and no other people in the world fulfill the many prophecies and characteristics of true Israel as foretold in Scripture and as delineated in this book.)

- National Witnesses -

Heraldic and Philological Proofs of True Israel

Let us again look to the characteristics the Bible gives us of God's *true* Israel people, and using the testimonies of the double witnesses of prophecy and history, let us, as intelligent investigators, see which people in the world, available for a *line-up* identification, bear the characteristics which fit this recorded description. As we saw, Scripture declares that God's true Israel people would have a new name, and no longer be called by the name of Israel (Psalm 83:4; Isaiah 62:2; 65:15; Hosea 1:10; 2:17; Romans 9:25,26; I Peter 2:10; Acts 11:26). Therefore, let us first look at the names by which God's true Israel people are *now* called.

The Israel identity of the Germanic peoples can be found in the *very names* of the Germanic tribes. First off, the word *German* itself comes from the Latin Germānus,[89] and means, "***genuine** or **authentic** (in relation to a family or klan of people; brothers, cousins; having the same parents; from the same race).*" Is it just a coincidence God warned us in His Word that not *all* who "claim" to be Israel, are in fact Israelites, and the very name by which all the European peoples are known (Germanic) means, "genuine or authentic people of the same race"?

More specifically, the words **Jute** and **Juteland** (ancient geographical area that now includes parts of Denmark and West Germany) are clearly derived from *Judah.* The Jutes also peopled the Isle of Wight.

(It should be remembered that in Old English (and other *Germanic* languages), *each letter* in a word was pronounced—***no*** letters were silent. For example: *knife* was pronounced "kə-nī′-fə." In German and Old English, as in Hebrew, the "j" was not pronounced as it is modernly; it was a "y." Therefore, the word *Jute* would properly be pronounced "Yū′-tə." *Judah* itself would be pronounced "Yū′-də." Any student of language knows that the "d" and "t" are interchangeable consonants, and therefore *Jute* and *Judah* are the same word.)

The origin of the words **Dane** and **Danemark** (Denmark) can easily be seen in the name of ancient Israel's most notable seafaring tribe: *Dan.* One of the ancient **Scottish/Irish** tribes was called the *Tuatha dé **Dan**nan*, which means the "Tribe of **Dan**nan," and **Scotland** in times past was called *Cale**don**ia.*[90] Wherever the Tribe of Dan went, it left its mark. It was no new thing for the Tribe of Dan to name places after its patriarch; for it did this in biblical times also (Joshua 19:47; Judges 18:12, 29).

The word **Welsh**[91] means "foreigner." If these related Germanic peoples called some of their own people "foreigners," obviously, these kindred peoples must have arrived from different lands at different dates. The Bible states that there were *Israelites* living in lands *other than Palestine*, who were "strangers;"

[89] *Indo-European Roots* in The American Heritage Dictionary of The English Language.

[90] —a place name: a legacy established by the seafaring Tribe of Dan who left their name throughout Europe and Asia in obedience to God who commanded them to set up waymarks (**Jeremiah 31:21**). Other examples of Dan leaving his name are: **Dan**mark, **Don** River, **Dan**ube (which means settlement of Dan) River, **Dan**astris River (**Dn**eister), **Dan**apris River (**Dn**eiper), Dar**dan**elles Straits, Rho**dan** River (now the Rhone), Eri**dan** River (now the Po), Co**dan** Gulf (Baltic), **Dan**zig, **Dan**nemora (opposite the Gulf of Finland), Swe**den** (Svea-**dan**), **Don**castewr, **Dan**nonia (Devonshire), **Dun**dee, Aber**deen** (mouth of the Don), Mace**don**ia, Sar**din**ia (the dispersed of Dan), etc.

In Hebrew, the word translated *Dan* is #1835, Dân (dawn) and is a variation of #1777 dîyn (deen) or dûyn (doon). This is proof that vowels were interchangeable: dan, den, don, din, etc. This can also be understood by recognizing how *drastically different* many words are pronounced by the English, Americans, Scottish, etc. (as well as the different regional accents within each of these nations). *Dan* means "judge." (See **Genesis 30:6; 49:16.**) Dan was one of Jacob's sons; however, Jacob also had a daughter: Dinah [#1783 Dîynâh (dee-NAW), which means "justice," from #1777].

The Danites also travelled through Spain, leaving their name in the old Spanish title of **don**, meaning "master." *Master* and *judge* are similar in their meaning. In Geoffrey Chaucer's Canterbury Tales, (written in Old English in the 1300's), Chaucer refers to Solomon as "Daun Solomon." Daun is Dan in Middle English; both mean "master".

[91] —as does *Volcae* (Celtic), *Walloon* (Latin), *Weahl* (Old English), and *Gall/Gaul* (Irish Gaelic).

thus, it was a common word used to distinguish *racial brethren who came from a different region.*[92] God also said the Israelites would be cast out of the land of Israel into a land that neither they nor their fathers knew, a land to the north in which Israel and Judah would be joined again; whence God would one day lead them back to the land of Israel, once He had purged the land of all the Canaanites (Jeremiah 3:18; 16:13-15; Joel 3:17; Matthew 13:41; 15:13).

The word **Ruthenian (Ukrainian)** comes from **Rus**[93] and means "seafarer." No doubt, Ruthenians descend from the seafaring tribes of either Dan or *Zebulun* (Genesis 49:13). The Zebulunites were also known to be valiant warriors (Judges 5:18).

The word **British** (from the ***Brits***) is derived from the joining of two Hebrew words, *Beriyth* (#1285, ber-EETH), meaning "covenant," and *ish* (#376, eesh), meaning "man" or "people." Thus, the word ***British*** means "People of the Covenant."

The word **English (**from the ***Angles*)** itself is derived from the two Hebrew words *AY-ghel* and *ish*. *AY-ghel* (#5695 (Jeremiah 31:18); feminine form #5697, eg-LAW; Hosea 10:11) means, "a male calf, bullock, steer (frisking or nearly grown)," or "a female calf, heifer (nearly grown)." Thus the word ***English*** means "People of the Bull." The Israelites' sacrificial system was symbolized by the calf and the bull, and God often referred to Israel as a *calf* or *heifer* because they had not reached maturity and they were prone to rebellion and backsliding (Psalms 29:5-6; Isaiah 11:6; 27:10; Jeremiah 34:18-19; 31:18; 46:21; Hosea 8:5-6; 10:11).

John *Bull* has long been a British symbol, similar to our Uncle Sam. The words **Britain** and **England** are also each formed by two Hebrew words: *Britain* is formed from the joining of *Brith* with the Hebrew word *am* [#5971], which means "a people, tribe, nation." Thus ***Britain*** means "Nation of the Covenant," and ***England*** means "Nation of the Bull."

The word **Aryan** itself *quite possibly* comes from the Hebrew word **Ariel** (#740/739, ar-EE and #410, AYL), which means "Lion of God." Ariel was another name for the city of Jerusalem.[94] By joining the root of **Ariel** (#738, ar-YAY or #717 aw-RAW, which means "lion") with the Hebrew word **am**, we get the word *Aryay-am* or *Awraw-am*, meaning "(God's Mighty) People of the Lion." As we already saw, the lion was declared by God to be the symbol of *not only* the Tribe of Judah but of ***all*** *Israel*. The lion is the "king of beasts," a royal, noble animal. The word "Aryan" is more recently traced to the Sanskrit *ārya-in* meaning "noble," coming from the Indo-European root *āryo-in*, meaning "lord or ruler."

The word **Scot** comes from ***Scythian***, which we saw came from the Hebrew word for "tent dweller." The origin of the word *Scotland* is also associated with the Hebrew Princess *Scotia*, (who was named after her people, *Skuths*) who was

---

[92] The Bible uses different words for "stranger"; these words (even "jew" and "Gentile") can only be understood *in context*: There can be "strangers of your *own* people" and "strangers not of your people." See Apologetic Expositions...Isaiah 56 by Balaicius/STM.

[93] similar tribes were *Prus*(*si*) and *Borus*(*si*), from Old Norse Rōthsmenn: "seafarers."

[94] —the city of the Great King, the Lion of the Tribe of Judah (Christ); the city in which David dwelt (**Isaiah 29:1-7**). See Davis Dictionary of The Bible.

transported to the British Isles by the Prophet Jeremiah by way of Egypt and Spain (together with her sister Tea Tephi) to replant the monarchy of King David in their new home (Jeremiah 1:10; 31:28; 41:10; 43:6; Ezekiel 17:22-24).

Anciently, **Spain** was called ***Iberia*** (meaning "land of the Hebrews"); so is a region of southern Russia in the Crimea (modern **Georgia**) through which the Israelites passed on their route to Europe as the Scythians and Cimmerians.

Ireland was originally called ***Hibernia*** (which also means "land of the Hebrews"), ***Inis-Fail***, ***Erin***, and ***Scotia***.[95] Mr. N. Nielsen, in works he submitted to the *American-Israel Message* (c. 1950; then headquartered in Knoxville, Tennessee), claimed that the word ***Erin*** came from a Hebrew word *yarin*, which means "far away," and that the word **Irish** is derived from *yarish*, meaning "far away people." Nielsen also states that the Romans referred to Ireland as "the end of the earth." This is interesting, for God said that He would call, and save, His people from afar, from the Isles afar off, and the uttermost parts of the earth (Jeremiah 30:10; 31:10; 46:27; Mark 13:27; Acts 1:8).

One group of *islands off the coast of Scotland* is still known as the ***Hebrides***, which means "isles of the Hebrews." Similarly, off the coast of Australia there are also Islands called *New Caledonia*, *New Ireland*, and the *New Hebrides*. There is a group of Danish islands off the coast of Scotland that are called the *Faeroes* (pronounced by some as "faries"), pointing to possible descent from *Pharez*, one of Judah's twin sons.

Another ancient name for Britain was ***Albion***; the Scots were known as ***Albans***; and the names of the ***Albanians*** and the tribe of ***Alans*** all share the same meaning: "white." Another interesting fact, is that there are two islands off the coast of England: the *Isle of* ***Wight*** and the *Isle of* ***Man***. *Wight* (pronounced *white*) is a Middle English word which comes from the Old English *wiht* (which comes from the Germanic root *wihti-*, stemming from the Indo-European root *wekti-*), and means "human being." The term *Albanian* itself is actually Latin; the Albanians, in their own language, refer to themselves as **Shqiperia**, which means "children of the eagle." As we have seen, the eagle is very significant in Bible prophecy concerning Israel.

Byelorussian means "white Russian," and **Balt** means "white." The Byelorussians possibly descend, in part, from the Lithuanians.[96] The Lithuanians had

---

[95] Even as the Scythian Israelites were known by the name of Sakae (and many other names) they were also known as *Habiru, Abiru, Abiri*. When the Israelites arrived in Ireland from Spain, they were known as Iberians, from which Ireland attained its name of Iberne, the Latin form being *Ibernia* or *Hibernia*. All are obviously forms of the word "Hebrew." The name "Iberne" was later shortened to *Erne*, thus providing for the old Irish title of *Erin*. In similar manner, the ancient names of *Eire* and *Eirland* are derived from the final syllable of the word *Abiri* and from the name *Iberia*, which the Iberians (Israelites) brought to Ireland by way of Spain. *Inis-Fail* was the very first name of Ireland, meaning the "Land of Destiny." *Scotia* was its second name.

[96] See The Lithuanians: The Overlooked Nordic Tribe by Balaicius/STM (due out in 2001). The Lithuanian language is the oldest and purest European language and is credited by philologists as being the original tongue of the Aryan race. The Lithuanians are credited as those having best claim to being the original Aryan parent-stock. This book will have exciting information on the Lithuanian language, racial type, history, origins, and customs.

their origin in the first wave of Scythians, who settled on the Baltic shore and were the progenitors of the true Balts. Lithuania's history reveals they are direct descendents of the Scythians and that they came to the Baltic from the east, as their God told them to travel west until they again reached the sea. The Latvians themselves are a tribe of Lithuanians, as were the ancient (or Old) Prussians (Borussi), who were exterminated in the 13th century by the Teutonic knights.

Nielsen claims the word **Gael** (Gaul) itself is Hebrew, meaning "sons of the Living God." *El* is the Hebrew word meaning "the Almighty or Mighty God." This would be appropriate since God declared,

> ...It shall come to pass, that in the place where it was said unto them, ye are not My people, there it shall be said unto them, ye are the *sons of the Living God*.... the children of Judah and the children of Israel be gathered together, and appoint themselves one head... (Hosea 1:10-11).

(However, I have not been able to locate any Hebrew word *Ga* or *Gay* meaning "sons." What I did find was *gaw-AL* (#1350), which means "to redeem or do the part of a kinsman"—literally, "to be the next of kin.")

The word **America** comes from two Gothic words *Amel* and *Rich*, meaning "Kingdom of Heaven." This was declared by professor Miskovsky of Oberlin College in Ohio, based upon evidence from the 1500's from a geographical treatise done by Martin Waldseemüller, an exceptional German geographer and cartographer (c. 1470-1513) who lived most of his life in Alsace (northeastern France). Waldseemüller is credited with giving America its name from his Latin treatise *Cosmographiae introductio...* and its accompanying map, both published in 1507 in Saint Dié, France. The name *America* caught on and became so popular that Waldseemüller himself could not extinguish its usage, which he attempted to do years later when many people were confusing the origin of the name of America with the similarly sounding name of the Italian explorer *Amerigo Vespucci.* (Waldseemüller concluded that Vespucci's accomplishments were not as great as some people had thought, and decried the misassociation.) The famous German explorer, naturalist, and statesman Alexander von Humboldt (1769-1859) recognized the importance of Waldseemüller's work and again brought its existence to the attention of the academic world. In 1901 Humboldt's recognition of the importance of these documents caught national attention, and thus began a great search for the Waldseemüller maps. Only one or two copies still exist.

Let us now look *individually* at some of the white Anglo-Saxon nations that comprise God's true Israel people. The symbols of Israel are clearly evident in the coat of arms of each nation. We shall also discuss some enlightening historical and archaeological facts that prove the Israel identity of these Anglo-Saxon nations.

(We will not be able to list all of the Anglo-Saxon-Celtic and related nations; neither will space permit us to list all of the symbols of those nations we will discuss.. Other nations and symbols can be found in full color in Symbols of Our Celto-Saxon Heritage, by W. H. Bennett F.R.G.S., as well as in These Are Ancient Things, Association of the Covenant People, and Lifting Up An Ensign To The Nations, Ida M. Ferguson.)

The United Kingdom

Great Britain

Britain's coat of arms is full of Israel symbols (lions, unicorn, David's harp). The French motto on the scroll, *Dieu Et Mon Droit*, means "God and My Birthright." The Latin motto on the belt reads, *Honi Soit Qui Mal Y Pense*, meaning "Blame to Him who Thinks Evil of It." Scripture tells us,

> It is not of him that willeth...but of God...[who chooses according to His Will]...**who art thou that repliest against God?** Shall the thing formed say to Him that formed it, Why hast Thou made me thus?...[God hath chosen one people alone for His glory] (Romans 9:14-23).

Joseph had two sons, Ephraim and Manasseh. Ephraim received the double blessing, and God declared that he would be greater than Manasseh and that he would become a multitude of nations (Genesis 48:19). The Hebrew word for "multitude" [#4393 (mel-O)] actually means "fullness"—and never has any nation been characterized as a "fullness of nations in the earth" more than the British Empire, which stretches forth to every corner of the globe and at its peak was more than *five times larger* than even the Roman Empire, which before Britain was the greatest empire the world had ever known.

Never have any people been characterized as a "fullness" more than the people comprising the British Empire have; for they ruled the world and had at their disposal every natural resource the earth had to offer. God declared the glory of the power of Israel, and specifically Ephraim, would be like a strong *unicorn* who "by his power would push together the people to the ends of the earth" (Deuteronomy 33:17). What other people have ever fit this description? Have the "jews"?

The British flag (the *Union Jack*) itself has ancient origins. When Jacob blessed his grandsons Ephraim and Manasseh (the sons of Joseph), he crossed his arms, one over the other, placing his hands on the heads of the young lads in this manner (Genesis 48:8-20.). It is claimed that *Jacob's cross* (the crossing of his arms) is the origin of the name *Union Jack*. (Jack is a nickname for Jacob.) Interestingly enough, the Union Jack is also the superimposition of two Hebrew letters representing God's Name. Most people are probably familiar with Christ YeHoWSHuWaH's statement in the Greek New Testament, "I am Alpha and Omega, the Beginning and the End" (Revelation 1:11; 21:6; 22:13). (This title itself explains the very name YaHWeH: the "self-existing one.") Alpha and Omega are the first and last letters of the *Greek* alphabet. In the *Hebrew* (Isaiah 41:4; 44:6; 48:12), however, this name would be represented by the first and last letters of the *Hebrew* alphabet: *Aleph* and *Tau* (a and t), which in ancient Hebrew were written: "x" and "+". Superimposing these two letters creates the Union Jack, "✳," or an eight-pointed star. In Scripture, the number 8 represents a *New Beginning*, which is Christ Himself; even the numerical value of YeHoWSHuWaH's name is "888." (See any of the numerous books available on *Bible numerics.*) For centuries, the name of Christ has been represented by the superimposition of the first two *Greek* letters of the Greek word for Christ, (#5547) Χριστός (*krees-TAHS*): Chi (X) and Rho (P): " ☧." This symbol is still seen throughout Christian churches. It is fitting that Ephraim, the leader of the House of Israel, would choose a symbol (the Union Jack) that represents the very name of their God YaHWeH, in fulfillment of Scripture: "In the Name of YaHWeH we will set up our banners" (Psalm 20:5).

The British flag, the Union Jack, is no modern symbol. As we saw, it was the Saka, the blond and fair Israelites, who also travelled east to India to build that once great culture. Commander (and Rev.) L. G. A. Roberts, on page 63 of British History Traced From Egypt To Palestine (1927), displays a picture of *The Topez of the Sachi* (Sakae), a rock carving found near Bhopal in India, which is dated to the 4th century B.C.

This carving contains the very symbols of Britain (Ephraim): a lion, a unicorn[97] (any large-horned animal), a banner with 5-pointed stars, a banner with two Union Jacks, as well as another Union Jack symbol in the form of a wheel.

Haberman interestingly stated concerning the **Early Britons**:

> Strabo, the Greek geographer, and the contemporary Kymbelin, left us a good description of a Briton of his time:
>
> He came, clad not in skins like a Scythian, but with a bow in hand, a quiver hanging on his shoulders, a plaid wrapped around his body, a gilded belt encircling his loins, and trousers reaching from the waist down to the soles of his feet. He was easy in his address; agreeable in his conversation; active in his despatch; and secret in his management of great affairs; quick in judging of present accuracies; and ready to take his part in any sudden emergency; provident withal in guarding against futurity; diligent in the quest of wisdom; fond of friendship; trusting very little to fortune, yet having the entire confidence of others, and trusted with every thing for his prudence. He spoke Greek[98] with a fluency, that you would have thought he had been bred up in the Lyceum, and conversed all his life with the Academy of Athens (Tracing Our Ancestors, p. 107).

The dolichocephalic (long-headed) Hebrews had been in Britain since c. 1800 B.C., under the name of ***Habiru***. Sir Arthur Keith relates in regard to Britain's early history of repeated invasions by Nordic peoples,

> With one important exception, no strange or new racial stock was added to the British Isles: all were apparently branches of the human stock which still occupy the north-west of Europe—men of the Nordic type—or as I prefer to call them, the North Sea breed.... In all these invasions and colonizations,

[97] The unicorn spoken of in Scripture had more than one horn (**Deuteronomy 33:17**). It most likely was a wild bull or bison; however, it can be symbolized by the mythical unicorn or any creature with prominent horns, not antlers.

[98] It is also recorded that the early Scots farmers and herders—the common people, not only the university educated—also spoke Greek fluently. Why would the early Scots and Britons speak Greek—and fluently?

there is only one which was not drawn from the North Sea stock. That invasion took place in the second millennium before Christ, when the round-headed [brachiocephalic] stock of Central Europe broke through the Nordic belt, reached the shores of the North Sea, and invaded Britain (from *Nationality and Race*, 21st lecture given by Robert Boyle before the Oxford University Junior Scientific Club on November 17, 1919).

There are many historical landmarks in Britain that point to Israel ancestry. F. Wallace Connon, in Documents of Destiny (1958), records,

The west window of Westminster Abbey, which is over the main door, has four rows of panels. The three at the narrow top contain the figures of Abraham, Isaac, and Jacob; the next two rows of seven each contain figures of Reuben, Simeon, Levi, Judah, Zebulon, Issachar, and Dan; Gad, Asher, Napthali, Joseph, Benjamin, Moses, and Aaron; and the bottom row contains the emblem of Moses and the emblem of Aaron at each end, but in the centre the Lion of Judah, and the Bull of Joseph, the Arms of Britain.

The Coronation service throughout is an intensely interesting study, but two extracts will have to suffice:

When the Monarch is anointed on the head by the Archbishop the following words are used:

Be thy head anointed with holy oil, as Kings, Priests, and Prophets were anointed, and as Solomon was anointed by Zadoc the priest and Nathan the prophet, so be you anointed, blessed, and consecrated King over the peoples whom the Lord your God hath given you to rule and govern. In the name of the Father, and of the Son, and of the Holy Ghost. Amen.

Then shall the King go to his throne, and be lifted up into it by the Archbishops and Bishops, and the Archbishop standing before the King shall say:

Stand firm, and hold fast from henceforth the seat and state of royal and imperial dignity, which is this day delivered unto you, *in the Name*, and by the *Authority of Almighty God*.... And the Lord God Almighty, whose ministers we are, and the stewards of His mysteries, establish your throne in righteousness, that it may stand for evermore, like the sun before Him, and as the faithful witness in heaven. Amen (from the Official Book of the Coronation Service.) (pp. 106-107).

Ida M. Fergusan, in her book, Lifting Up An Ensign To The Nations, quotes from chapter 17 of Old and New London concerning James I's coronation:

King James entered London by the Gate of the Elders...Aldersgate, there is no longer any archway and gate there, all London gates have been removed: Aldersgate in 1761; but a bronze replica of the arch about to be described is still to be seen on the gate of St. Botolph's Churchyard, just off Aldersgate Street.

Over the Arch of the wateway the authorities of London erected two figures facing North, the direction from which King James would come. The figures were of the prophets Samuel and Jeremiah, and under each a biblical declaration: under Samuel the words were: "...Samuel said unto all Israel, Behold I have hearkened unto your voice...and I have made a king over you." (Israel's first king: Saul.) Under Jeremiah the words were, "Then shall there enter into the gates of this city kings and princes sitting upon the Throne of David, riding in chariots and on horses, they, and their princes, the MEN OF JUDAH, and the inhabitants of Jerusalem...this city shall remain for ever" (p. 84).

(Is it just a coincidence that statues of the prophets Samuel (who first gave Israel a king by God's appointment) and Jeremiah (who by God's appointment transferred this throne to the British Isles) were symbolically involved in the very coronation procession of Britain's kings—especially in their re-uniting under James?)

In regard to Britain being the "isles afar off" as recorded in the Bible, John D. Baldwin, A.M., in his Pre-historic Nations (1869; Harper & Brothers), states that in the ancient Sanskrit books the *British Islands* were referred to as "the Sacred Isles of the West" and were considered the abode of the Mighty, and the home of the "mighty ones" (p. 379).

Connon records the experience of an English chaplain in Cologne:

> [Rev. Glover asked the Rabbi] to write the word "England" in Hebrew.... Hebrew is written from right to left and Mr. Glover expected...the Rabbi would write England backward, beginning with the *D* in Hebrew and ending with an *E*, but...he wrote from right to left Mih-Iia," pronounced *Yaii-Yaiim*, the very Hebrew phrase used by Isaiah which we translate as "Isles of the Sea"...[adding] When we speak of the United Kingdom we say *Yaii-Yaiim* as if spelt *Aii-H'Im*. No educated Jew would write his meaning in any other form (Documents of Destiny p. 112). (Brackets mine.)

Evidence shows that Christ Himself founded the early church in Britain during the years between His early childhood and His recorded biblical ministry—the period about which the biblical record is silent. Greater evidence exists that Joseph of Arimethea,[99] a handful of the disciples, Mary the mother of Christ, and others migrated to Britain and strengthened the church. St. Andrew became the bishop (and patron saint) of Scotland. The Apostle Paul in his missionary journeys travelled to Britain. There are dozens of well-documented books on this topic. One of the best is The Drama of The Lost Disciples (1961) by George F. Jowett. A few historical proofs are listed below:

St. Augustine, in 600 A.D., wrote,

> In the western confines of Britain there is a certain royal island of large extent, surrounded by water, abounding in all the beauties of nature and necessities of life. In it the first neophytes of catholic (universal) law, God beforehand acquainting them, found[ed] a church constructed by no human art, *but by the hands of Christ Himself*, for the salvation of *His* people (Spelman, *Conecilia*, p. 5). (Emphasis and brackets mine.)

Gildas (Albanicus) the Wise (425-512 A.D.), a British historian, wrote: "Christ, the true Sun afford[ed] His light, the knowledge of His precepts, to our Island in the last year...of Tiberias Caesar" (*De Excidio Britanniae*, sec. 8, p. 25). (Brackets mine.)

Eusebius (260-340 A.D.): "The Apostle [Paul] passed beyond the ocean to the Isles called the Britannic Isles" (*De Demonstatione Evangelii*, Lib. III). (Brackets mine.)

William of Malmesbury (1080-1143 A.D.) was asked by the monks of Glastonbury to write their history. He recorded that after Christ's crucifiction and resurrection, Joseph of Arimethea arrived with 11 missionaries from the holy land, the king gave them 12 Hides of land (*De Antiquitate Glastoniae*, chapter I).

[99] —Christ's uncle, a wealthy tin merchant. Britain was known in antiquity as the *Cassiterides*: "the Isles of Tin."

Polydore Vergil (1470-1555): "Britain, partly through Joseph of Arimathea...was of all kingdoms the first that received the Gospel" (Lib.II).

* * * * * * * * * * * * * *

Ireland

The national coat of arms of Northern Ireland contains a lion, a deer, David's harp, the red hand of Ulster[100] and the flag of the patron saint of Ireland, St. Patrick.

Old Irish manuscripts provide much information concerning the Tuatha dé Dannan. Two excellent works on ancient Irish history are The General History of Ireland (1620) by Jeoffry Keating (translated by Dermo'd O'Connor, 1841; two vol. in one ed.) and *Annala Rioghachta Eireann* (1636) by The Four Masters (first complete translation (1851) as The Annals of (the Kingdom) of Ireland by John O'Donovan). These ancient histories record that the Dannans and Milesians[101] were of the same race and arrived in Ireland in different waves of migration from Greece, from Gothland (near the Euxine [Black] Sea), and from Scythia (near the Euxine and Caspian Seas). Migrations of Phoenicians and other people by way of Egypt are also recorded. Keating states that the Dannans migrated before the Milesians did, having left Greece after a battle with the Assyrians, and arrived in Ireland by way of Denmark and Norway (p. 40). The Milesians came to Ireland from Scythia by way of Spain.[102] The Four Masters indicate that the Dannans arrived in Ireland c. 1200 B.C. and the Milesians arrived c. 1000 B.C (p. 123).

Long before Israel was conquered and deported, remnants of several of the tribes had already begun migrating for various reasons. The Danites had left the land of Israel rather early, because they felt cramped in the land allotted to them (Judges 18). Further, the Tribe of Dan was an adventurous tribe and sailed all over with the Phoenicians (who were Hebrews and possibly also descendents of the Tribe of Dan themselves).

The renown naturalist, statesman, and explorer **Baron Alexander von Humboldt** (1769-1859) (whose scientific excursions laid the groundwork for the sciences of physical geography and meteorology) considered the Greeks to be Israelites, and he was certain that the early inhabitants of Ireland were pure Hebrews and that most of them came to Ireland by way of Spain from Greece. Humboldt stated that the Greeks, when they used the word "Phoenicians," included the Israelites as the same with these people.

If the Dannans arrived in Ireland c. 1200 B.C., this would have been about 85

---

[100] —usually with a red band around the wrist or a red rope encircling the hand, a symbol of the scarlet thread tied around the wrist of Judah's son Zarah **(Genesis 38:28-30).**

[101] —who are also sometimes called *Gadelians*; whose banner was a dead serpent on the staff of Moses (Haberman; p. 119).

[102] Ingersoll states the Tribes of Dan (Dannans) and Simeon (Simonii) came to Ireland, Scotland, and Wales. The main part of Simeon probably remained in Spain with the remnant of Zarah-Judah.

years after a great battle in which several prophecies were made concerning various of the tribes of Israel. One of these prophecies was that *Dan would **abide** in ships* (Judges 5:17), thus sailing all over the world. Even more illuminating is the fact revealed by Farley Mowat in his The Farfarers: Before the Norse (2000),

> ...that it was an ancient custom to convert ships that had served their time at sea to this final purpose [of placing them upside down on top of structures making them into barns and houses]. "Many Shetlanders *...had been conceived, lived, and died under or in a boat*" (p. 12). (Brackets and italics mine.)

Moses also prophesied about Dan's great journeying: "Dan is a lion's whelp; he shall leap from Bashan" (Deuteronomy 33:22). (Young lions are very adventurous and travel all over.) If the Milesians arrived c. 1000 B.C., this would have been around the time of King David and about 70 years before Israel was split into two kingdoms after Solomon's death.

(King Solomon was the wisest man who ever lived; however, he made many terrible mistakes when he followed the desires of the flesh rather than seeking to please God. Solomon taxed the Israelites excessively. His son, Rehoboam, planned on *increasing* the taxes—*against* the wise counsel of his older advisors. Since Israel already had a navy (I Kings 9:26-27; 10:11,22), it is possible some Israelites became dissatisfied with the government of their country and left before things got worse—even as the Puritans left Britain and travelled to Holland and America to escape persecution; even as many people left Russia before the Bolshevik Revolution; even as many people have fled Hong Kong since they know that British rule, peace, and safety are past. Many whites for a decade have been fleeing African nations, as barbarism has been imminent.)

Keating states that the Dannans and Milesians spoke the same language. Gawler refers to sources that indicate that this language, Gaelic or pure Irish (Erse), as spoken up until the 1700's, was identical with Hebrew (which was identical with Phoenician). Gawler further quotes a revealing statement from Phoenician Ireland (*Ibernia Phoenicea, seu Phoenicum in Ibernia incolatus, ex ejus priscarum coloniarum nominibus, et idololatrico cultu demonstratio, Auctore Doctore Joachimo Laurentio Villanueva*) by Joaquin Lorenzo Villanueva (1757-1837) as translated by Henry O'Brien (1831, Dublin, p. 184). Villanueva recorded,

> I recollect that in the Phoenician language is to be found the word *danihain*, signifying illustrious, generous, noble, or rather Danirfor Danani, or Danita, *the inhabitants of the city of Dan at the foot of Mount Lebanus, the spot where the Phoenicians* [Israelites] *worshipped the graven image given them by Micah, and where Jeroboam erected the golden calf* (See Judges xviii. 22-31) (Gawler, p. 31). (Emphasis and brackets mine.) (See Also Judges 17 and I Kings 14.)

Professor C. A. L. Totten, in his book, Our Race (c. 1896), recorded that the eminent Irish historian and antiquarian Colonel Charles Vallancey (1721-1812), based upon concrete evidence (which he recorded in his book, An Essay on The Antiquity of The Irish Language, 1772), firmly believed that Irish and Punic[103] were the self-

---

[103] Punic was the Phoenician dialect of Carthage. In Our Race, Totten also stated the Carthagenians, who nearly destroyed Rome, were Israelites mainly of the Tribe of Dan and Judah (mixed possibly with other Shemites). DeBurgh in The Ancient World* recorded that the Phoenicians were Shemites (p. 26). (* presumably William George De Burgh (1866-1943) Legacy of The Ancient World (1924).)

same language, or that they were branches of the same language, having their origin in a common mother-tongue.

(Though his name has been nearly erased from history of the modern era, Vallancey's discovery and decipherment of what has come to be known as *Ogam* script, according to Barry Fell, were "brilliant." Fell went so far to say that, "He was the first of a long line of linguists who have been responsible for virtually every major decipherment in archaeology" (America B.C. (1976) p. 11). **Charles Vallancey** went on to become Brigadier-General and Chief Engineer of Ireland.)

Haberman states the Milesians (Gadelians) were of the tribe of Judah and constituted the aristocracy of Ireland. He also shows that the Scots and Irish Gaelic, as well as the Welsh and Manx languages, are branches of the Phoenician/Hebrew language.[104] Haberman further states,

> It is most striking...that one of the old names for the Irish should be "Leagael," or in Hebrew, a stammering people, the double word representing the left to right Phoenician and the right to left Hebrew (p. 120).

The Four Masters also state that the Cuath di Dannan gave Ireland the name *Inis Fail* (The Isle of Destiny), in connection with the Lia-Fail (The Stone of Destiny)—the remarkable stone that they brought with them. This *mirror quality* of a word represented by both languages can again be found in this word *Liafail.*

Haberman, quoting the Irish historian O'Halloran (presumably Sylvester O'Halloran (1728-1807), Honorary Member of the Royal College of Surgeons, Ireland, from his books Complete History of Ireland, An Introduction to and An History of Ireland, or Ierne Defended), relates an ancient Irish law regulating how many colors a person's coat could contain, depending upon his caste or status:

> Here again do we find evidence of a descent from Joseph, whose father made him a coat of many colours.... Probably the plaid, according to the colours of which the Scotch clans were distinguished, originated in Joseph's Coat of many colours (p. 116).

Haberman also references Vallancey, who indicated there were *Priests of On*[105] in Ireland; that the ancient wells of Ireland were considered sacred in memory of the well into which Joseph's brethren cast him (before selling him into slavery, which carried him into Egypt) (Genesis 37:24-28); and that the ancient Irish stone circles were originally called *Bothals* in memory of the stone pillar Jacob made, which he called *Bethel*, meaning "House of God" (Genesis 28:18,19) (p. 116).

Connon records the introduction of an ancient poem from the Royal Irish Academy library "The Kings of the Race of Eibhair" (Heber, the ancestor of Abraham):

> The use of [Coats of] Armes and Escouchions [family shields] is anciently obserued by the Irishy in imitation of ye Children of Israell, who began to vse them in Egypt (at which time the ancestor of all the Irishy, called Gaoidhil, or Gathyelus there liued) which Armes, the Israellits at their passing through ye Redd Seas, vnder the conduct of Moyses did carry in their severall Banners.

[104] For more proof that the Celtic languages are identical with Hebrew, see **Appendix E** and Why Did God Create Other Races? and The Theocentric, Scientific Evolution of the Modern Nations and Languages of Israel by Balaicius/Sacred Truth Ministries.

[105] While in Egypt, Joseph married Asenath, the daughter of the *Priest of On* (a pure Adamite, Shemite, and possibly even Hebrew), who bore him Ephraim and Manasseh (**Genesis 41:45**).

They were Twelue Tribes, and each Tribe had a certaine number of men vnder his own command with Distinct Banners and Armes; then follows a list of the banners of Israel, of which the two in which we are interested for the present are Judah—a lion, and Joseph—a bull (Documents of Destiny, p. 106). (Brackets mine.)

One of the oldest names of **Ireland** is ***Erinn***. One of the sons of Ephraim was *Eran*, who was the father of an entire clan called *Eranites* (Numbers 26:36-37). In British History Traced..., Roberts relates that the Spanish-born Roman geographer Pomponius Mela (A.D. c.50) asserted (in his *De Situ Orbis...*, which was translated into English as The Cosmographer (1585) by Arthur Golding) that some of the earliest inhabitants of Ireland were "jews" [sic, Israelites] and gave the name *Erin* to the country.

The Book of Armagh, the old Irish Chronicles from the early 800's A.D., has a symbol for each of the gospels: a *man* for Matthew, a *lion* for Mark, an *ox* for Luke, and an *eagle* for John. These are the symbols of the 4 brigades of Israel (Ezekiel 1:5-20; 8:15; 9:4; 10:6, 18, 20-22; Revelation 4:7; 7:11; 14:3; 15:7; 19:4). These are also the symbols for the gospels as listed in the Latin Vulgate Bible (c. 400 A.D.). Other ancient books (c. 600-1000 A.D.), such as *The Books of Durrow, Lindisfarne, Kells*, and *Cathach*, also contain translations from the Latin Vulgate into Welsh, Celtic, Irish, and Scots Gaelic and contain the same symbols. Is it just a coincidence that the historical records of the European peoples have been called *The Irish* ***Chronicles****, the Anglo-Saxon* ***Chronicles****, the* ***Chronicles*** *of the Kings of Britain*, etc., even as the Israelites termed their history books as listed in the Old Testament? (See I Kings 14:19; II Kings 14:28; 15:31.)

* * * * * * * * * * * * *

Scotland

The national coat of arms of Scotland has 2 unicorns and *3** lions (*symbolizing the Trinity?: the lion on the flag representing the Holy Spirit (wind)?), thistles, chains, and the flag of their patron Saint Andrew. The Latin motto above the coat of arms reads *In Defens*, meaning "In Defense;" the Latin motto below reads *Nemo Me Impune Lacessit*, meaning "No One Attacks Me With Impunity (implying *—without being punished*)." This might be in reference to God promising Israel,

...I will...curse him that curseth thee.... No weapon that is formed against thee shall prosper...every tongue that shall rise against thee in judgment thou shalt condemn. This is the heritage of the servants of YaHWeH...their righteousness is of Me, saith YaHWeH.... Who shall lay any thing to the charge of God's elect? It is God that justifieth (Genesis 12:3; Isaiah 54:17; Romans 8:33).

Gawler quotes a footnote by Owen Connellen in (the first English translation (1846) of the second part of) The Annals of Ireland by The Four Masters indicating the kings of Scotland and the House of Stewart descended from the Irish Milesians (p. 32).

According to The Scottish Declaration of Independence (1983) by E. Raymond Capt, M.A., A.I.A, F.S.A., Scot., Scotland's most precious possession is its Declaration of Independence, known as the ***Declaration of Arbroath***. It was written to Pope XXII on April 6, 1320, at the bequest of King Robert of Scotland (Robert de Brus [the Bruce], Seventh Lord of Annandale) by Bernard de Linton, Abbot of Aberbrothick, and affirmed by the 25 members of the Scottish Estates in parliament, who affixed to it their respective noble seals. The letter described King Robert, who attempted to free his people and heritage from the hands of the enemy: Robert "arose like **another** *Joshua* or *Maccabeus*,[106] and cheerfully endured toil and weariness, hunger and peril." (Emphasis mine.) Consider the following testimony of the ancient Scots, from the Declaration of Arbroath (1320):

> Most holy Father and Lord, we know, and from the chronicles and books of the ancients we find that among other famous nations our own, the Scots, has been graced with widespread renown. They journeyed from *Greater Scythia* by way of the Tyrrhenian Sea and the Pillars of Hercules, and dwelt for a long course of time in Spain among the most savage tribes, but *nowhere could they be subdued by any race*, however barbarous. Thence they came, ***twelve hundred years after the children of Israel crossed the Red Sea***, to their home in the West where they still live today.... In their kingdom there have reigned one hundred and thirteen kings of their own royal stock, the line unbroken by a single foreigner.... The high qualities and deserts of these people, were they not otherwise manifest, gain glory enough from this: that the King of kings and the Lord of lords, **our Lord Jesus Christ**, *after His Passion and Resurrection,* ***called them***, even though settled in the uttermost parts of the earth, almost ***the first to His most holy faith***. Nor would He have confirmed them in that faith by merely anyone but by the first of His Apostles by calling—though second or third in rank—the most gentle Saint Andrew, the Blessed Peter's brother, and desired him to keep them under his protection as their patron forever (p. 23). (Emphasis mine.)

A few years before this declaration, just before a battle to conquer oppressors, on Sunday morning, June 24, 1314, King Robert the Bruce addressed his men:

> For us, the name of the Lord must be our hope of victory in battle. This day is a day of rejoicing.... With our Lord Jesus Christ as commander, Saint Andrew and the martyr Saint Thomas shall fight today with the saints of Scotland for the honour of their country and their nation (p.16).

Four years after the declaration, King Robert's wife bore him a son: David.

* * * * * * * * * * * * *

Wales

The symbol of the dragon dates back about 2,000 years. However, W. H. Bennett F.R.G.S., in Symbols of Our Celto-Saxon Heritage (1976), indicates that originally the symbol was a red rampant *lion* but was later changed to a red passant dragon (p. 169). The king of the ancient Welsh Silurians was called the *Pendragon*, meaning chief dragon; the symbol of the dragon was taken from this title. The dragon seems to be a *hybrid*

---

106 —a most valiant High Priest of Israel who delivered the Israelites from oppression in the Second century A.D. Detailed in the Apocrypha and Josephus, his line was the last of the true Israel Priests in the land of Palestine—the rest were Edomite usurpers.

symbol combining the *lion*, the *eagle*, and the *serpent*. The serpent is a symbol of wisdom—but most often, *dark* wisdom. Christ instructed His disciples to be "wise as serpents yet harmless as doves" (Matthew 10:16). The lion and the dragon are also closely associated in Scripture and are possibly interchangeable (Psalm 91:13). The serpent is primarily a symbol of the Tribe of Dan: God said Dan would be the *judge* (ruler) of all Israel (Genesis 49:16,17). The lion, a symbol of power, is also the chief symbol of the Tribe of Judah—the Royal Tribe. It is possible that the hybrid symbol of the dragon symbolizes a *special union* of the Tribes of Dan and Judah. God declared Judah was a lion, and the scepter (ruling authority) would not pass from Judah, nor a lawgiver from between his feet, until Christ returned (Genesis 49:8-10). It seems likely that *Dan* is this "lawgiver" between Judah's feet (appointed in authority under Judah). The Tribe of Benjamin was also to be closely connected with the Tribe of Judah (as we shall see when we discuss Iceland). *Judah and* ***Benjamin*** were to be in close association, as were *Judah and* ***Dan***, therefore, Benjamin and Dan *would also* ***have to be*** in close association. William the Conqueror, with his fellow Normans,[107] brought *Danelaw* (Dan's Law) to England. From this Danelaw (based upon the 10 Commandments) English Common Law was derived. American Common Law was, in turn, formulated from it. Thus, Dan has judged Israel: for all of our nations have been founded upon Dan's Law.

(It must be noted that the serpent is used in a special context in European heraldry, for the serpent is also the symbol of the *occult world* and of most false religions in their evil quest for power, dark knowledge, and false wisdom.)

The symbol of the dragon *may also be* a remnant of a larger symbol, which is found in other European nations' heraldry—a remnant of St. George[108] on a white horse slaying the dragon with a lance, spear, or sword. This dragon, of course, represents Satan, that old Serpent, the Devil (Revelation 20:2). This story can also be found in the Old English saga *Beowulf*. This symbol of St. George killing the dragon can be found in the coat of arms of certain provinces of the original Russian empire and several cities of Lithuania. Perhaps the serpent is a remnant from the brass serpent that God commanded Moses to affix to a rod (Numbers 21:8) and that would appear to be flying when wrapped around a pole and hoisted into the air. Scripture reveals that this serpent on the pole, of all unlikely things, was a type of *Christ* (John 3:14). Scripture also shows us how Israelites *corrupted* things that God intended for our good (II Kings 18:4; Exodus 32:2-4; the body of Moses was even buried in a secret place so the people would not one day dig it up and worship it). Ancient Irish and English records indicate that this rod of Aaron was taken to the British Isles, where it was planted, took root, and grew. As we already saw, one of the symbols of the early Irish was the Rod of Moses with a serpent.

---

[107] The Normans (Northmen) were Vikings, predominately Norwegians, Danes, and Icelanders. After the arrival of the Normans, England not only experienced a "fine tuning" of English law by the Danelaw (which included the introduction of the jury, based on the number 12), but they also experienced a revival in learning and a rebirth of spiritual fervor.

[108] It should be pointed out that the stories of Saint George and King Arthur are no mere legends. (See Saint George (1909) by E. O. Gordon.) Arthur himself descended from Joseph of Arimathea, Christ's uncle. (See The Pedigree of Arthur (1971) by Sir Ian Stuart-Knill, Bt., published by Kingdom Revival Crusade (England).)

The line of Zarah-Judah founded the Roman empire and the city of Troy and then moved to the British Isles and founded the city of London, which was first called Caer Troy or New Troy, later Londinum, and finally London. The Welsh Bardic literature records:

> And when Brutus had finished the building of the city and had strengthened its walls and castles, he consecrated them...made inflexible laws for the governance of such as should dwell there peacefully, and he put protection on the city and granted privilege to it. At this time, Beli [Eli] the Priest ruled in Judea, and the Ark of the Covenant was in captivity to the Philistines [c. 1050 B.C.] (*The Welsh Bruts*; from Prehistoric London (1914) by E. O. Gordon). (Brackets mine.)

Brigadier-General George N. Wilson, in his Coincidences: Pointers To Our Heritage (c. 1960), records:

> Caswell's* History of England states, "Druidical rites and ceremonies were *almost identical* with Mosaic ritual." Also "the Chief (Arch) Druid and the Israelite High Priest were *similarly arrayed*—even to the Breast Plate of Judgement with the twelve stones representing the Tribes of Israel and the Holy Name [YaHWeH] on the headgear." Charles Hubert (AD 1825), in his Religions of Britain, writes, "so near is the resemblance between the Druidical religion in Britain and the Patriarchal religion of the Hebrews that we would hesitate *NOT to pronounce their origin the SAME*" (p. 10). (* sic, presumably (John) Cassell's History of England (c. 1890) in 9 Volumes.) (Bracket mine.)

(Interestingly, the Welsh have a term for the *right-hand* (*deheulaw*) and it actually means the "*south* hand." This is ancient (eastern) terminology, since the right hand is only the "south hand" when facing *east* (from History of the Anglo-Saxons, Turner, Vol. 1, p. 66, fn. "a"). The Israelites used the very same concept. *Benjamin*, one of Jacob's sons, the founder of the Israelite Tribe bearing his name, means "son of the right hand." However, the Hebrew word actually carries the meaning of *south*, though it has not been translated in this manner since most people would not understand the meaning. The Hebrew word for *south* tay-MAWN (#8486) also means "right hand" and comes from the root yaw-MEEN (#3225), which is part of Benjamin's name *bayn* (son of) *yaw-MEEN*: Benjamin. The Druidical Priests were also exempt from war and taxes, as Hebrew Levitical Priests were. See also *The Welsh Triads* and Celt, Druid, and Culdee, Elder.)

* * * * * * * * * * * * * *

Canada

Canada's coat of arms is very similar to Britain's. The arms represent the original groups that make up Canada: England, Ireland, Scotland, and France. The Latin motto *A Mari Usque Ad Mare* means "From Sea To Sea." The Canadian flag of the 1920's (bottom right) was much different from the modern flag (top right), which simply bears a red maple leaf; but the maple leaf itself is significant. Scripture tells us:

> Blessed is the man...[who is not a friend of the world...but delights in God's ways]. He shall be like a *tree* planted by the rivers of water...his **leaf** also *shall*

*not wither**...whatsoever he doeth shall prosper.... Blessed is the man who trusteth in YaHWeH, and whose hope is in YaHWeH. For he shall be like a tree planted by the waters...[whose] **leaf** shall be green (Psalm 1:3; Jeremiah 17:7-8). (Brackets mine.) (* —also implying being *green*.)

The ***original*** maple leaves at the bottom of Canada's coat of arms (contained in the fly of the older Canadian flag, c. 1920) were ***green*** maple leaves, which were changed to red in 1957 (Symbols of the Nations (1973), A. Guy Hope and Janet B. Hope; p. 48).

Of all the nations of the world, Canada is *the only* nation that has been known as a ***Dominion***. Scripture declares, "Judah...His sanctuary, and Israel His *dominion*" (Psalm 114:1-2). Is Canada's motto just another *coincidence*, considering the fact that God said that Israel's *dominion* would be "From Sea to Sea"? (Psalm 72:8; Zechariah 9:10) The individual shields of Canada's *12* provinces and territories also contain: a bison, a ship, lions, unicorns, a wolf, lilies, and leaves.

* * * * * * * * * * * * * *

The United States of America

The coat of arms of the United States contains a pillar of a cloud encircling 13 stars, an eagle with 13 arrows, and an olive branch with 13 leaves and 13 olives. The original flag of the U.S. contained 13 stars and 13 stripes. The number 13 was the number of Manasseh. (The tribe of Joseph was divided among Joseph's two sons, Ephraim and Manasseh.) The number 13 in Scripture represents "rebellion." In a sense, this *rebellion* of Manasseh occurred when the colonies pulled away from Britain to form the United States. *Manasseh* means "forgetful"—and if ever any nation has been forgetful of its own origin and its God, it is the United States. The Israelites were commanded to teach the law to their children and not to forget it (Deuteronomy 6:1-9; 8:11; 9:7). As prophesied, rebellion against this command produces forgetfulness (blindness/ignorance). Is it merely a *coincidence* that the motto of the United States is ***E Pluribus Unum***, which means "One Out of Many"? Remember that God called Abraham out from among all the peoples of the world (even from among his own family) to be a special people, set apart unto Him as His chosen.

When the Pilgrims came to the New World, they proclaimed they were *led here by God*. God said He had appointed a place for His people where they would no longer roam and that He would plant them in this land (II Samuel 7:10; I Chronicles 17:9). In fulfillment of prophecy, America is this *Second Promised Land* in which His true Israel people were to finally come to rest; they would no longer have to roam throughout the earth. America clearly is this *Last Frontier*: peoples from every Israelite (Caucasian) nation have migrated to America. Very few have ever migrated *from* America. The forming of America was, at that point in time, one step toward the eventual regathering of all true Israel. All the tribes of Israel (each European-descended nation) have been gathered in America (Jeremiah 3:14-18) and continue to come here for rest and safety as the end of this evil age approaches.

We saw that the throne of David was transplanted to the British Isles. The

Celtic, Germanic, and Scandinavic peoples, which flowed out from the British Isles, were planted in America, also in fulfillment of the prophecy that Joseph would be like a *fruitful bough by a well whose branches run over the wall* (national borders) (Genesis 49:22). Britain, the Isle of Ephraim, is the bough by a well (surrounded by water) that grew so prosperously her branches went over the wall, spreading to America, Canada, Australia, South Africa, and *all over the world.* No other race has spread across the globe—*prospering enormously wherever it set roots*. God likened the transplanting of the throne of David to a cedar tree in which an eagle took the uppermost tender twigs (the king's daughters) to a distant, mighty nation where they would be replanted (Jeremiah 1:10; Ezekiel 17:22-24). True to prophecy, they grew mighty and prosperous and lived separate from the rest of her European brethren, in Britain, Australia, New Zealand, South Africa, Canada, the United States, and her other colonies.

America is mentioned in the prophecy given to Joseph's sons. God said after the fruitful bough grew over the wall (to America) the archers hated and grieved him, shooting at him (Genesis 49:23). These *archers* might represent the American Indians who waged bloody and hateful war against the colonists. They might also represent the Zulus in Africa, who savagely attacked the Boers.[109] God promised these lands to *His* people. Those who refuse to recognize God's sovereignty and His plan for His people say that the white man *stole* the land from the Indians. This is malicious propaganda. Dr. Barry Fell of Harvard University, in his three books, Bronze Age America, Saga America, and America B.C., proves that there were Norse Viking (as early as c. 1700 B.C.), Celtic (as early as c. 1000 B.C.), Phoenician (as early as c. 300 B.C.), and Hebrew and Roman (as early as c. A.D. 225) expeditions and settlements in America before the time of Christ. Further, the Indians *themselves* stole the land from those who inhabited the land before their arrival—by their own admission.

God promised if we obeyed His law, He would bring incredible blessings upon us, and the illegitimate inhabitants of the land would wane before us (Exodus 34:10-11; Deuteronomy 33:17; Isaiah 60:12). This occurred when we obeyed God's laws in the early days of America. But as we have turned from God's ways, other peoples have outpopulated us. God said if we forsook His law, curses would befall us and our enemies would become the head and we would become the tail. Every tragedy that has befallen us in America is a result of our sin and was predicted in Scripture—even cancer and AIDS (Leviticus 26; Deuteronomy 28).

America, "The Kingdom of Heaven," suffers violence by those third-world peoples who are entering her by force and demanding to be supported and given equal status with true Americans. These people are bringing their pagan gods and evil ways with them into our land (Matthew 11:12; John 10:1; Revelation 18:2-3), and America shall soon collapse under the burden. God is again using our enemies to chasten us to repentance.

(We are a sinful enough people ourselves. We do not need the added burden of

---

[109] The white Dutch farmers were in South Africa ***long*** before the blacks had migrated that far south.

having other peoples to teach us new avenues of idolatry and immorality. The Old Testament clearly records how the "mixed multitude" led Israel astray (Exodus 12:38; Numbers 11:4). However, it was the Israelites themselves who were to blame for allowing the mixed multitude to be among them. Likewise, **we** are primarily to blame. It was our sin in allowing them to enter, and our sin in allowing them to be given equal status. No other people allow foreigners to move among them *en mass*, gain equal or greater status, and then change the laws to their own benefit, to the detriment of the founders.)

One of the foremost symbols of the United States, the *Liberty Bell*, bears the inscription, "Proclaim Liberty throughout the Land...LE.XXV.X" (Leviticus 25:10). The Liberty Bell still resides in Philadelphia, Pennsylvania—our nation's first capital. *Philadelphia* means, "The City of Brotherly Love." Its very name has its origin in the Scriptures, being one of the few New Testament churches of whom Christ had anything good to say (Revelation 3:7). Christ said, "If you love Me, keep My Commandments" (John 14:15).

It should be pointed out that "brotherly love" is only possible when one lives among ***brethren***—and when these brethren follow the laws of God. God said our blind brethren would know we were His People by our love (John 13:35). True love is defined as obedience to God—following His ways, not man's.[110] God is righteous, holy, and just; He is a God of order, and God is love. Therefore, righteousness, holiness, justice, order, and love are defined by God's decree in His Holy Word—which does not change.[111] True love is displayed by *actions*, not mere words (lipservice). (See Proverbs 20:11 and Matthew 15:7,8.)

(For proof that true love is shown by obedience to God's Law, see John 14:15 and I John 2:5; 5:2-3. Further, understand *in context* the following verses: Psalm 66:18; Proverbs 28:9; Romans 8:28; 10:17; I Corinthians 2:9; I Thessalonians 1:3; Hebrews 6:10; James 2:5,17; I John 3:1,16-17,22; 4:7-11,16,20-21; Revelation 12:17; 14:12; 22:14.) Understanding this is *essential* to being sealed by God and to being part of the remnant that will survive the *wrath to come*. Please look them up now and return to God on *His* terms. God has set before us life and death. He desires that we choose life (Deuteronomy 30:19; Proverbs 14:12; 16:25; Hebrew 11:26; II Peter 3:9). Christ is the only way to life, and the terms are non-negotiable. Works play no part in *salvation*, they are a product *of* salvation: they show the inner man. (See Ephesians 2:10, II Corinthians 5:17, and I Peter 1:15,16.)

The Bible says in Hebrews 11:6, "But without faith it is impossible to please God: for he that cometh to God must believe that He is,[112] and that He is a rewarder of those who diligently seek Him." First of all, those who would come to God must believe that His record is true and unchanging. Second, those who seek God must do so *diligently*. How can one seek God?—only through obedience! Romans 10:17 says that faith comes solely from what God has revealed and decreed in His Word; and James 2:17 says that faith without works is dead. God can only bless *obedient* children who demonstrate *true* love.

---

[110] God established what is good, and what is evil—and pronounced a curse on those who would attempt to switch the two (**Isaiah 5:20**). We ought to obey God rather than man (**Acts 5:29**).

[111] What man determines to be good or evil changes almost daily (based upon how many perverts are "elected" each year); however, God and His Word never change (Psalm 100:5; 117:2; Malachi 3:6; Matthew 5:18; 24:35; Hebrews 13:8; James 1:17; I Peter 1:23; 2:5).

[112] *—that He is God, that He is just as He said He is, and that everything He has said is infallibly true, exactly what He intended to say, and constant.*

George Washington descended from royal blood himself. He was 54 generations from Odin, the first king of Scandinavia (from whom Queen Elizabeth also descended). When the government of the United States was formed, the people wanted George Washington to become the king, whereupon he declared, "We have no king but Jesus Christ." The fact that the United States elects its officials is also a fulfillment of prophecy (Hosea 1:11). Britain retains the monarchy promised to David. Although America also could have legitimately maintained this monarchy, according to God's divine plan, she chose to elect her officials.

Christopher Columbus declared that Isaiah 49:1-12 was fulfilled in his discovery of America. The Pilgrims who came to America referred to this new land as *The Wilderness* and *New Canaanland,* and they referred to themselves as *the children of Abraham, Isaac, and Jacob/Israel.* (See **Appendix G**.) When the early colonists arrived, they built a church in the community—even before they built their own houses—just as the children of Israel assembled the Tabernacle (God's dwelling place) among themselves first. Further, the 10 Commandments and the laws of the Bible were the first and only law of the early colonies, and all laws that were later created were based upon the Bible. In the early United States (and until recent times), in order to hold public office one was required to be a man of *European descent* who *professed Christ* and whose life was a reflection of this profession. This foundation upon the Word of God was the cause of America's greatness and has so been noted by many famous people.[113] It is the departure from God's law that is the cause of America's decline and demoralization. When our forefathers developed the Constitution, they did *not* establish the freedom of just *any* religion. They extended freedom and protection *solely* to ***true denominations of Christianity in the worship of the one true God.***

On October 16, 1746, the early colonies were about to be invaded by an irate France. When the colonists (who were few in number) heard this, they assembled and called for a national time of fasting and prayer. To make a long story short, the entire French fleet was wiped out by various disasters before it even got to the colonies. Upon learning of the defeat of the French navy, the colonists assembled to praise God, and the newspapers recorded that God had delivered His people in America, even as He had previously delivered His people out of the land of Egypt, drowning the armies of pharaoh in the Red Sea. (From a sermon preached (ironically) by a Rev. Jonathan *French* on November 29, 1798, recorded in The Christian History of The American Revolution (1976) by Verna M. Hall.)

In Scripture, the number *12* represents **Divine Governmental Perfection**. There were 12 tribes of Israel (assembled into 4 brigades of 3 tribes each; not counting Levi, the priestly tribe that was dispersed among the tribes for ministration). God commanded Israel to have a system of *just* weights and measures (Leviticus 19:36). America (Manasseh) and Britain (Ephraim) follow their own system of weights and measurements based on a factor of 12. (All other white nations utilize a system based on a factor of 10. The number 10 in Scripture symbolizes **Divine Ordinal Perfection**.)

Shortly after our Republic was formed, there came the call for an official seal.

---

[113] See America, Christianity, Liberty & Truth: What Famous Men Had To Say, by Balaicius/STM.

Thomas Jefferson and Benjamin Franklin, working independently, both suggested that the United States' official seal be fashioned after *the Israelites crossing the Red Sea with pharaoh's chariots drowning* (at left). After many proposals, this was seriously considered for the *reverse* of the seal, with the *obverse* (at right) containing a shield with the symbols of the 6 *original nations* that formed America: the rose (England), thistle (Scotland), David's harp (Ireland), eagle (Germany), lily (France), and lion (Holland) (Our Great Seal, Capt).

God ordained that Joseph would live apart from his brethren (Genesis 49:26b; Deuteronomy 33:16b; Psalm 80:2). Ephraim (Britain)[114] and Manasseh (the United States)—the House of Joseph—do in fact live *separate* from the rest of their European brethren. Even in their minds the English are separate, from Europe for they adamantly maintain they are not Europeans but *British*. Many British people opposed the building of the Chunnel[115] from the start, for they wanted the French and the rest of Europe to remain *in Europe*.

God used Joseph in Egypt to save all Israel from famine and death. History has a way of repeating itself: Ephraim and Manasseh (the Tribe of Joseph) have continually been used by God to save all Israel (all white nations), and the entire world,[116] from all sorts of famines, wars, calamities, and natural disasters. In fact, the United States of America feeds the entire world, even as Joseph was used by God to feed Egypt, as well as the family of Israel, during great famine.

Some symbols on early colonial flags were: lions, troops, horses and riders, eagles, sheaves of wheat, and even David and Goliath. Most of the mottos had a central theme: *trusting God* and having the *Lord as the leader or sovereign ruler*. One motto in particular is interesting—"Jehovah-Nissi: The Lord Our Banner."[117]

* * * * * * * * * * * * *

Scandinavia

The above flags bearing Christian crosses are (left to right): Norway, Iceland, Sweden, Denmark, and Finland. Originally, flags were hung down from a crossbar atop a pole so that the flag's emblem was visible regardless of whether the

---

[114] —and other nations under the *Crown*: Canada, Australia, New Zealand, and South Africa.

[115] The tunnel that was constructed under the English channel which connects England and Europe for mass transportation.

[116] In the Bible, Egypt is a symbol of the world.

[117] Some versions of this flag read "An Appeal To Heaven." German and English Bibles sometimes translate God's Name, Yahweh, as *Jehovah*.

wind was blowing. The full beauty of this sight was vividly portrayed in the 1992 Olympics, in which these flags were raised in triumph in their *original* positions. While other flags looked odd being raised in an inverted position, the Scandinavian flags looked perfectly normal—in fact, it was a moving sight.

(Although, *technically*, Denmark and Iceland are not Scandinavian countries, they are closely related. For this reason they are included in this section.)

Norway

Although the *lion* (dating back to the late 1100's) and the *battle ax* are the main symbols in the coat of arms of the Kingdom of Norway (*Kongeriket Norge*), the *wolf* is also an old symbol of Norway and the *Norvegrs* (*Northmen, Normans*), as is the *eagle*. Professor Herbert Bruce Hannay, in European and Other Race Origins (1914), says that a part of the Tribe of Benjamin left the East (c. 300 A.D.) and migrated to what is now Norway. Howard La Fay, in The Vikings (1972), states, "The pre-Viking North was a self-contained society.... Swedes, Norwegians and Danes spoke a common language, shared a common culture..." (p. 22). Runic characters first appeared in Scandinavia c. 200 A.D. and reportedly came from the Roman or Greek alphabets. Since the Greek Israelites migrated to Denmark, after leaving Greece, it is no surprise that Runic was derived from *Greek*. However, it is also possible that the Runic alphabet was derived from the *Punic* alphabet (as the names themselves clearly point to some relation), which was the Phoenician dialect of Carthage. We know that both the *Phoenicians* and the *Vikings* sailed all over the world and that they both left colonies in the British Isles and along the coasts of Italy, Spain, Portugal, and Africa. Is there any doubt that the two were one and the same—or of common origin?

Sharon Turner, in The History of the Anglo-Saxons (1870) (Bk. 2, ch. 8, fn.j.), tells us the Vandals (weakest of all the Viking nations) invaded Spain and passed victoriously into Africa, where they set up a kingdom, challenging the Roman Empire's province there. Rome's colonies were the most debauched and immoral of the day, but the Vandals were known for the *chastity* of their manners. Instead of the Vandals *becoming corrupt*, living among such depravity as found in Carthage and other towns of northern Africa, they *became its moral reformers*. They encouraged prostitutes to marry, made adultery a capital offense, and punished immorality so severely that great moral change transpired in all the provinces they conquered. Where did *barbarians* acquire such morals?

The physical descriptions of the Phoenecians and Vikings are also identical. Both were the best shipbuilders of their day. In fact, we are told that the Viking ships were so well designed that even with modern technology it is impossible to design a more seaworthy craft of its type. The Vikings built their ships without blueprints or plans—merely by "eyeing the craft up" as they built it.

(Even today, only one or two people in all of Scandinavia keep this dying art alive, building beautiful boats by eyeing them up, using a simple hand-forged ax and the nearly forgotten Norse measurement called the *alen* (about 21 inches). Is it a *coincidence* that the Egyptian Royal cubit (20.67 inches) which was identical to the ancient Hebrew long cubit, is roughly the same as the Norse *alen*?)

Norway was greatly responsible for colonizing Iceland, the Orkneys, Shetland, Faeroes, Hebrides, and the Isle of Man. The Faeroes Islands and the Isle of Man retain their Old Norse languages: Faeroes and Manx, respectively. La Fay records an illuminating piece of information about the Faeroes Islands in The Vikings:

> In the village of Kvívík on Stremoy, I paid my respects to a Faeroese patriarch, 92-year-old Graekaris Madsen. Fresh from a nap, Mr. Madsen received me in traditional attire: black knee breeches and black vest trimmed with silver buttons. He was interested to learn that I was an American. New York City, he said, owes the name of one of its boroughs, the Bronx, to a Faeroese, Jonas Bronck.
>
> Mr. Madsen incarnates the long continuity of Faeroese culture and the tenacity with which the islanders nurtured it during centuries of Danish domination. "When I was a boy," he told me, "we had no school in Kvívík. We'd never had one. My grandfather taught me to read and write and **to obey the laws of God....** He said, **'Honor thy father and thy mother** and all the ancestors from the very first to have settled here, **and you will live long in the country'"** (p.119). (Emphasis mine.) (See Deuteronomy 4:40; Ephesians 6:2,3.)

* * * * * * * * * * * *

Iceland

One of the oldest symbols of Iceland (Ísland) is the *wolf*; which was said to be one of the banners under which William the Conqueror entered the harbor to conquer England. It was the symbol and even the *name* of William's nephew. The *falcon* (eagle) and the *horn* are also symbols of Iceland. The coat of arms of Iceland contains a *bull*, an *eagle*, a *dragon*, and a *man*. As we already saw, the dragon was originally a *lion* and might symbolize the joining of the lion, eagle, and serpent. These four symbols of Iceland are the very symbols of the four *brigades of Israel* (as also described in Ezekiel 1:10 and Revelation 4:7).

Now we come to Iceland's ancestry as the tribe of Benjamin. Benjamin is a unique tribe, a special tribe that God set apart for His glory to be a light for Judah (and the *rest* of Israel too, since Judah rules over all Israel). Benjamin (the younger brother of Joseph) was Joseph's *favorite* brother, for they had a common mother. The tribe of Benjamin is represented today *chiefly* by Iceland. Scripture states that the dwelling place of the throne of David was to be *between the borders* of Judah and Benjamin (Ezekiel 48:22). England (where the throne of David resides) is between the borders of Germany (Judah) and Iceland (Benjamin). Scripture declares that Benjamin was to dwell in safety (Deuteronomy 33:12). For centuries Iceland never spent a penny on national defense, and yet it had never been invaded by a foreign nation. Scripture says Benjamin was to dwell between the shoulders of Ephraim and Manasseh (Deuteronomy 33:12; Psalm 80:2). Iceland is located above and between England (Ephraim) and America (Manasseh)—the shoulders (strength) of the world.

Benjamin was to be the light-bearing tribe for Judah—to lead the way for

Judah to rule (I Kings 11:35-36; 15:4; I Chronicles 21:6). Of the 12 disciples, only *Judas Iscariot* was a "jew." *The other 11 disciples* were *Israelites* of the Tribe of ***Benjamin***, as were *Matthias* (who replaced Judas) and the *Apostle Paul.* How apropos that Christ said unto them, "Ye are the light of the world" (Matthew 5:14). It was these light-bearing Benjamites who then took the Gospel into all the world to their dispersed Israel brethren. Since God ordained Benjamin to be the light-bearing tribe, it is only fitting the disciples and the Apostle Paul were *Benjamites.*

In His foreknowledge and faithfulness, God prepared a way to preserve the Tribe of Benjamin so they would always be there to lead the way out of darkness. Before Babylon came to conquer and carry Judah and Benjamin away, God warned the Benjamites to flee Jerusalem (Jeremiah 6:1), and many of them did. Josephus confirms this (Complete Works of Flavius Josephus, *Wars*, II, 19, 7). These Benjamites returned when it was safe and repopulated the northern land of Israel in Galilee. The Temple Dictionary of The Bible states under the heading "Galilee" that the terms *Galileans* and *Benjamites* are synonymous. Professor Hannay also states that the Galatians of Asia Minor were Benjamites, who escaped captivity in Babylon and Media, the name *Galatia* coming from the Babylonian word *Galutha,* meaning *prisoner.* There is a province in southeastern Poland and northwestern Ukraine called *Galicia.* This is the general area in which the Scythian Israelites settled once they left captivity. (This area was also known as *Crimea* or *Scythia.*) There is also a region in northwestern Spain called *Galicia*, whose ancient name was *Gallaecia.* Since the early church fathers and other respectable scholars attest to the fact that the epistle to the Galatians was written to the Galls (Gauls/Gaels) of France (*Gallia*), is it such a coincidence that a region of northwestern Spain bordering France is called *Galicia*? George F. Jowett, on page 66 of Drama of the Lost Disciples (1961), indicates that this is supported by St. Epiphanius (315-407 A.D.); Theodoret (393-458 A.D.); Cardinal Baronias (1538-1607); and Rev. Lional Smithett Lewis, M.A., (Vicar of Glastonbury, the leading church historian of his day: St. Joseph of Arimethea (1922) and Glastonbury: Her Saints (1925)). Tertullian (155-222 A.D.) also stated that the various parts of Gaul (as well as Spain and Britain) had received the religion of Christ (*Tertullian De. Fidei*, p. 179). The book of Galatians is considered to have been written c. 50 A.D. It does not seem farfetched that 100 years or so later a church father would state that the region of France (Galatia) had already received the religion of Christ.

Later, to again preserve this Benjamite remnant, Christ gave them the same warning to flee before the Romans would sack Jerusalem in 70 A.D. (Luke 21:20-24). Oxonian (W. H. M. Milner), in Israel's Wanderings (1900), states that the "Christians [of Asia Minor] of the first two centuries were mainly of the Tribe of Benjamin." The Benjamites eventually migrated north and became known as *Dacians*, settling in Scandinavia. This is confirmed by Eusebius Pamphilus of Caesarea (260-340 A.D.) in his *Historia Ecclesiae* (Ecclesiastical History) (Book 111, 5, 2).

The Icelandic language is one of the purest European languages. A linguistic cousin to English (a Germanic language), it has also greatly influenced English. Many of the most important words in English are Icelandic: father, mother, brother, sister, ill, glad, die, etc. Iceland began the production of literature in 1117 and was one of the first European nations to write in its own language. Up until then, most literature was written in Latin, thus keeping the average person in *darkness*. The first book published in Iceland contained the laws of Iceland; the second book contained its history. After this, Iceland began to produce more books per capita than any other country in the world. Is it just a coincidence that the very first books of the Bible are the *laws* and *history* of the Israelites?

The people of Iceland have, as a shining example to the rest of Israel, preserved the purity of their race and kept from intermarrying. It is the only Germanic nation that is still approximately 99 percent white. Further, in Israel tradition, they have kept intricate genealogies. Dr. Jón Stephásson says, "We possess the records and genealogies of many hundreds of the most prominent of these settlers in the *Book of Land-takes* (*Land-námabók*). No other nation possesses so full and detailed records of its beginnings." Adam Rutherford, F.R.A.S., F.R.G.S., was present at the day of Iceland's independence, and reportedly many Icelanders in parliament confessed to him their knowledge that they descended from the Tribe Benjamin.

The Tribe of Benjamin was the smallest tribe of Israel, and Iceland is the smallest white nation. Benjamin was the last of Jacob's sons to be born, and Iceland was the last European country to be settled (9th century), the last European nation to be formed (1918), and the last to become independent (1941), making it the youngest European nation. Iceland was first colonized (c. 785 A.D.) with Celtic Culdees, then Albans from Scotland (See The Farfarers: Before The Norse, by Farley Mowat, which centers on the obscure Albans), then peoples from Ireland and greater amounts of Norsemen from Norway (c. 850). Is it any wonder, that the Icelanders keep such careful genealogies, seeing how the Scots themselves have also preserved their family clan genealogies for over a millennium?

Iceland, the land of Benjamin, the light-bearing tribe, is also geographically known as the *Ring of Fire* and the *Land of Fire*, for it contains some of the most active volcanoes on the face of the earth. In fact, the whole island of Iceland was formed by volcanic eruption and lava flow. Iceland is also the land of the **Northern Lights** (the *Aurora Borealis*). How *illuminating* that the Prophet Isaiah declared,

> They shall lift up their voice, they shall sing for the majesty of YaHWeH, they shall cry aloud *from the sea*. Wherefore glorify ye YaHWeH *in the **fires***, even the Name of YaHWeH God of Israel *in the **isles of the sea***. From the ***uttermost part of the earth*** have we heard songs... (Isaiah 24:14-16).

The Hebrew word translated "fires" in this passage is *oor* [#217], which means "fire, flame, or lights." Unfortunately, many fine translations *erroneously* render the word as the "east," since the sun rises in the east. Thus, to balance the verse out, they render *uttermost parts of the earth* as the "west." As we saw, however, Ireland was known as *the land afar off*, and as *Ultima Thule* by the Romans, which we saw means "the uttermost parts of the earth." If the British Isles can be described thusly, even more would the title apply to Iceland. Interestingly, even Sir Richard Burton, in his voluminous work about Iceland titled Ultima Thule (1875), describes Iceland as "the Canaan of the North." The Welsh Burton himself believed the Welsh and their kin to be descended from Israel. According to some, Burton celebrated Passover in his home.

(Information on Iceland drawn in part from Iceland's Great Inheritance (1937), Rutherford; Encyclopedia Americana (1950), Americana Corporation, New York, Vol. 14; Symbols of Our Celto-Saxon Heritage (1976), Bennett.)

* * * * * * * * * * * * *

Sweden

The Kingdom of Sweden (*Konungariket Sverige*) dates back to the 9th century. The flag of Sweden (Svea-***dan***) dates back to 1448. Individual provinces of Sweden have the following symbols: bull, deer, moose, man, eagle, and gryphon (a creature, with the top half of an eagle and the bottom half of a lion; it might symbolize two different tribes of Israel or a brigade and the tribe within it). The *lion* in the coat of arms dates back to 1200; the emblem of 3 crowns (representing Swedes, Goths, and Wends) dates to 1364. The shield contains a silver urn (or chalice), a gold eagle with silver stars, and a silver twin-turreted castle. The chalice or goblet (in conjunction with other factors) seems to indicate that Sweden represents the Tribe of Asher, which was said to be fat (rich) and yield royal dainties (Genesis 49:20), of which wine is included. (Wine was the traditional drink served in goblets.) The Tribe of Asher was prophesied to live on the seashore and abide in his (or possibly *Dan's*) breaches (Judges 5:17). (The Moffatt, Smith/Goodspeed, and Moulton translations of the Bible render *breaches* as "creeks.") The Hebrew word translated *breaches* is *mif-RAWTS* (#4664), meaning "a break in the shore, a haven or breach;" it comes from *paw-RATS* (#6555), which means "to burst (or break) out (or abroad), to spread, scatter, grow, increase." It is well known that the Swedes sailed all along the coastlines of the world and navigated the Danube and other rivers inland to explore, conquer, and establish settlements. Yet they always kept their homeland close to their hearts. The fearless Swedish Vikings braved wild and uncharted rivers through Scythia and funneled into the Black and Caspian Seas. The Gulf of Bothnia above Sweden was originally called the Co**dan**us Sea. The Normanist School maintains Swedish Vikings founded the true Russian Empire in the 9th and 10th centuries, with its capital of Novgorod, called Holmgård by the Norsemen. The first rulers of Kiev were Scandinavians.

The Swedish Rus and the Normans also produced some of the most mighty and distinguished mercenary forces ever known: the *Varangian Guard*. The most famous of these were 8 sons of Tancred de Hauteville (an obscure Norman knight) who founded the kingdom of Sicily and southern Italy—considered by many the greatest kingdom of its time. The Normans also established a kingdom in France bearing their name (*Normandie*), which was the springboard for William the Conqueror's conquest of England.

In The Racial History of Scandinavia: An Outline, Bertil J. Lundman, Ph.D (born 1899; professor of Physical Anthropology at the University of Uppsala, Sweden), records that German immigration into Sweden continued into the 18th century and that more than one third of the nobility was of German blood. Lundman reported "the most capable of recent migrants [to Sweden] are the often intellectual refugees from the small Baltic nations."

* * * * * * * * * * * * *

Denmark

The kingdom of Denmark (*Konigeriget Danmark*) is nearly 1,200 years old. Denmark's flag, the *Dannebrog*, means "Dan's Cloth" and dates back to the early 1200's. A few items on Denmark's coat of arms are two men guarding and supporting the shield; the main shield contains in its quadrants (clockwise from top left): 1) three blue, crowned lions (the 12th century state emblem); 2) two blue lions (Schleswig); 3) one blue lion with red hearts (ruler of Wends) and a Wivern (dominion over the Goths); and 4) three golden crowns (union of Denmark, Norway, and Sweden), and a ram (Faeroes); there is also supposed to be a falcon (Iceland). The middle shield contains a gold horse head (Lauenburg) and a gold armored rider on a white horse (Ditmarsh).

Keating and others showed us that the Danite Israelites left Greece after a battle with the Assyrians and sailed north settling in Denmark. The Danish historian **Saxo** (called) **Grammaticus**, in his *Gesta Danorum* (also called *Historica Danica*) (1188-1201), tells us that two brothers, Angel and Dan, settled in what is now Denmark and that some of Angel's descendents then migrated to England (translation by Jorgen Girik, Vol. 1, pp. 66-67). The **Venerable Bede** (673-735), the famous English church historian left a similar record in his Ecclesiastical History of the English Nation.

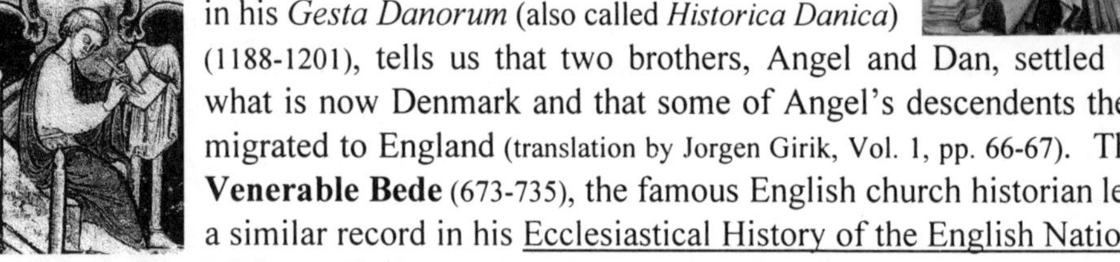

La Fay, in The Vikings, displays color photographs of a Viking-age graveyard in Jelling, Denmark, that contains various stone monuments, one of which is a stone bearing the Runic inscription, "Danmark," that dates to c. 980 A.D. Jørn Bie, an expert on the stones, says the stone is "Denmark's birth certificate" (pp. 64-65).

In Judah's Scepter and Joseph's Birthright (1902), Bishop J. H. Allen reveals that shortly before 1650 A.D., a Danish peasant and his daughter were following their plow in the field when something bright and glittering was turned up. The object turned out to be a golden trumpet ornamented with a lily and a pomegranate. It was taken to the authorities and identified by experts to be one of the *seven Golden Trumpets* of the ancient Israelites used in Jerusalem in their Temple altar services. This trumpet is in the National Museum in Copenhagen (p. 265).

Some of the symbols of the provinces of Denmark are castles, trees, bulls, horses, ships, water, horns, eagles, wheat, (olive) branches, lions, and stars.

* * * * * * * * * * * * * * *

Finland

The Finns seem first to have inhabited the area around the Volga, but they were driven from that area by the Bulgars (c. 7th century A.D.), and so they migrated north to the land they now occupy, driving the Lapps living in the area even further north. The Finns were converted to Christianity (c. 12th century) by the Swedes

Finland's coat of arms was developed in the 16th century, upon becoming a grand duchy (having previously been jointly ruled for more than 400 years with Sweden), by King Johan III. Its flag was originally similar to the coat of arms.

More recently, Finland had been ruled by the tsars of Imperial Russia until 1919 (after the Russian Empire fell following the assassination of the tsars by the Bolsheviks). Civil war broke out between the *Red Guard* (pro-Bolshevik Finns aided by the Bolsheviks) and the **White Guard** (pro-German Finns and White Russians). It is reported that before the Finnish General, **Baron Carl Gustav Emil von Mannerheim** (1867-1951) (who was of Swedish-Finnish descent) led the White Guard (and 12,000 German troops) victoriously against the Red Guard, Mannerheim inspired his men with a moving speech, inciting them to fight for victory, calling them, "men of ***Issachar***" (one of the tribes of Israel). Finland soon thereafter became an independent republic (*Suomen Tasavalta*; meaning "Land of a Thousand Lakes"). Finland's flag and coat of arms originally had a dark red field; however, they abandoned the red shield to avoid any association with the *Bolsheviks* (who later adopted the color of blood upon which their despotic dynasty is founded). The nine silver roses symbolize the original provinces that formed Finland. The lion trampling the Russian scimitar symbolizes the desire to remain free and independent.

* * * * * * * * * * * *

The Balts

According to Alfred Bilmanis, in his History of Latvia (1951), scholars agree that the root *-balt* means "white" and that the Baltic region (and peoples) acquired their name because the region was

> settled by blond, blue-eyed tribes who contrasted with the darker Finno-Ugric[118] peoples to the north. These light-skinned prehistoric settlers were called *Balts*, or Whites, whence *Baltia*, the name...the Roman geographer Pliny the Elder, who wrote of his journey to the north of Europe in the first century A.D., uses to describe the land which he affirmed was similarly denominated by the Phoenician merchant Pytheas of Massilia, who had visited it in the fourth century B.C. Wolfstan, the geographer of Alfred the Great, called this country "Whitland," an obvious translation of *Baltia*. This latter term, then, appears to be much older than the name of the Baltic Sea, which was first used, in the form *mare balteum*, by the eleventh-century chronicler Adam of Bremen (p. 4).

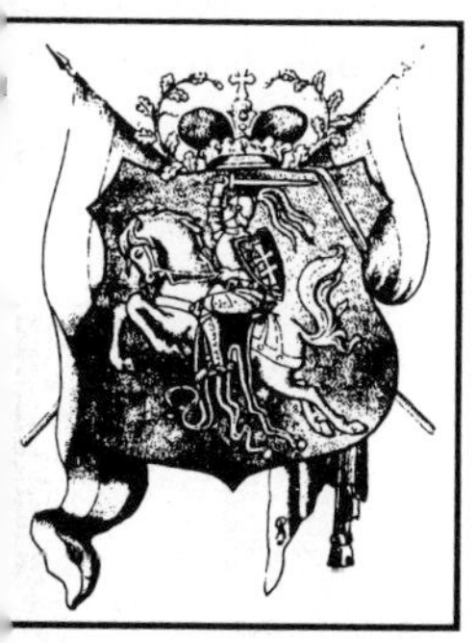

Lithuania

The coat of arms of Lithuania (*Lietuva*), considered one of the oldest European coat of arms, features an armed rider on a white horse (the *Vytis*; the only one of its kind in European heraldry) and dates back to the early 1200's. The double cross (‡) (commonly called the *Vytis Cross*) is also unique to Lithuania. (Though it does appear on the

[18] The Estonians (a Baltic nation above Latvia) are related to the Ugric Magyars of Hungary (Huns) and the aboriginal Lapps of Finland, are not Caucasian, but Turko-Mongol. However, many people living in Estonia are actually descended from Latvians, Lithuanians, Germans, and Danes.

Collar of the Order of the Seraphim hanging below the coat of arms of Sweden, it does so because the Swedish king Sigismund Vasa III's mother was the Lithuanian Grand Dutchess Caterina, daughter of Žygimantas II.) The *Vytis*, *might* point to the Tribe of Dan, or a confederacy of the other tribes of Israel. Scripture records:

> Dan shall judge his people, as one of the tribes of Israel. Dan shall be a serpent by the way, an adder in the path, that biteth **the horse heels, so that his rider shall fall backward** (Genesis 49:16-17).

The *Vytis* symbol *might be* a fragment from St. George slaying the dragon, which is the official symbol of the cities of Marijampolė, Prienas, and Varniai. St. George slaying the dragon is also an old symbol England and Imperial Russia.

The iron wolf (*Vilkas*) is also an important symbol of Lithuania (dating to the early 1300's). According to the eminent Swiss Professor Dr. Joseph Ehret, in Lithuania: The European Adam (translated into English from the German in 1973), the Lithuanian word *vilkas* (wolf) is philologically related to the Indo-European root *welk*, "which means 'to drag away.' It is an animal that drags away its plunder" (p. 24). God said that Benjamin would ravin as a wolf (Genesis 49:27). The word *ravin* in Hebrew [#2963 (*taw-RAF*)] means "to pluck off or pull to pieces." Lithuania primarily represents Benjamin. Having always had a strong priesthood, however, there is probably a good portion of Levi. Other symbols of Lithuanian provinces are: bulls, lions, eagles, battle axes, ships, deer, lilies (officially as early as 1611), swords, spears, bow and arrows, griffins, sheep, wheat, rose, unicorn, angel slaying a dragon, and bison.

The Lithuanians are direct descendents of the Scythians. Tacitus in the first century A.D. and Herodotus in the fifth century referred to the Lithuanians as "Aistii" (*Aestiorum gentes*), which means *honorable people*. They were so called because they were highly respected by all their neighbors. The Lithuanians were first called Lithuanians in 1009 A.D. in the *Annals Qedlinburgenses*. Although there were many different Lithuanian tribes, the major tribes were Lithuanians Proper, Latvians, and Old Prussians (Lithuania Minor: *Prussi*; exterminated by the Catholic Teutonic knights in the 13th century). In 1434, under Grand Duke Vytautas, the Lithuanian Empire was so vast, it ruled all of Poland, the Ukraine, Rumania, Prussia, the east Baltic coast, and all the way to Moscow and to the Black Sea. It covered 350,000 square miles (today it covers 26,000), and thus was the largest empire in all of Europe. (See The Lithuanians: The Overlooked Nordic Tribe by Balaicius/STM. Due out 2001.) Lithuania is considered one of the purest white nations left on earth (accompanied only by Latvia and Iceland).

* * * * * * * * * * * * * *

Latvia

The Latvians (Letts or Latgallians) are a tribe of Lithuanians. The symbols on the national coat of arms of Latvia (*Latvija*) are lions, griffins, the sun and stars, and oak branches. Latvians today sometimes refer to their country as *Baltija*, but they refer to themselves as Latviji (*Latweeschi*). The ancient Latvians believed themselves to be sons and daughters of the sun. Their history shows a remarkable military prowess. The head of the Latvian family was the father, who also acted as supreme *judge* and *priest.* The oak tree was considered to be the abode of the souls of ancestors. Ancient Latvian paganism tells of a great world flood. The pagan Latvians did not worship idols but believed in a God and the spirit world. Modern Latvians are of sturdy peasant stock, with great loyalty to the traditions of their race. Traditional Latvian musical instruments are the harp, flute, drum, and bagpipes. Many parallels can thus be seen between the Latvians and the ancient Israelites.

* * * * * * * * * * * * *

The True Rus

Imperial Russia

The Russian (*Rossiya*) civil flag of 1914-1917 (top right) was white, blue, and red with a *bicephalic* (double-headed) eagle (which dates to at least the late 1400's) occupying the canton. The coat of arms (top left) is that of one of the tsars (or *czars*). As with the Russian Imperial arms (at right), the numerous crests contain symbols of the individual coat of arms of various Russian cities, nobles, provinces, or districts. They contain: crowns, orbs, scepters, wiverns, St. George slaying the dragon, eagles, swords, lions, armed riders, horses, bow and arrows, and deer.

The original Rus were most likely Swedish Vikings, who with Rurik the Great founded the great dynasty of the true Russian Empire, siring some of the godliest rulers Europe and the world would ever know—the Romanov Tsars (or *Czars*). The Zionist Bolsheviks assassinated the Romanovs, initially one at a time, then finally *en masse*, because they stood in the way of the Bolshevik effort to destroy Christianity and overtake all of Europe. The royal houses of Europe so intermarried that the tsars boasted that *every dynasty of Europe was married to a Russian princess*. (See Professor R. G. Latham's Native Races of the Russian Empire (1854) for a more in-depth understanding of the racial elements that make up present-day Russia.)

Bottom right: Tsar Nicholas II and his family shortly before their gruesome and tragic execution: Empress Alexandra is seated on *Nicholas'* right; in front of her is Alexei; behind her from left to right: Maria, Tatiana, Olga, and Anastasia.

Tsar Nicholas II

* * * * * * * * * * * * *

Central Europe

Germany

The eagle has been a national symbol of Germany (*Deutschland*) since the 9th century. At times, the eagle was bi-cephalic (double-headed) to symbolize both the royal and imperial dignities. Germany's present flag is made up of black, red, and *gold* horizontal stripes of equal size. Originally, however, the colors were black, *white*, and red—proposed by Prince Bismark. At times, the eagle on a gold shield was also included on the flag. Flags of 4 German provinces are displayed below: (from left to right) Hamburg, Saar, Lower Saxony, and Baden-Württemberg, emblazoned with lions and a white horse.

The modern Germans (*Deutschen*), in great part, have descended from the Saxons (sons of Isaac) and the Teutons, as well as the Jutes (Judah). The Teutons lived in Jutland until c. 100 B.C. We have seen that the Latin word *Germānus* means, "authentic or genuine people...from the same race, the same parents, or grandparents;" and comes from the Indo-European root *gene-*. The Latin word for Teuton, *Teutonī*, means "of the whole tribe." The Indo-European root for Teuton is *teutā*, which became the root *theudā-* in the Germanic meaning "people," which became *duutsch* in Middle Dutch, meaning "Teuton (German)." The suffixed form *teut-onōs* means "they of the tribe," which became the Germanic tribal name of *theudanōz*, which was borrowed from Celtic and later appeared in Latin as *Teutōnī*. As we already saw, Ortelius recorded more than 300 years ago that Israelites migrating through Europe took the name *Gauthei*, which means "the people of God" (shortened to *Goth*), and that Tacitus called them "Teutones Gothones." The Goths founded the Pannonian Empire, ruled Italy for a time, and founded a Kingdom in Spain. Ferdinand and Isabella of Spain, as well as many of the leaders of the arts in Italy (Raphael, Vivaldi, etc.) descended from the Goths.

According to Turner, in The History of the Anglo-Saxons, the Saxons were proud of their descent. They were anxious to preserve and perpetuate themselves and were thus averse to marriages with other nations. Starting around the 8th century, the *Saxons* were governed by 12 Ethelings (nobles) of equal rank. During wartime, one of the 12 was chosen king. When the war was over, the war-king then returned to equal rank (Bk. 2, pp. 143, 145, 146).

The Germans are the epitome of the creative genius, industrious ethic, and honest, hospitable nature with which God created Adamkind in general, and Israel specifically. (To learn the truth about what *really* happened during World War II, send SASE to Sacred Truth Ministries or the distributor of this book.)

* * * * * * * * * * * * * *

Belgium

Belgium owes its name to the Belgae, a people from ancient Gaul. The Franks also appeared here in the 3rd century A. D. The Flemings (Teutonic) and Walloons (Celtic) are the two major ethnic groups today. The motto on the Belgium coat of arms is written in both French *L'Union Fait La Force* and Flemish (a Dutch language) *Eendracht Maakt Macht*, and both mean "Union Provides Strength." After gaining independence from the Netherlands in 1830, the lion was chosen as the *official* national symbol, though it had existed *unofficially* before then. (Is it not interesting that the lion was employed as a national symbol by nearly *all of the Germanic nations of Europe* from the earliest of times—even though the lion *has not existed in Central or Northern Europe for about 5,000 years*? However, it was well-known to the Israelites in the Middle East.) The flags above the canopy are of the Belgian provinces; most contain lions, although there are some eagles, bi-cephalic eagles, and castles.

* * * * * * * * * * * * * * *

Netherlands (Holland)

The French motto on the coat of arms of the Kingdom of Netherlands (*Koninkrijk der Nederlanden*) *Je Maintiendrai* means, "I Will Uphold." The coat of arms was *officially* adopted in 1815. The lion on the shield has a bundle of 7 arrows in one talon and a sword in the other. The unicorn and a horn are also old symbols of the Netherlands, as is the ship. Certain provinces of the Netherlands also have the double-headed eagle as a symbol, as well as rams, lions, castles, horns, crosses, horses, men, and stars.

Holland's ***Ship of State*** (1579) features a ship with the Bible on the prow, 7 arrows on the sail, 7 shields (one for each province) with lions and other symbols on them. The flag by the crow's nest also contains a lion. The ship's sails contain the motto of the Netherlands and what is presumably a *Dutch* version of Belgian's Flemish motto, "Eendracht Maakt Macht" (though not fully visible). The motto encircling the seal, *Saevis Tranquillus In Undis Vigilate Deo Confidentes* means, "Trusting God in the Midst of the Savage Waves."

The old ***Dutch Fisher's Seal*** features a ship with a *lion* as the captain holding two royal scepters. The old arms of Hoorn (c. 1630) featured a horn supported by a lion and a unicorn. Bennett, in Symbols of Our Celto-Saxon Heritage, preserves the translation of an inscription found on a plaque gracing an old house in Hoorn that commemorated victory over invading Spanish forces in 1573. It reads,

> O, happy times, O grand gold message; Everyone who remembers it must rejoice: The country shakes and trembles, the enemy is drawing near, with the help of *Amalek* he wants to destroy all ***Israel*** (p. 149). (Emphasis mine.) (Possibly the Spaniards had joined with the Moors to invade Holland.)

* * * * * * * * * * * * * * *

Austria

Austria was occupied by the Celts and the Suebi when the Romans conquered it (c. 15 B.C.-A.D. 10). Charlemagne conquered the area in 788 and used Lower Austria to halt the inroads of the Avars (a Mongol people). The eagle of Austria (*Republic Osterreich*, meaning the "Republic of the Eastern Kingdom") dates back to the 1100's. In the 14th century, the eagle was bi-cephalic. Even as Germany supposedly took its eagle from the (Israelite) Empire of Western Rome, Austria supposedly took its double-headed eagle from the (Israelite) Empire of *Eastern* Rome (Byzantia). The hammer and sickle in the talons of the eagle were adopted *long before* the Bolsheviks began to use these as their symbols of Communist despotism. The broken chains and the tri-towered castle-crown are also significant symbols. The ruling houses of Austria (Hapsburg, Bebenburg, and others) provide other significant symbols.

* * * * * * * * * * * * *

Ancient Bohemia

The Bohemians (*Böhmen*, meaning "home of the fighters") were descended from a Celtic tribe called the *Boii*. The old arms of Bohemia feature a crowned rampant lion (which dates back to the early 1200's) and are from a rock carving from the "Pulver Turme" at Prague from the late 15th century. The Bohemians were overcome in the first century B.C. by the *Marcomanni*, an ancient Germanic tribe, who were in turn overcome by other Celtic and Teutonic tribes in the 4th or 5th centuries A.D., and the Czechs eventually settled in the land. Later a part of the Austro-Hungarian Empire, it became a province of Czechoslovakia in the early 1900's. The Boii most likely also migrated to Bavaria, where they were known as *Boiarii* and *Baiuoarii*.

* * * * * * * * * * * * *

Ancient Czechs and Slovaks

The coat of arms of old Czechoslovakia contains several lions, eagles, and crosses. The motto *Pravda Vitezi* means "Truth Will Prevail." Some Czechs and Slovaks are possibly of Swedish descent, since part of the region of modern-day Ukraine was once a Czechoslovakian province called Carpatho-Ukraine (1918-1939). Some Ukrainians may be descended from the Swedish Rus. Although Czechs and Slovaks are generally classified as *Slavic*, no doubt a good portion are actually Celtic, Teutonic, and Scandinavian in their ancestry. Bohemia, Slovakia, and Moravia were the main regions of the old country.

* * * * * * * * * * * * *

Poland

The eagle has been a symbol of Poland since the late 900's. It was the symbol of Lech, an ancestor of Poland's first ruler, Mieczyslaw I. The symbol was firmly established nationally by the 1200's, and was originally crowned. After about 1400, as a result of Poland's union with Lithuania, the majority of Poland's aristocracy, prominent artists, military leaders, writers, etc. were actually Lithuanians who *Polanized* their names and even moved to Poland to retain their nobility status. The most prominent of these was Brigadier-General Thaddeus (Tadeusz) Kosciuszko (in Lithuanian, Tadas Kosčiuška) (1746-1817), the famous "Polish" patriot and freedom fighter. A prominent military leader, Kosciuszko helped train and command the American Revolutionary forces in America's war for independence from Britain. In 1947 the *Polska Rzeczpospolitz Ludowa* chose to retain the national symbol, although without the crown, since they no longer had a monarchy.

Tadas Kosčiuška

* * * * * * * * * * * * *

South Eastern (Latin) Europe

The original builders of these modern nations, which were once world powers, were of pure Israel (white) stock. The portraits of the early monarchs, artists, explorers, scientists, etc. clearly show this. Sadly, the majority of these peoples are no longer white, but mixed, due to heavy intermarriage with indigenous Indian populations and imported slaves. However, there is still to be found a small remnant of pure blood within these countries and within other countries of the world to where the original Italians, French, Spaniards, etc. migrated.

France

The arms in the *center left* are of two ducal lines (1890) of Savoy-Aosta and Savoy-Genoa. Savoy is a province in southeastern France bordering Switzerland and Italy. It was a duchy in the Middle Ages and was later part of the Kingdom of Sardinia (1720-1860). Aosta was a province of northwest Italy, and Genoa a port city. The arms in the *center right* are those of the Principality of Andorra, a tiny city high in the Pyrénées mountains that was granted independence by

Charlemagne in the 9th century. In 1278 it came under the dual protectorship of France and Spain. The postage stamps (on the previous page) are of Gascogne (left) and Normandie (right). Stamps of other provinces and cities bear similar Israel symbols. The *fleur-de-lis* (lily), the most popular symbol of France, dates back to the 12th century and can be found on flags and arms.

The original French were a *Germanic* people. Charlotte M. Yonge, in her (Young People's) History of France (1874), says the early Franks were Kelts, primarily Gaels (Gauls) and Kymry, and that they had to move periodically, when stronger tribes pushed them from their lands. She revealingly records,

> ...They would turn to the south into Greece or Italy.... One set of them, in very old times, even managed to make a home in the Middle of Asia Minor, and it was to their descendents that St. Paul wrote his Epistle to the Galatians (p. 12).

This is also documented by numerous church fathers and historians. The Ante-Nicene Fathers record,

> The Gauls...were from ancient times called Galatians, from the whiteness of their body; and thus the Sibyl terms them. And this is what the poet intended to signify when he said,—'Gold Collars deck their milk-white necks,' when he might have used the word *white*. It is plain that from this the province was called Galatia, in which, on their arrival in it, the Gauls united themselves with the Greeks, from which circumstance that region was called Gallograecia, and afterward Galatia (Vol, VII, p. 323, *Fragments of Lactinius*).

The French also had a good portion of Viking blood from the Norsemen (who came to be known as *Normans*), who founded the province of *Normandie*. Sadly, few pure Frenchman are to be found today in France. Upwards of 95 percent of Parisians are of Moroccan (African Moor) descent. This resulted from Napoleon sending most of the pure, young blood of the country off to die in war. Remnants of the pure French blood are to be found in some regions of France, as well as parts of southern Belgium and southwestern Germany, as well as parts of western Switzerland, northwestern Italy, and the eastern coast of Britain. Since France was once a strong participant in worldwide colonization, it is possible that there are still some pure French communities left in various regions in Africa and elsewhere.

* * * * * * * * * * * * * *

Italy

The flag of the Kingdom of Italy was originally divided into three vertical segments, with a shield bearing a cross in the center. The flag at the left is that of the ***King of Sardinia*** (1800's). It contains several lions, crosses of various styles (including one in the *Union Jack* pattern), eagles, crowns, a horse, and olive branches. The stamps (on the following page) depict the Province of Modena in Italy. They feature a crowned eagle, oak and olive branches, and a cross on a crowned shield. In 1852, when the first postage stamps were issued,

Modena was under the rule of Duke Francis V, of the House of Este-Lorraine. In June 1859, Francis was overthrown, at which time the duchy was annexed to the Kingdom of Sardinia, which itself became the Kingdom of Italy in March 1861.

Many original Italians were most likely predominantly of the Israel Tribe of Gad, although there was an infusion of other tribes. The Gaddites also migrated elsewhere, such as northwestern France (Armorica, Brittany). Turner, in The History of the Anglo-Saxons, relates that there was a tribe of Gauls known as *Bagaudæ*. Turner indicated that *Bagad* in Welsh means "a multitude" and *Bagat* in Armoric means, "a troop or crew"; and that *Bagach* means "warlike" in Irish and "fighting" in Erse (Vol. 1, Bk. 2, Ch. 8, p. 131, fn. "h"). One of the tribes of Israel was *Gad*. The name *Gad* (#1410) means, "a multitude or a troop" from the root (#1464) "to crowd upon, attack, invade, or overcome" (Genesis 30:11; 49:19). Since we have seen that the Welsh and Celtic languages are nearly identical with ancient Hebrew, it is no mere coincidence that the name ***Gad*** appears in this Gaulic tribal name (*Bagaudæ*) and its root words (*Bagad*, and *Bagat*) and that they mean the same thing.

The high-school history text The Ladder of History (1945; MacMillian & Co.) says the early inhabitants of Italy came down from the north and were a blue-eyed, fair-haired people like the early Greeks.

(For an in-depth study of the early inhabitants that settled Italy, the various Germanic peoples who founded the Italic Kingdom, and those peoples that later invaded and conquered the debased Roman Republic, see Race or Mongrel (1908) by Alfred P. Schultz.)

Later, after the Roman Empire had begun its decline due to mass immorality, it was the Goths and Vandals who again descended and conquered this mongrelized nation (made up of at least 20 different racial strains, predominately African and Mediterranean) whose evil degeneracy they despised.[119] The eastern branch of the Roman Empire, Constantinople (also called the *Byzantine* Empire), lasted longer because it retained its racial purity longer. In its decline, however, it too fell under Norman conquest by 1042. Despite enormous evidence that national greatness, morality, and success are related to racial purity, liberal minds ridicule the idea as antiquated. But the truth never becomes outdated—it just becomes *unpopular*. Regardless, thousands of years of history, genetics, and Scripture prove it to be true. Scripture says that a kingdom or house divided against itself cannot stand (Matthew 12:25; Mark 3:24-25; Luke 11:17). In the Bible, it was often the *mingled peoples* who caused Israel to fall into sin (which leads to degeneracy) and caused *confusion of face*.[120]

---

[119] See p. 21 of The Ultimate World Order by Robert H. Williams (c. 1940; Major, Military Intelligence USAR and Captain AUS), which quotes from a lecture given to Oxford University in the 1870's by Dr. Charles Kingsley.

[120] See **Numbers 11:1-4 and Ezra 9:7**. As we saw, the word *Babylon* means "confusion by mixing." God will destroy the Babylonian system because of this racial (and moral) confusion (See **Jeremiah 25:9-38** and **Obadiah**). Sadly, most people think that because things have "progressed" so far, and because we have strayed so far from God's standard of holiness, that *God will have to change* His standard. This is the **great lie**. God cannot change His standard. There will just be far fewer accepted; this is why it is called a "remnant." (See Galatians 6:7 and Deuteronomy 30:19.)

The Lombards of northern Italy descended from the Vikings, through whom descended Columbus, Dante, Michaelangelo, and da Vinci, according to Madison Grant. If these men were of the Nordic Tribe of Benjamin, is it any wonder that they and others of their kin were the "*lights* of the Renaissance?" The Normans also infused their blood in the south of Italy and even in Sicily, although the Norman blood in Sicily was extinguished hundreds of years ago.[121]

The Normans invaded southern Italy and Sicily around the same time their Norman brethren invaded England (c. 1050-1150), but had earlier established their kingdom in Naples in 1016. **Houston Stewart Chamberlain**[122] (1855-1927), in his classic *Die Grundlagen des neunzehnten Jahrhunderts* (1899) (Foundations of the Nineteenth Century; English translation, 1910), also attests to Viking blood being responsible for the Renaissance and Italy's greatness in general. Sadly, the *vast majority* of the Italians of the modern world have *little or no relation* to the Old World Italians; modern Italians are largely African, Moor, Tartar, Saracen, and Indian.

Howard La Fay, in The Vikings (1972), states that Normans, in particular 8 sons of the Norman knight Tancred de Hauteville, founded "the most aggressive and splendid kingdom of its time" in southern Italy and Sicily (pp. 11-12). The Varangian Rus (Swedish Viking) was the most distinguished Viking force that conquered this region. Also, when the Goths were driven out of Scythia by the Huns, they established the Pannonian Empire in Italy and ruled the region there for a time.

* * * * * * * * * * * * * *

Spain

The official arms of Spain (at left) are set on a large eagle with the sun haloing its head. A bundle of five arrows appears at the bottom of the arms. On the shield, the gold castles on red represent the province of *Castile* (meaning "castle"), and the red lions on white represent the province of *Leon* (meaning "lion"). The *Spanish Imperial War Ensign* of the 18th century (at right), was replaced in 1785. It contains lions, eagles, castles, and arrows.

As we already saw, Spain and Portugal were originally known as *Iberia* ("Land of the Hebrews"). The original Spaniards were once a pure white people. For many years they kept the Moors from invading western Europe. Sadly, however, they eventually intermarried with the African, Indian, and Moorish

---

121 —it has been claimed that Canaanite "jewish" blood predominates in the crime families.

122 —British-born, he was the son of Admiral William Charles Chamberlain; yet became a German citizen and the son-in-law of German classical music composer Richard Wagner; Chamberlain also wrote his father-in-law's biography, Richard Wagner (1897). Two of Chamberlain's uncles were generals in the English army and a third was the well-known Field-Marshall Sir Neville Chamberlain. His mother was the daughter of Captain Basil Hall, R.N. (Royal Navy).

subcultures in their regions. The original Spaniards descended from several houses of Israel. In Spain there is still an old town called *Zaragossa*, (on the *Ebro* ["Hebrew"] River), meaning "Zarah's Stronghold," which was founded by the Zarah branch of the Tribe of Judah. The Tribe of Simeon also settled in Spain (and later Wales) under the name of *Simoni* (plural, *Simonii*). A good portion of the Tribe of Dan (Danite Phoenicians) also settled in the country and soon became prominent in their sailing, exploration, and shipbuilding and renown for their invincible navy: the Armada. King Ferdinand and Queen Isabella were fair and redheaded, since they descended from the Goths. Viking blood was common in Spain, since many descended from the Normans, Varagian Rus, and Vandals (from whom *Andalusia* gets its name).

Tarshish, the city mentioned in the Bible, was a flourishing Hebrew colony in Spain at the time of Solomon. It was located in southeastern Spain, centered in the modern port of *Cadiz*, formerly known as Gades, founded by the Tribe of Gad in 1100 B.C. This settlement was established along the *Guadalquiver* Valley. Guadalquiver is derived from the Arabic *wadi-el-Heber*, meaning "the river of the Hebrews." Also, a stone inscription from King Solomon to his tribute-bearer *Adoniram* has been found near Seville. This stone records in Hebrew, "This is the tomb of Adoniram, who came to collect tribute and died here." This is easily supported by Scripture. King Solomon developed a navy. Scripture says that "Dan remained in ships," and that Dan would spring forth adventurously from Bashan (I Kings 9:26-28; Judges 5:17; Deuteronomy 33:22).

Martin A. S. Hume records, in <u>The Spanish People</u> (1901), that the Phoenicians sailed to Spain 1,100 years before Christ. They came from the ports of Tyre and Sidon, and their crews were Danites—"the indomitable race of Shem." They came to Spain with the luxuries of the East and brought back to pharaoh and Egypt the raw materials from the West. By 1296 B.C. the Danites had developed a large shipping trade and had established many large shipping colonies outside Palestine.

The Spanish word *hidalgo* signifies "*nobleman*" but literally means "son of the Goth," according to Richard Kelly Hoskins in <u>Our Nordic Race</u> (1958) (p. 25). The old Spanish title **don** (as in *Don Juan*) means "master" or "lord." Clearly, some of the pure Spaniards were also of the Tribe of Dan, since **Dan** means "judge" or "ruler." Further, since God declared that Dan would judge or rule Israel, is it just a coincidence that we also get our words *domain*, *dominate*, *dominion, etc.* from the word *Dan*? (See Indo-European root *deme*[1].) That the *Conquistadores* under Cortés and others, who conquered the Atzecs of Mexico and the Incas of Peru, were of the white race is well documented in history. The Aztecs and Incas thought the Spaniards were gods, because the crude histories of these primitive Indians recorded that their civilizations were founded and built by a wise, peaceful, tall, bearded, white-skinned, blue/gray-eyed, fair-haired people from the North who sailed in ships across the sea. The Conquistadores and Columbus's men were not as evil and torturous as modern history books claim. It is recorded that they "massacred" some of the Indians—but *only when* they were discovered to be cannibals and daily offering human sacrifices to their gods. (See Columbus and Cortez: Conquerors For Christ (1992), John Eidsmoe, and In Quest of the White God (1961), Pierre Honoré.)

A Final Word About Race and Civilization

Elmer Pendell

Anyone who studies history will find that the zenith of all empires and civilizations of lasting impact occurred when the pure Israel (white) blood was in the majority and ascendancy. One will likewise discover that the downfall of these great empires was due to the mongrelization of the pure blood. (See Why Civilizations Self-Destruct (1977), Professor Elmer Pendell (Cornell), How The Greatest White Nations Were First Mongrelized, then Negroized (1965), Myron C. Fagan, and Makers of Civilization in Race and History (1929), Professor L.A. Waddell, LLD., C.B., C.I.E., (London University).)

Though such thinking is not modernly considered "politically correct," this does not change reality. Though the truth is unpopular, it is the truth nonetheless. Blind and evil people, although they choose to travel the road of destruction, cannot alter the destination of reality. Others do not have to follow in their fatal steps. Quoting George Santayana once again: "Those who do not learn from history are doomed to repeat it." This is the course America, Britain, and what is left of Europe now follow. Australia, Canada, South Africa, and other white nations have already fallen to third-rate nations. Scripture records that wisdom declares, "All those who hate me love death" (Proverbs 8:36).

Oddly, over the past several decades, many South American nations—including Uruguay, Brazil, Chile, and Argentina—have encouraged white European immigration in an attempt to revive the vegetative corpses of their nations. (See The Rising Tide of Color (1920) by Lothrop Stoddard, A.M., Ph.D. (Harvard), Our Nordic Race (1958) by Richard Kelly Hoskins, pp. 30-32; and Race or Mongrel (1908), Schultz.) (Egypt itself encouraged the same c. 100 A.D., which resulted in the large Hebrew/Israelite colony in Alexandria.)

Lothrop Stoddard

It has *not only* been the *Latinized* branches of the white race that have suffered mass-mongrelization. The other Germanic peoples of Europe have suffered the same, though on a lesser scale. Lothrop Stoddard, in The Rising Tide of Color (1920), points out that even Germany has been largely mongrelized with non-Nordic blood. Stoddard stated that this was due in large part to the *Thirty Years War* in the south of Germany, in which the vast majority of the pure German blood was exterminated. The same thing occurred in France (as well as most other white nations). War is one of the enemy's best tools to destroy the good blood of a nation. Departure from the ways of God will bring about judgment—from within *and* without. The myriad of tribal wars among the clans of Scotland, the various Viking tribes, and all other branches of the white race, within their own tribe and against their tribal cousins, has greatly diminished our numbers. More recently, our numbers have been decimated from the teeming millions of nonwhite immigrants flooding our nations, causing the size of white families to diminish (due to excessive taxation of white people to provide the welfare and aid to support the rest of the world). We are told the lie that "~~diversity~~ is our strength"—yet 6,000 years of history prove that the opposite is true: "***Purity*** is our strength." But that purity *cannot* be preserved unless we trust in *God's power* to keep us true to following His ways.

Only the northernmost countries in Europe, especially those protected by natural boundaries, and those that have maintained rigid bulwarks against immigration, have retained any degree of purity and strength. But mass-mongrelization and mass-immigration have left most nations teetering on the edge of extinction. Still, there remains a vestige of pure blood—those who have not been brainwashed or who are beginning to see the truth—that opposes international vandalism and interracial rape. (*Babylon* means "confusion by mixing." The mixed majority will soon attack the pure *Remnant* of God.) Those who are evil or blind will try to smear us as "racist," "prejudiced," and "hateful." But the issue is one of purity, love of family, ancestral pride, common sense, proven facts, obedience to God, and survival itself. No other race of people on earth will invite unwholesome, heterogeneous foreigners to invade its land and take control of its country. If any nation attempted to exterminate another race by war, there would be a universal outcry. Yet *the extermination of the white race by intermarriage*, although it produces the same results, barely causes a raised eyebrow. Even the current ***mass murdering*** of white farmers and their families in Africa is ignored as *insignificant* by the world. Environmentalists are frantic to protect all types of species threatened with extinction—*all except the most important species*, the one that guarantees the very existence of all others: the white race.[123]

We should not *hate* other races. However, wanting to preserve our own race and heritage is not *hate*. It is an inalienable right! All races ought to be able to live as they wish in their own country. We simply desire the same. Yet our people are taught to be ashamed of who they are—***if** they even **know** who they are*. Our nation was established as a ***Christian*** nation. Yet this truth is maliciously denied (despite indisputable proof) and true Christianity is about to be outlawed. Those who scoff at such a statement know *nothing* (but will soon learn). Many will not acknowledge the truth until the enemy overtakes them like a flood—but then it will be too late. God help us! Or as **Rudyard Kipling** (England's poet laureate) expressed: (Kipling was asked to write a poem to honor Queen Victoria on her Diamond Anniversary as Monarch of Britain. He produced the poem "REQUIEM" (The Quiet Sleep of the Dead), (June 22, 1897) which was not received too warmly by the British nobility.)

God of our fathers, known of old,
Lord of our far-flung battle-line,
Beneath whose awful Hand we hold
Dominion over palm and pine -
Lord God of Hosts, be with us yet,
Lest we forget - lest we forget!

---

[123] See America, Christianity, Liberty, and Truth: What Famous Men Had To Say by Balaicius/STM for profound statements on these topics.

The tumult and the shouting dies;
The captains and the kings depart:
Still stands Thine ancient sacrifice,
An humble and a contrite heart.
Lord God of Hosts, be with us yet,
Lest we forget - lest we forget!

Far-called, our navies melt away;
On dune and headland sinks the fire:
Lo, all our pomp of yesterday
Is one with Nineveh and Tyre!
Judge of the Nations, spare us yet,
Lest we forget - lest we forget!

If, drunk with sight of power, we loose
Wild tongues that have not Thee in awe,
Such boastings as the Gentiles use,
Or lesser breeds without the Law -
Lord God of Hosts, be with us yet,
Lest we forget - lest we forget!*

For heathen heart that puts her trust
In reeking tube and iron shard,
All valiant dust that builds on dust,
And guarding, calls not Thee to guard,
For frantic boast and foolish word -
Thy mercy on Thy People, Lord!

[*—and lest we PERISH!] (Brackets mine.)

- Famous, Noble Witnesses -

Reputable, Personal Proofs, and Testimony of True Israel

"He who sees the truth, let him proclaim it, without asking who is for it or who is against it" (Harry George, The Land Question).

Some people seem to need a *security blanket* of sorts before they will commit to something not held by the majority. They need to know about prominent people who can lend credence to a particular belief. This list of *exceptional* people who once believed that the Anglo-Saxon peoples are the Israelites of the Bible, is presented for those people. This list is also presented for those people who may like to know simply as a matter of curiosity.

This list also serves to refute the claims of our dishonest, hate-filled opponents who have attempted to discredit this truth by *demonizing* its proponents. Contrary to false propaganda, those who believe that the true Israel peoples are the Anglo-Saxon and related peoples are *not* feebleminded, imbalanced, talentless misfits, nor rabid, militant hate-mongers. This list, brief though it is, presents *merely a fraction* of the distinguished people who confessed belief in the fact that the Anglo-Saxon peoples were indeed the very Israel people of the Bible.

True Israel Hall of Fame

(A far larger listing of this section will be offered in a booklet entitled, The Anglo-Israel Hall of Fame: They Shone the Light of Truth and Passed the Torch—Will You?)

Dean Jacques Abbadie, D.D. (1664-1727), of Killaloe, Ireland, Bishop of the Falkland Islands, considered one of the great scholars of his time, published in his *Le Triomphe de la Providence et de la Religion* (1723, in Amsterdam):

> Unless the Ten Tribes of Israel are flown into the air or sunk into the earth, *they must be those ten Gothic tribes that entered Europe in the fifth century, overthrew the Roman Empire, and founded the ten nations of modern Europe* (Emphasis mine).

Alfred the Great (849-899), king of the West Saxons (Wessex, England) and overlord of Kent, Surrey, Sussex, and Essex was a deeply religious man. He translated the Bible from Latin into Anglo-Saxon and he formed the Common Law of England from the Old Testament itself. Although his native tongue was Saxon, he learned Latin and English and translated many classics into English. He strengthened the monarchy, the church, and learning. He declared to his subjects, "Be ye kind to the stranger within thy gates, **for ye were strangers in the land of Egypt**" (Exodus 22:21). Alfred himself designed the boats a team of Frisian boatwrights constructed, with which he successfully defeated the Vikings in A.D. 872.

H.R.H. Princess Alice, Countess of Athlone, chief patron of the British-Israel World Federation (1920).

Bishop John Harden Allen, was the pastor of Wesleyan Methodist Church (California). He authored Fact and Fiction Concerning Israel and Judah, Judah's Scepter and Joseph's Birthright (1902), The National Number and Heraldry of the United States of America (1919), and The National Rebirth of Judah (1920), and was a popular speaker.

In review of Allen's Judah's Scepter and Joseph's Birthright the ***Baptist Messenger*** reported (c. 1902),

> This is one of the most interesting volumes we have read in many a day...and we confess...the arguments produced by Mr. Allen seem to be unanswerable. It is more thrilling than Western fiction. The description of the scarlet thread, the royal remnant, and the part played by Jeremiah in the preservation of the ruler for David's throne will cause you to lose sleep rather than go to bed without knowing the outcome.

Archbishop Bond (Montreal) stated, "I strongly advise a study of the Scripture prophecies upon British-Israel lines" (Facets of the Great Story (1954, South Africa), H. Robin Tourtel, p. 138).

The Book of Common Prayer of the Anglican Church (Church of England) is so replete with Israel word and structure, it would be absurd, were not the Anglo-Saxon peoples, in fact, God's Israel people. However, the Book of Common Prayer, published with the authorization of the Anglican Church originally in March 1549, was revised in 1927-28, removing a significant amount of phraseology indicative of Israel ancestry. Astonishing is the revelation that,

> The continuity of our Church is seen in Archbishop Cranmer's statement to Parliament (1549) that the Prayer Book, then being authorized, contained the same prayers that had been in use in Britain for over 1,500 years—from the days of Joseph of Arimathaea and the Apostles. (from The British Reformers, Vol. VIII, p. 271. Also in the Proceedings of the House of Lords, in the British Museum.)
>
> William Byrd (1543-1623), in his Sacred Music work of Anglican worship titled "The Great Service," is made up of six movements that are all a part of the prescribed Anglican ritual for the celebration of Mattins, Evensong, and Communion. Part of "The Great Service" is as follows:
>
> O Lord, make thy servant Elizabeth our Queen rejoice in Thy strength. Give her her heart's desire and deny not the request of her lips; but prevent her with Thine everlasting blessings and give her a long life.... Sing joyfully unto God our strength. Sing loud unto **the God of Jacob**.... **Blow the trumpet in the new**

moon, even in the time appointed and at our feast day.... This is **a statute for Israel**, and a law of **the God of Jacob**. (Emphasis mine.)

Premier John Bracken (born 1883), Prime Minister of Manitoba, Canada.

Charles Bradlaugh, M.P. (1833-91) was an able king's counsel and Member of Parliament for many years. He one day stood before a great audience in London with a Bible in his hand. He proceeded to read out of the Scriptures portions of the great covenant God made with Abraham—the covenant God later confirmed by His very oath and still further later reaffirmed to his seed. Bradlaugh, upon completing his readings from the Scripture, asked, "Have those promises ever been fulfilled to the Jews?" There were no replies in the affirmative. He then said, "And you tell me the God of that Book is a God of truth? I don't believe it." Bradlaugh went on to become one of the most active infidels and opponents of Christianity in his day. Initially barred from Parliament because of his atheism, he later won the appeal and his seat. Later in life, however, he was introduced to the Anglo-Israel message and embraced the Bible as wholly true, attending many Anglo-Israel lectures. He once declared, "I love to come: It is most wonderful what light British-Israel truth throws on the Bible" (*Thy Kingdom Come*, Vol. 5, No. 3, March 1992, pp. 34-35; Association of the Covenant People, 7730 Edmonds Street, Burnaby, British Columbia, V3N 1B8 Canada).

Premier Thomas Bavin (c. 1929, of New South Wales, Australia); Prime Minister.

Pastor Lawrence Blanchard, M.Div., graduate of Denver Theological Seminary, missionary in the Philippines for 6 years, authored: Is The Judeo-Christian Gospel The Biblical Gospel? (2000), One Nation Under God (1995), Standing on the Premises: A Presentation of 38 Biblical Propositions of Christian-Israel Identity Theology (1998), and *Evidences of Israel's Identity* (seminar presentation).

Lieutenant Richard Brothers (1757-1824), was one of the earliest proponents of the Anglo-Israel truth to write on the topic (1792-1795). He was also one of the earliest proponents to be ridiculed, misunderstood, and persecuted. He served faithfully in the British navy but lost his pension when he refused to swear the required oath.

Jonathan David Brown, a contemporary Christian music writer, singer, and producer, was raised believing the Israel message. He is one of the most notable contemporary Christian music producers and recording engineers. In his career he has produced dozens of award-winning albums for individual artists, each of which has sold more than 100,000 units (some selling more than 500,000). He is the only Christian producer to have produced 4 of the "Top 25 Christian Records of All Time." He has also produced 35 "Number-One" songs and dozens more in the "Top 5." He is the only producer to have produced the same song ("Unto the Least of These,") for three separate artists (Bob Bennett, Phillip Sandifer, and Glen Campbell) within a 12-month period, all of which have received successful radio airing. (The song was written by the first two, but recorded on three individual albums.) Brown has produced albums for other notables such as: PETRA, Twila Paris, Steve Taylor, Bill Gaither Trio, Paul Smith (formerly of the Imperials), Trace Balin, Karla Worley, the Archers, Rob Frazier, Santa Fe, Kelley Willard, Tom Coomes, Roby Duke, Mark Heard, Laury Boone-Browning, Chuck Girard, Servant, Morgan Cryar, Steve and Annie Chapman, First Call, David Meece, Russ Taff, Jamie Owens-Collins, and Daniel Amos. He also produced some of the well-known *Praise* and *Praise Strings* series and *Maranatha!* series.

Not only is Brown an acomplished producer, recording engineer, and musician, he also has an incredible voice. He has sung backup vocals for many artists; for example: Twila Paris on "The Warrior Is a Child" (among *many* others). His first solo recording, *Sinners in the Hands of an Angry God* (1997), was titled after the famous sermon by the Puritan preacher Jonathan Edwards. (His second recording will hopefully be released in 2001.) Brown also wrote Keeping Yahweh's Appointments.

(Jonathan David Brown highly endorses books written by Balaicius/STM.)

His Honour R. R. Bruce (c. 1929), Lieut.-Gov. of British Columbia.

E. Raymond Capt, M.A., A.I.A., F.S.A., Scot., a prolific author and producer of dozens of documentary videos, he received his Masters of Arts in Christian History and Biblical Archaeology from Covenant College, Lake Wales, Florida, and has his California State teaching credentials in biblical archaeology and history. He is a Member of the Archaeological Institute of America and Fellow of the Society of Antiquarians in Scotland (1972). He received an honorary Doctorate of Literature from the Accademia Testina Per Le Scienze (established A.D. 450), in Pescara, Italy. Capt has appeared on numerous television shows as an expert on the pyramids. Some of his books are: The Glory of the Stars (1976), The Great Pyramid Decoded (1978), Jacob's Pillar (1977), King Solomon's Temple (1979), Missing Links Discovered in Assyrian Tablets (1985), Our Great Seal (1979), Petra (1987), The Scottish Declaration of Independence (1983), Stonehenge and Druidism (1979), Study in Pyramidology (1986), and The Traditions of Glastonbury (1983).

(Raymond Capt endorses Your Inheritance by Balaicius/STM.)

Major-General Count Arthur Cherep-Spiridovich (1858-1926, assassinated), was a direct descendent of Prince Rurik (one of the founders of the original Russian Empire; c. 800 A.D.). He was a personal friend of President Teddy Roosevelt (at whose request the photo at left was taken). He authored The Secret World Government: The Unrevealed in History (1926).

Christopher Columbus (1451-1504), was the very same Genoese (northern Italian) explorer and navigator of worldwide fame. He wrote in a letter to King Ferdinand of Spain in 1502, in regard to his discovery of America: "Fully accomplished were the words of Isaiah..." (See Isaiah 49:1-12).

Rev. Bertrand Comparet, A.B., J.D., D.D., was a lawyer and Deputy District Attorney for San Diego County, California (1926 to 1932), and Deputy City Attorney for the City of San Diego, California (1942 to 1947). When he was 22 years old he was on the debate team at Stanford University (from which he graduated with his Law degree), and won the Joffre Gold Medal (the highest Pacific coast debate award). He successfully defended Royal Raymond Rife (inventor of the Rife Microscope and the Rife Generator, which reportedly cured cancer) against Philip Hoyland (who had a high-priced attorney, and reportedly the backing of the American Medical Association operating behind the scenes). (See The Cancer Cure That Worked (1987), Lynes, p. 96). He later became a minister and preached faithfully for many years, delivering many of them over the radio. Several hundred of his sermons were later printed.

Rev. Charles E. Coughlin (1891-1979), was a Canadian-born, Roman Catholic priest who spoke out against the Zionist purposes behind World War II, the Zionist control of money, the economy, and the government. He had a huge audience for his radio broadcasts in the 1930's and was considered one of the greatest orators of his day. He put out a magazine called *Social Justice*. He was opposed by the U.S. "government" and the Catholic Church itself. At the end of his life, near his deathbed, the true Israel message was presented to him, and upon hearing the evidence maintaining that the Anglo-Saxon and kindred peoples were the factual Israelites of the Bible who were in national blindness and that the "jews" were the Canaanites of the Bible, he declared, "That's it! That's it! That's the missing piece of the puzzle!" He authored Money: Questions and Answers, numerous booklets, pamphlets, and radio messages (many of which were transcribed).

Brigadier-General Sir Standish G. Crawfurd, Bart., C.B., C.M.G., C.I.E., D.S.O., wrote Our Celtic Heritage.

Alexander Cruden, in the 1761 edition of his Cruden's Complete Concordance To The Bible (including the Apocrypha) in the dedication to King George III of England, pronounced the following blessing and declaration,

> May the great God be the guide of your life, and direct and prosper you, that it may be said of the present and future ages, that King George III hath been an Hezekiah to our ***British-Israel***. (Emphasis mine.)

Colonel Dan Daniels is a full Colonel retired from the Regular U.S. Army. He is also retired from being the Sheriff of Polk County, Florida. Colonel Daniels is the Publisher/Editor of a patriotic paper out of Eagle Lake, Florida entitled *The Eagle*. Colonel Daniels is also very involved in various patriotic causes, and he is a field writer for the *Patriot Press*.

(Colonel Daniels endorses Your Inheritance by Balaicius/STM.)

David Davidson, Esq., C.E., M.C., F.R.S.A., M.I.Struct.E. (1844-1956) was born in Scotland. He was a famous British structural engineer who was an avowed agnostic. After seeking to disprove the validity of Bible numerics and the history of the Bible contained in the measurements of the Great Pyramid, he not only received Christ as Saviour, but also became a firm believer in the Israel identity of the Anglo-Saxon peoples. A popular lecturer, he wrote many articles for the *Covenant Report*. He authored many books on the subject which have never been refuted (the first of which appeared after 20 years of painstaking research), a few being: The Church and State in The Great Pyramid's Prophecy (1930), The Date of the Crucifiction and The Era of The New Birth (1934), The Domination of Babylon: Literal and Symbolic (1939), Early Egypt, Babylonia, and Central Asia (1927), The Exodus of Israel: Its Date and Historical Setting (1933), The Great Pyramid: Its Divine Message (1924), The Great Pyramid's Prophecy and Its Fulfillment, The Great Pyramid's Prophecy Concerning the British Empire and America (1932), The Great Pyramid's Prophecy: On The Current Economic Oppression (1931), The Great Pyramid's Prophecy: The Age of Gold and The Golden Age, Herschel's Geometric Inch (1938), The Hidden Truth In Myth and Ritual and in The Common Culture Pattern of Ancient Metrology (1934), The Judgment of the Nations in The Great Pyramid's Prophecy (1940), Miracles of History (1947), Nebuchadnezzar's Seige of Jerusalem: A Study in Chronology (1938), Palestine: Esau Claims Possession (1947), The Path To Peace in Our Time (1942), Relationalization of the Gold Standard (Sweden, 1933), Through World Chaos To Cosmic Christ (1944), and Unto A Land Unknown (1947). Davidson stated,

> I proclaim with humility...yet...confidence...the Pyramid's Message establishes the Bible as the Inspired Word of God...testifies that Jesus Christ, by His Displacement, paid the purchase price of man's redemption, and effected the Salvation of all who truly believe in Him (Great Pyramid: Proof of God (1932), by G. Riffert, p. 22).

In his book The Domination of Babylon (p. 67), Davidson wrote,

> The great German commentator, Dr. Delitzsch, in his commentary of Isaiah's prophecy of the return of Israel for the final occupation of Palestine, identifies the origin of the movement with the geographical location of the British Isles.... Britain...likewise fulfills all the prophecies concerning Israel's spiritual and physical characteristics, material possessions, and geographical location and distribution promised to Israel as her inheritance for the 20th century of our era. The fact of this identity rescues the Old Testament prophecies from the realm of myth, imagination, and legend to which modern theological criticism has banished them; and shows how fallacious could be the conclusion of such an eminent Hebrew scholar as the Rev. Professor S. R. Driver, who, failing to realize the fact of this identity, sadly confessed that, in his opinion, the Old Testament prophecies concerning Israel never had been fulfilled, and that in this late stage in history, never could be fulfilled. The time, however, is fast approaching, when, according to the prophecies, the identity of lost Israel is to be disclosed to all nations together with the Revelation of God's purpose

concerning Israel's relationship to all other races....

Let me...reiterate, as a fact that can be confirmed by a comparative study of prophecy and history...every promise given to Israel to be fulfilled down to the current year, has been fulfilled down to the current year in the history of the British race in the British Empire and the United States of America. Let me also reiterate that the succession of constitutional crises through which the British Commonwealth of nations and the United States...have passed and are passing constitutes the initial stage in the preparation of the English-speaking peoples for the coming of our Lord Jesus Christ as King, and for the entrance of those peoples into the full inheritance promised to Israel from ancient times.

If this is not the truth that I have spoken, then may I ask you, what hope have we of survival in the chaotic world conditions of our time? If the restraining, aiding and guiding influence of our race fails humanity, what hope has humanity of survival? (I Believe God (1942), Frederick A. Kent, pp. 117-118).

The Rt. Hon. Sir Joseph Dimsdale, P.C., K.C.V.O., Lord Mayor of London in the coronation year of King Edward VII.

Sir Francis Drake (1540-1596), the English navigator who sailed around the world and commanded the naval defeat of the Spanish Armada, while on a voyage, wrote a letter to Rev. John Foxe (author of the famous History of the Christian Martyrs; commonly known as Foxe's Book of Martyrs) with the prayer that,

...God may be glorified, His church, our Queen and country preserved, the enemies of truth vanquished, that we might have continual peace in ***Israel***. Our enemies are many, but our Protector commandeth the whole earth (Emphasis mine).

H.M. King Edward VII (ruled 1901-1910) was the son of Queen Victoria and King of the United Kingdom, Emperor of India; his reign marked a peak of prosperity and power of English history.

H.M. Queen Elizabeth I of England and Ireland (ruled 1558-1603) was known as "the Light of Israel." She commissioned the translation and printing of the Bishops' Bible, which was to be used by the clergy to instruct the people in God's ways. She had the following as one of her prayers:

O Lord God Father Everlasting, which reigneth over the kingdoms of men, and givest them of Thy pleasure: which of Thy great mercy hast chosen me, Thy servant and handmaid to feed Thy people and Thine inheritance: so teach me, I humbly beseech Thee, Thy Word, and so strengthen me with grace, that I may feed Thy people with a faithful and true heart; and rule them prudently with power. O Lord, Thou hast set me on high, my flesh is frail and weak. If I therefore at any time forget Thee, touch my heart O Lord that it may again remember Thee. If I swell against Thee, pluck me down in my own conceit. Create therefore in me O Lord a new heart and so renew my spirit within me that Thy Law may be my study, Thy Truth my delight; Thy church my care; Thy people my crown. [O would that our rulers *today* had such a heart and mind and conscience toward God and man!]

Everard and **Winstanley**, two prominent members of the Levellers (a Puritan political reform movement in England in 1647, closely associated with Cromwell's New Model Army) were known to believe that the Saxon peoples were the Israelites.

Lieutenant-Colonel Francis P. Farrell, USAF (Ret.), received the Bronze Star and the Distinguished Flying Cross from Brig.-Gen. Smith of the First Infantry Division for his combat accomplishments beyond the call of duty in South Vietnam.

Brigadier-General William Henry Fasken, C.B., wrote: Britain: The Racial Aspect (1943), Cimmerians and Scythians (1936), The Great Pyramid (1932), and Israel's Racial Origins and Migrations (1934).

Admiral Lord John Arbuthnot Fisher, Baron of Kilvorstone, was a noble-born Briton who rose quickly to fame. He served in the Crimean War and China War (1859-60); was the Commander of the *Inflexible* in the bombardment of Alexandria in the Egyptian campaign (1882); Director of the Naval Ordinance (1886-91); Lord of the Admiralty (1892-97); Commander-in-chief in North America and West Indies (1897-99); British Naval Representative at the peace conference in the Hague (1899); Commander-in-chief in the Mediterranean (1899-1902); First Sea Lord (1904-10). He was the pioneer in the introduction of the all-big-gun ships, modern-day battleships, the dreadnoughts and battle cruisers, and he converted the fleet from coal to oil. Recalled from retirement in 1914, he resigned in 1915 in protest of the implementation of Churchill's *Dardanelle Program* (which turned out disastrous) instead of his *Baltic Plan*. If not for his efforts prior to World War II, Britain would not have won. At one time, he was the most famous sailor in the world.

In the *Times* of May 7, 1919, he stated, "Why we win, in spite of our incredible blunders, is that we are the lost ten tribes of Israel" (Our Great Heritage With Its Responsibilities, W. T. F. Jarrold, p. 187).

Major Fred T. Foort (Canada, Indian Army), wrote Children of Laughter [Sons of Isaac]: a Story Which Is Both Biblical and Historical... (1942).

Henry Ford, Sr. (1863-1947), the world-famous American automobile manufacturer and Christian-American patriot. Ford published (between 1920 and 1927) a series of articles in his small-town newspaper, the *Dearborn Independent.* These articles were written by the editor of the paper, William Cameron. (They were later also published in a book called The International Jew.) In them, the root of international conspiracies in finance and government (including wars) were exposed. Ford, of course, was vilified and demonized as an "anti-Semite," which was entirely untrue in both spirit and fact. In 1928, Cameron formed the Anglo-Saxon Federation in America, located in Detroit, Michigan, and began publishing the magazine *Destiny*. Several years later, Howard Rand took the magazine's office to Merrimac, Massachusetts.

Lieutenant-Colonel William Potter Gale, AUS (died 1988), served under General Douglas MacArthur in World War II in the Philippines. He later became a preacher for the true Israel message. Some of his sermons were printed. (See details of his life in The Committee of the States (1991), Cheri Seymour.)

Colonel John Garnier, R.E. (born 1838), authored: The Coming Dominion of Rome in Britain (1918), The Coming End of the Times of the Gentiles (1918), The Foretold Falling Away of Apostacy (1926), The Future of Britain (1912), The Great Pyramid: Its Builder and Its Prophecy (1905), The Identity of Romanism and Paganism (1914), The Kings of the East and the Great Day of Jezreel (1906), The Secret of the Cross: Or How Did Christ Atone? (1902), The Ten Tribes From Captivity Until Now, The True Christ and the False Christ (1900), The Worship of the Dead (1904), Coming Prophetic Events (1873), England's Enemies: A Warning (1900), Israel in Britain (1911), Present Dangers and Coming Conflicts of the British Race and Empire, and Sin and Redemption (1893).

Colonel John Cox Gawler, Keeper of the Crown Jewels, wrote Dan: The Pioneer of Israel (1880), Heir of the World, Our Scythian Ancestors (1875), The Two Olive Trees (1880), and The British Line in the Attack, Past and Future (1872).

Rev. William Pascoe Goard, L.L.D., F.R.G.S., F.R.E.S., was born in Cornwall, England. He would have entered the ministry early in life, but his father insisted he study law, which he did. Upon the death of his father, the family moved to Canada where he studied for the ministry graduating from Wesley (Methodist) College in Winnipeg. He was first introduced to the Israel message in 1892 after having met Professor Edward Odlum and Captain (and Rev.) Merton Smith.

In 1912 Goard accepted the position of pastor of the Knox Congregational Church (later renamed Grandview Congregational Church after it relocated to another district of Vancouver). He was the vice-president of the British Israel World Federation in 1921 and editor of the *National Message* when it was founded in 1922. He was also secretary general of the British Israel Association in Canada in 1922 and president of the Canadian British Israel Association in 1926. During 1924 and 1925 Goard helped establish a teaching college in London at the headquarters of the British Israel World Federation. In 1933 the Harrow Weald Park College (named after the former estate purchased for this purpose) was officially opened for the training of speakers and leaders for the British Israel message. This college continued until 1939, when it was commandeered by the Armed Services during wartime. Its operation was later resumed, and it was renamed the Garrison Bible College, with Goard still as president. In 1930 Goard attended a special ceremony at the College of Laws in Chicago, where he was awarded by Chancellor Du Bois the degree of Doctor of Laws and Logic in recognition of excellence of scholarship for his book The Law of the Lord: The Common Law (1928) (reprinted by Sacred Truth Ministries). While in Britain in 1930, Goard prepared a manifesto of the world conditions of the time titled "The Present Menace and How To Meet It." This manifesto was published in 21 newspapers in Britain in the month of June. In 1931 he wrote his second manifesto, "The World Crisis," which was also printed in many newspapers in Britain. During the last half of 1936 he travelled over 50,000 miles crossing Canada and the Pacific. He also travelled many miles in the U. S., Australia, and New Zealand. Within three months of returning home to the college in England, in February of 1937, he passed from this life to his eternal reward at the age of 74, having spent more than 40 years in faithful ministry in the Methodist Church. "His life and personality were of such a quality that it is not possible to put that spirit on paper. One had to know the man, it is not possible to read about him. All British Israel students thank God for William Pascoe Goard." (Material drawn from 70 Years Old: An Outline History of Our Work Since 1909, by **M. Alma Hetherington** (right), Association of the Covenant People; photo 1942.)

He authored Armageddon and the Battle of the Great Day, Bethesda or Jesus Christ? (1933), The Bible and Science (1926), The Book of Revelation (1926), The Crisis of the Ages, Crossing the River (1930), Documents of Daniel (1940), The Empire in Solution (1931), The Epistle to the Romans (1947), Esther: A Keystone of the Bible (1933), Isaiah (1937), Is It the End of the Old or the Beginning of the New Era For the World? (1933), Jesus Christ Triumphant (1926), The Kingdom Law of Divine Healing (1932), The Kingdom of God (1928), The Law of The Lord: The Common Law (1928), The Man (1937), The Names of God (1929), The National Message of the Bible (1925), New Light on Old Paths and the Fifth Gospel (1917), Our Heritage: The Bible, The Post-Captivity Names of Israel (1934), The Present Menace and How To Meet It (1930), The Races of the Bible (1926), The Revelation of St. John the Divine; The Second Coming of Our Lord (1958), The Simple Truth (1926), The Shekinah Glory, The Statesmanship of Jesus: A Study in the Wonderful Epistle to the Hebrews (1929), The Two-Fold British Race: In Britain and Palestine, The World Crisis (1931), and others.

Surgeon-General, Dr. J. M. Grant, M.D., wrote Israel In The New Testament or Proofs of The National Conversion of The Ten Tribes To Christianity, and The Origin, Progress, and Establishment of The Kingdom of God In The World (1896).

Sir George Grey, K.C.B. (1812-1898), was born in Lisbon, Portugal. He began his military career serving in Ireland (1830-36). He led the expedition for settlers in Western Australia (1837-39). A very competent statesman, he was Governor of South Africa (1841-1845); Governor of Cape Colony, South Africa (1854-60); Governor of New Zealand (1861-68); and Premier of New Zealand (1877-1879).

Lieutenant-Colonel James "Bo" Gritz, is the *most decorated* Vietnam Green Beret Commander. He has been the role model for several movies. He ran for president in 1992 on the Populist Party ticket; he authored A Nation Betrayed (1988) and Called To Serve; he is a seminar speaker, patriot radio talk show host, and the instructor of the nationwide "S.P.I.K.E." self-defense training program.

(Colonel Gritz endorses books written by Balaicius/STM.)

Dr. Grattan Guinness, F.R.G.S., F.R.A.S. (1835-1910), was an Irish evangelist who travelled around the world preaching for 12 years, and then again later in life for 5 years in world missionary tours. He was the Director of the Livingstone Inland Mission (1880), and the Founder and Director for the East London Institute for Home and Foreign Missions (1873-1910). He founded the missions magazine *The Regions Beyond* in 1878. He later founded missions in 5 other countries, which consolidated with the East London Institute as the Regions Beyond Missionary Union. He authored several books, two being The Approaching End of The Age and Light For The Last Days (1886).

Dr. Mordecai Fowler Ham, D.D. (1877-1961), was an 8th generation Baptist preacher who was converted to Christ by the famous professional baseball player-turned-evangelist, Billy Sunday (America's greatest evangelist). Ham was awarded his honorary Doctorate of Divinities from Bob Jones University. He was a radio evangelist, published a newspaper, *The Old Kentucky Home Revivalist*, and wrote several books: Believing a Lie, The Jews, The Sabbath Question, and The Second Coming of Christ (1945). Ham travelled extensively preaching as an evangelist, and had the practice of inquiring who was the most notorious sinner in any community, then finding him and preaching to him. This of course brought threats of physical harm and police arrest, as well as the occasional conversion. Ham led Billy Graham himself to Christ in 1934. In Macon, Georgia 13 brothels closed because all the prostitutes were converted by Ham's influence.

Nathaniel Brassey Halhed, Esq., M.P. (1751-1830), a gifted genius who possessed rare literary talent, was an Oriental scholar and later a Member of Parliament (under the sponsorship of the Treasury). He first gave the West correct notions of Sanskrit and initiated the movement that caused Indian studies and comparative linguistics to bloom, and who set the Bengal Renaissance on its course. He assisted Richard Brinsley Sheridan (1751-1816, English dramatist) in Sheridan's first literary ventures, and was one of Warren Hastings' (1732-1818, the first Governor General of British India) most faithful intimates. He wrote: A Code of Gentoo* Laws or Ordinations of the Pundits from a Persian Translation Made From The Original Sanskrit Language (1777), A Grammar of The Bengal Language (1778; reprinted in 1980 in Calcutta, India), Essay on the Slain Lamb of Revelation... (1795), and 1) The Whole of The Testimonies To The Authenticity of The Prophecies of Richard Brothers As Prince and Prophet to The Hebrews...2) A Calculation on The Commencement of The Millennium: With Observations on The Pamphlets Entitled, "Sound Arguments..." (1795), as well as several titles on British rule in India. (See Orientalism, Poetry, and The Millennium (1983) by Rosane Rocher, or the earlier, Sketch of the Life and Character of Nathaniel Brassey Halhed, Esq., 1795.) (* Gentoo is an alternate form for the word *Hindu*.)

Professor Herbert Bruce Hannay, Esq., of the Inner Temple, Barrister-at-Law, Advocate of the High Court of Juricature in Calcutta, India, wrote European and Other Race Origins (1914) which was printed in London. His other books which were printed in Calcutta at the University, have his name spelled "Hanna***h***": Ancient Romic Chronology (1920), Culture and Kulture Race-Origins or The Past Unveiled (1919), and A Grammar of the Tibetan Language (1912; reprinted in 1978 and again in

1996). Hannay stated,

...that the British are the modern representatives of the ancient Beth Sak (House of Israel) is...not open to doubt, except by minds that deliberately refuse to accord just weight to the fact, inferences, and probabilities upon which that hypothesis is based (from *The National Message*; 11/13/26, p. 712).

Ty Hardin (born Orson Whipple Hungerford) was the actor who played the leading role of Bronco Lane in the TV series "Cheyenne" (1959) (replacing Clint Walker). He starred in the classic movie "PT 109" (1963) (with Cliff Robertson and Robert Culp). He also starred in "Merrill's Marauders" (1962), and in many other movies, with notable actors such as Joan Crawford, Stephanie Powers, and Robert Conrad (among others).

Rev. George T. Harding was a Canadian minister, Incumbent of Durham.

Having become fully convinced of the truth of our identification with the ten tribes of Israel, I felt it to be a duty to acknowledge boldly my belief. It is my opinion...these truths...[are] spreading very rapidly in Canada (July 23, 1879).

Reader Harris, K.C. (1847-1909), a competent lawyer who was an active infidel and antagonist of Christianity was brought back to a full faith in the Bible when clearly shown that the Anglo-Saxon peoples were the true Israelites of the Bible and that not a single prophecy of Scripture nor a single promise of God has failed. He authored The Case Against Atheism, The Lost Ten Tribes (1907), and many booklets and pamphlets. Commenting on the wrecking of the faith of Charles Bradlaugh (see separate entry in this section), due to similar disenchantments as a result of not understanding who God's Israel people actually are—and as a result of false teaching to the contrary, Reader stated,

Do you not see the pity of it? And whom do you consider is the more to blame? Truth-seeking and candid Bradlaugh, or his teachers? I appeal to you to inquire into the matter for yourselves. You will be amply repaid. You will be surprised how much more easily you will be able to read your Bible with this new light thrown on its mysteries. And watching events of the world sharpen themselves as foretold, each day you will be more convinced that the Anglo-Saxon race is in very truth God's Chosen Servant Race for the evangelizing and subjugating of the world for Christ—and I challenge contradiction. (From *Thy Kingdom Come* (Vol. 5, No. 3, March 1992, pp. 34-35, Association of the Covenant People, 7730 Edmonds Street, Burnaby, British Columbia, V3N 1B8 Canada.)

Harris also stated,

The discovery and acknowledgment of the lost ten tribes would revolutionize the whole world, give impetus to Scriptural study, and encourage man in a wonderful degree to believe the promises of God.

(See **Appendix K** for the sad record of other great men who turned from the truth because God's prophecies concerning Israel were not fulfilled in the "jews.")

Surgeon-General, Dr. Thomas Hastings, F.R.C.S.

Hon. L. H. Hollins, Australian statesman.

Not only has the mantle of Israel fallen on Britain, but the British are, in literal fact, the long lost tribes of Israel, which were to be found, as the Bible tells us, in the Isles north and west of Palestine (Only One Road, 1950).

Richard Kelly Hoskins, graduated Fishburn Military School (1947); received his B.A. in history from Lynchburg College, VA; attended Hampton Sidney College and William and Mary Law School; served in U.S. Air Force, Air Force Intelligence, 100th Division, Airborn Division, receiving the rank of First Lieutenant; was a member of the Air Force Pistol Team and competed in Nationals in 1952; served in the Richmond Light Infantry Blues (as did many generations of his ancestors; some serving under Patrick Henry); he also worked on Wall Street for 33 years. He is a respected lecturer and author of several fine books: In The Beginning..., Our Nordic Race, Vigilantes of Christendom, War Cycles Peace Cycles, and The Wolf and the Sheep; he produces a financial investment portfolio and *Hoskins' Report.*

(Richard Hoskins highly endorses Your Inheritance written by Balaicius/STM.)

Rev. Thomas Rosling Howlett, B.A., A.M., pastored North Pearl Street Baptist Church (later called Immanual Baptist Church), Albany, N.Y.; Calvary Baptist Church, Washington, D.C.; and Berean Baptist Church, Philadelphia, PA. He authored, Anglo-Israel, The Jewish Problem, and Supplement: The Ten Lost Tribes of Israel, Found and Identified in The Anglo-Saxon Race (1892).

H.M. King James VI of Scotland (James I of England) (ruled 1566-1625), who commissioned the King James Bible, claimed in 1603 that the Lord had made him king over *Israel.* In his coronation procession to enter London, he passed through the Gate of the Elders, or Aldersgate. Over the arch of the gateway were two statues facing north, the direction from which King James would come. These two figures were the prophets Samuel and Jeremiah. Under each was a Biblical declaration. Under Samuel: "And Samuel said to all Israel, Behold, I have hearkened unto your voice in all that ye said unto me, and have made a king over you." Under Jeremiah: "Then shall there enter into the gates of this city, Kings and Princes, sitting on the Throne of David, riding in chariots and on horses, they and their princes, the men of Judah, and the inhabitants of Jerusalem; and this city shall remain forever" (Old and New London, chapter 17).

It should be noted that while God used Samuel to set up the first king of Israel, it was Jeremiah whom God used to *transplant* the throne to the British Isles through the daughters of King Zedekiah. In the niches of the British law courts of London are many statues. In the back of the courts is Carey Street. Overlooking it are four statues: Moses, Solomon, Christ, and Alfred the Great.

King James, in his book *Basilikow Dorow*, also claimed to have traced the royal lineage of the kings of Britain back to the House of David, the king of Israel. Regardless of King James' reputation as being less than moral in some areas, this does not mean that he was not descended from Israel. Most of the kings of Israel mentioned in the Bible (as well as the kings and queens of England, etc.) were wicked and godless. However, God's truth is revealed to all, and God's truth will make itself known even in spite of wicked men. Evil men might even have hidden motives that are less than honorable, yet to accomplish His purpose God will often turn *to good* what men might have intended for evil.

A gold sovereign (coin) issued in 1640 called the *Jacobus* (Jacob) or the *Unite*, was ordered to commemorate the union of England, Ireland, and Scotland. The obverse displayed King James with the Latin: *IACOBVS. DGMAG. BRIT. FRAN & HIB. REX* ("James, the King of Britain, France and Hibernia"). The reverse had the royal standard and the Latin inscription: *FACIAM EOS IN GENTEM VNVM* ("I will make of them one nation")—the prophecy of Ezekiel 37:22.

During the 16th century, the Welsh Tudors ruled England. An old manuscript can be viewed in the British Museum, in the Harleian Collection, that traces the Tudor monarchy to Anna, a descendent of Joseph of Arimathaea (Christ's uncle). (See also The Pedigree of Arthur, Sir Ian Stuart-Knill.)

Thomas Jefferson, one of the founders of our nation, upon remembering the death of George Washington (1799) (in a letter to Dr. Walter Jones in 1814), wrote, "I felt on his death with my countrymen, that verily a great man hath fallen this day in Israel." In his Second Inaugural Address, he further stated, "I shall need too, the favor of that Being in whose hands we are, who led our fathers as Israel of old, from their native land and planted them in a country flowing with all the necessities and comforts of life." Jefferson also suggested that the great seal of the United States should be Moses leading the children of Israel through the wilderness with the pillars of fire and clouds.

Jefferson was one of the greatest intellects of his time. He began studying Greek, Latin, and French at the age of 9. He entered the College of William and Mary at the age of 16 and graduated at the age of 19 and began five intensive years of study under George Wythe, the first professor of law in America. When Wythe examined him for the bar, Wythe afterwards confessed that it seemed as if Jefferson knew more than those examining him. Jefferson also learned the Anglo-Saxon language. He studied the Bible and the Greek and Roman classics, as well as European and English history—often in the original languages, not wishing to lose anything in the translation.

Of noted importance, consider the following: While studying the history of ancient Israel, Jefferson made a significant discovery. He saw that at one time the Israelites had practiced the earliest and most efficient form of representative government. As long as the Israelites followed their fixed pattern of constitutional principles, they flourished. When they drifted from it, disaster overtook them. Jefferson referred to this constitutional pattern as the "ancient principles."

Jefferson was surprised to find the Anglo-Saxons had gotten ahold of these "ancient principles" and followed a pattern almost identical to that of the Israelites, until c. 8th century A.D. (Taken from The Making of America: The Substance and Meaning of The Constitution (1985), W. Cleon Skousen, National Center For Constitutional Studies; Washington, D.C., pp. 27-28.) (Emphasis mine.)

"Jewish" Testimony (See **Appendix B**).

George Fiusdale Jowett (1891-1969), was born in England. When he was 9 his parents were told he would never walk again, and he was not expected to live past the age of 15, due to an accident he suffered when he was 6 months old. He recovered and eventually wrote books on fitness, invented and manufactured sports equipment (the revolving plate-loading barbell, the coil-spring chest expander, etc.), and went on to become an amazing, ***champion***, ***world-class*** *athlete.*

He became the international gymnastics champion in his age group and by the age of 18 he had won world titles in boxing in feather, light, and welterweight divisions. He also won titles in junior weight lifting and catch-weight. In 1907 in Bradford, England, the town auditorium was packed in anticipation of a professional wrestling bout between light-heavyweight world champion Joe Carrol and the local Yorkshire champion. The crowd was growing restless as they had paid good money to watch the match, and neither of the two had yet shown themselves. The crowd was starting to turn into a mob when Joe Carrol appeared and announced that the local champion would not be able to make it for the match. Carrol then asked if someone from the audience would like to take his place. If any man could last 15 minutes in the ring with him, he would go home with the 2nd place prize money. A solemn silence fell over the auditorium as the men in the crowd sheepishly glanced at each other. Then George Jowett stood up. A wiry, high-school youth, George was only 5’5” with a thick head of wavy blond hair. It was a scary mismatch, with Carrol not only being taller, but 30 lbs. heavier. The free-style bout was fought to a stalemate by the time the bell rang. Once Carrol could catch his breath, he shouted to the audience, “There’s no doubt about it, George Jowett is the strongest man I’ve ever met.” George accepted his winnings and slipped quietly out the back. The age-old question of *who would win between a wrestler and a boxer* was later settled when George stepped into the ring with Alfred Baxter, a leading European welterweight boxer. George easily dodged Baxter’s punches, while he waited for the right opportunity. It was soon over and Baxter, on his way to the hospital, swore that he would never again step into the ring with a wrestler. In 1921 in Pittsburgh George defeated the world champion wrist wrestler Eugene LaRocke in a grueling 30-minute match.

He moved to Canada at the age of 19 and began his research, while toiling as a blacksmith. He also served in Canadian Expeditionary Forces in WWI. He gave lessons in wrestling, weight-lifting, boxing, and judo. When he weighed 154 lbs. he became the first man in America to lift *double* his body weight; when 176 lbs., he lifted 340 lbs. in a clean jerk; and at 192 lbs. he became the first man in North America to one-arm swing 210 lbs. Over the course of his life he won some 300 medals. At local fairs he performed amazing strong-man feats. He would eventually win 4 international titles, including, “Best Developed Man in England, and “Most Perfectly Developed Man,” and “World’s Best-Developed Body.” He trained Joe Wieder (and Wieder’s brother) as well as Johnny Weissmuler (the future Olympian athlete and “Tarzan,” who was so impressed he endorsed Jowett’s products for free). He would come to be known as the “Father of American Weight Lifting.”

He later founded the *Jowett Institute For Physical Culture* in both Philadelphia and New York. He founded a mail-order business and wrote numerous health and exercise booklets (which inspired Charles Atlas): one sold over 25 million copies (Molding Mighty Muscles; at .25 cents each). By the late 1930's he controlled 5 corporations with offices in Australia, New Zealand, Britain, Europe, and the Far East. In 1940 he broke his back in an accident, and he moved toward retirement, but amazed people at the age of 64 when he lifted a 245 lb. dumbbell over his head with one hand. He was the Chairman of the Board of Planning and Development of the *St. Lawrence Seaway Project* (which was his last, among many, eminent positions in civic affairs); he worked tirelessly for his community since it was destined to be flooded by the Seaway; and he was the People's Warden of Holy Trinity Anglican Church, and led the drive to move the 200-year old church stone-by-stone to its new location.

He came from a prominent literary family, and he also founded a large publishing house in New York and Philadelphia. In addition to writing many books on health and exercise, he also wrote a book which has become a classic: Drama of the Lost Disciples (1961). It reveals the Israelite origin of the Anglo-Saxons, and details Christ's early life in Britain, the apostles in Britain after Christ's death, Britain's conversion to Christianity by Christ Himself, and much more concerning the First-Century Church in Palestine and beyond. He also wrote Dominion, a small booklet showing Canada's position in the Covenant, representing one of the 12 tribes of Israel. The year before his death he was honored with the *Molson Trophy* in Montreal, distinguishing him as the man who had contributed more than anyone else to bodybuilding. He is buried at St. Lawrence Seaway Union Cemetery. His gravestone reads, in part, "a humble man who carried his meritorious achievements with quiet dignity and thanksgiving."

Dr. Willem A. and **Helene W. (van Woelderen) Koppejan,** though citizens of the Netherlands, chose to be married in 1970, in Glastonbury, England where Christ and the early Apostles first established Christianity.

Willem studied medicine at Leijden University, and developed a large medical, psychological, and pedagogical practice based upon Christian principles. An ardent student, his library contains over 30,000 titles.

Helene was born in Flushing, Holland, the daughter of the burgomaster, and is of Huguenot descent on her mother's side. She graduated from Amsterdam University with her degree in social education. She authored, Strange Parallel (1984), showing that the Dutch people are descended from the Israelite Tribe of Zebulun; she wrote many articles for various Israel publications in both Dutch and English, and was a contributor to several Dutch magazines.

John Leech, M.A., LL.B., K.C., a distinguished lawyer, who was listed in the Who's Who of his day, gave up his career (1926) devoting the remainder of his life to witnessing for the British-Israel truth and the Message of the Kingdom.

Counsellor LeLoyer, the French Magistrate, declared in his The Ten Lost Tribes Found (1590), "The Israelites came to and founded the English Isles." The *Petit Parisien* on June 24, 1913, published a review of his work and declared, "He has found the Israelites, and that to-day they form the English People."

Mrs. Milton "Larry" Lent (born Aileen Lawrence in 1904 in Summit, New Jersey), a profound believer of the Anglo-Israel truth, descended from a long line of patriots, including a gentleman who accompanied Roger Williams in the founding of the Colony of Rhode Island. In the 1940s she was a secretary in Naval Counter Intelligence, and later a clerk in Intelligence. She worked for the Senate Internal Security Subcommittee (1952-54), then under Senator McCarran. She worked directly under special counsel Robert Morris during the IPR investigation and hearings. She was Assistant Secretary to Senator Joseph McCarthy (Wisc.), and transferred to Senate Permanent Investigations Subcommittee to continue working under McCarthy, its new Chairman.

(Mrs. Lent is a personal friend, and a dear godly lady who, although now blind, continues to live a fruitful life in glory to God. Her autobiography, My Travels Through This World, was recently completed. Larry knew nearly every politician from Huey Long to James Forrestal, and every Christian-Israel preacher from Swift and Comparet to Gerald L. K. Smith, as well as every patriot such as Father Charles Coughlin.)

Sir Oliver Joseph Lodge (1851-1940), the eminent English physicist, stated,

> We too, are a chosen people. It were blasphemy to deny our birthright and responsibility. Our destiny in the world is no small one. We are peopling great tracts of the earth and carrying thither our language and customs. The migrating of that primitive tribe from Ur of the Chaldees under the leadership of that splendid old chief, Abram, into the land of promise, was an event fraught with stupendous results for the human race.

John Alvin Lovell (1907-1974) received his B.A. from Hardin Simmons University, Abilene, Texas (1931). As a student, he drove 95 miles to pastor Oak Grove Baptist Church, Cadds, Texas (1928-1931). He founded and pastored numerous other churches: Trinity Baptist Church, Abilene, Texas (1928-1931); Calvary Baptist Church, Ranger, Texas (1933-1939); the Kingdom Fellowship Churches in both Long Beach, and Los Angeles California (1940-1946), and finally the First Covenant Church, Dallas, Texas (1947-1974) (now pastored by Michael Spradlin, in Irving, Texas). He also founded the radio program *America Awake* (1932), pioneering in the "new" thing of radio with a one-hour daily Gospel broadcast (11:00 a.m. to noon on KFPL, Dublin, Texas; 1931-1936). Since there were few radio stations in existence at the time, coverage was extensive. He founded *Kingdom Digest* magazine (1940) which is still issued monthly from Irving, Texas by his wife Vada and son Jan.

Lietenant-Colonel William Gordon MacKendrick, D.S.O. (Canada), a.k.a. the "Roadbuilder," authored, Destiny of the British Empire and the U.S.A. (1921), God's Plan for Freedom of the Seas (1929), God's Commonwealth's: British and American (1928), God's Economic Plan for the Empire (1935), Jews Not Israelites According to Scripture (1931), and This is Armageddon: God Wins This War, for Britain and America: How, When and Where (1942).

Commander Donald Henry MacMillan, M.B.E., R.N.R., F.R.I.S., F.I.N. (c. 1960, Britain), wrote The True Ecclesia (1955) and forewords to The Second Coming of Our Lord by Goard and to Intelligence Work and The Bible (rev. ed.) by McQueen.

Rear-Admiral Sir Errol Manners, K.B.E. (c. 1949, Britain), wrote the foreword to first edition of Intelligence Work and The Bible by Lt.-Colonel J. A. McQueen.

Sir Charles Marston, K.St.J., J.P., F.S.A. (1867-1946), was son and heir of the industrialist John Marston (who found great success as a metalworker and japanner), who founded and owned Sunbeam (as well as Villiers Cycle Component Company) that first made the finest bicycles that money could buy, and then fine quality and innovative cars and motorcyles. Charles who became an eminent archaeologist said,

> Great Britain was the first of all nations to adopt Christianity. Bible study and the result of the Great War are forcing me to the certain conclusion that to-day we, as a nation, represent the Lost Sheep of the House of Israel...We are in the peculiar position that is upon us—both as a Church and a People—may depend the whole future civilisation of the world. (*From The National Message and Banner*, 2/9/29, from a speech he delivered at Caxton Hall, Westminster; taken from Facets of the Great Story, Tourtel, p.140.)

Marston authored: The Bible Comes Alive (1937), The Bible is True (1938), The Christian Faith and Industry (1927), Lands (1938), New Bible Evidence (1934), New Knowledge About The Old Testament (1933).

The Hon. William Ferguson Massey, P.C. (1856-1925) was Prime Minister and Minister of Lands and Labour of New Zealand (1912-1925). Although born in Ireland, his father moved the family to Aukland in 1870. He was raised farming with his father and before he was 20 he became independent, married, and soon became prominent in civic affairs, local, and then national government. He declared, "British-Israel truth is God's truth. It is therefore bound to win, *it is winning all along the line*" (Facets of the Great Story, Tourtel, p. 140).

Dr. James S. McGaw, D.D. was a Scottish Covenanter who was a life-long minister in the Reformed Presbyterian Church and represented the National Reform Association for 17 years, which took him on speaking engagements in 46 states. McGaw was travelling through a small Midwestern town and was on his way to the train depot, when he stepped into a haberdashery store, that turned out to be owned by a "jew." McGaw tried every approach he could to convert him without any success, and in desperation blurted, "The Jews are God's chosen people and Jesus was a Jew, therefore, you ought to accept Him as your own personal Saviour!" The "jew" replied that McGaw was mistaken. Bewildered by the declaration, McGaw himself replied, "Well if the Jews are not the chosen people I'd like to know who are." The "jew" replied, "If you really want to know who the chosen people are, read Judah's Scepter and Joseph's Birthright, by Bishop Allen." The conversation affected him greatly, but he was able to obtain a copy of the book after a year's searching. In the quietness of his room he took the book, as well as his Bible, and with his Greek and Hebrew texts beside him he began to read the book. Though he read deep into the night, he could not put the book down, and as the rays of the early-morning sun began to shine into the room he finished the book a confirmed believer. He later prepared two studies himself, *Outline Studies in The Covenants of The Bible* and *The State Religion of Israel, or Symbolism of The Old Testament Ritual*, which are profoundly conceptualized and set forth. He declared:

The revelations brought to me through the study of the 'Israel Truth,' have definitely established my faith in the Bible as the inspired Word of God and proved to my complete satisfaction that God is a God of order, manifested in a mighty plan and program unfolded in the eight covenants, the prophets, and the Gospels, and fulfilled in and through the special creation of His chosen people Israel. With this vision, the sixty-six books of the Bible are seen to be a complete disclosure of God's love, and a marvellous unit, symmetrical, co-ordinated, harmonious and progressive from Genesis to Revelation.

I thank the 'Israel Truth' for making the Bible a new book to me and for a fully rounded Gospel of Salvation for the individual and redemption of the nation to be preached in these last days of a dying age, linked with a lively realization of the coming Kingdom of God on earth. I shall never cease to be thankful to...Judah's Scepter and Joseph's Birthright (pp. 2,3 Suppose We Are Israel: What Difference Does It Make?, McGaw).

Rev. Peter S. McKillop, wrote Britain and America: The Lost Israelites (1902, St. Albans, VT). In it he quotes Mr. Streator, M.A., asserting:

If the destiny of our race has been foretold and guaranteed by the Eternal God in an ethnical covenant promise, it becomes us as patriots as well as Christians to investigate and understand as fully as possible every feature of it (p. 22).

McKillop also shares Mr. J. G. Taylor's observation:

Men have been looking for a community like the Jews in appearance, having "Jewish features,"...investigation proves that the so-called Jewish features are a late and restricted growth;" while Holman Hunt declares that the Anglo-Saxon type of countenance bears a closer resemblance to the Ancient Hebrew physiognomy than any other modern form (p. 505).

Lt.-Colonel J. A. McQueen, D.S.O., M.C. (Military Intelligence) authored Intelligence Work and The Bible: A Digest of Kingdom Truth (1949).

Dr. F.(rederick) **B.**(rotherton) **Meyer** (1847-1929), was an English Baptist pastor, evangelist, and expositor. Considered one of the most knowledgeable and influential scholars of the late 19th and early 20th centuries, he authored more than 70 books and 35 booklets and edited several magazines. He pastored many churches. Two of these he started with a handful of people and built to congregations exceeding 2,000 people in just a few years. He started a local prison ministry that met all newly released prisoners. He personally fed an initial breakfast to over 5,000 newly released prisoners and counselled them. He provided a place for them to live and started several businesses (cutting firewood, washing windows) to provide work for them until they could manage for themselves. He attempted to convert them to Christ and keep them from crime. Spurgeon said, "He preaches as a man who has met God face to face." Although a Baptist, he was not fond of denominationalism. In a letter he wrote to the *Jewish Chronicle* dated February 18, 1916, he confessed,

In my opinion, the gist of the present upheaval is the Jewish question, and the inevitable result will be the restoration of Jerusalem and Palestine to the Hebrew race. I confess, also, without absolutely committing myself to it, a strong attraction to the view that the Saxons have close affinities with that ancient stock.

Rev. W. H. M. Milner, M.A., F.R.G.S., A.V.I. (whose father was the Rector o

Middleton-in-Teesdale), authored (some under the pen name of "Oxonian"): The Ancestors of the Cymry: An Exposition From the Testimony of Ethnologists of the Israelite Origin of the Ancient British, British Israel Truth, Dynasty of King David Established in Britain, Ephraim the Scot: An Argument Identifying Israel with Britain, History is On Our Side: A Vindication from the Evidence of Historians of the Thesis that Israel is Found in Britain, History Fulfilling Prophecy; The Illustrious Lineage of the Royal House of Britain (1904), Israel's Wanderings (1892), The Royal House of Britain: An Enduring Dynasty (1902), Russia - Japheth: or The Muscovite, the Cossack, and the Mongol (1890), The Russian Chapters of Ezekiel (1902), Shiloh: The Site of Ezekiel's Temple, Tara: The Hebrew Episode in Irish History Verified (1903), and Verse By Verse From Genesis To Malachi: An Examination of the Old Testament Scriptures Bearing on the Discovery of Israel (1901). He also edited the monthly *The Covenant People*.

Lieutenant-Colonel Cyril W. Minett (USAF, Ret.), attended the University of North Carolina, the University of Southern California (postgraduate work), Arizona State University, and East Texas State University. He majored in journalism and history and his postgraduate work was in advanced management. He entered the USAF in 1953, graduated from aviation cadets in 1954, and was an instructor of single-engine jets for 4 years. In 1967 he began a 2½ year's tour in Vietnam as a fighter pilot, earning 4 rows of medals, including 4 Air medals and the Combat "V" (the highest medal awarded to a foreigner by Vietnam). Returning home in 1970 he was named editor of *Aerospace Safety Magazine*. He was later assigned Assistant Chief of Staff at USAF Headquarters, 12th Air Force, Austin, Texas. He retired in 1974. In 1979 he joined the board of FREE (Fund to Restore an Educated Electorate), in Kerrville, Texas, and became chairman of the board upon the death of its founder (Johnny Stewart). In 1992 he was the vice-presidential candidate who ran with Lt.-Col. James "Bo" Gritz on the Independent ticket. He is a frequent speaker at patriotic conferences.

(Col. Minnett highly endorses Your Inheritance, by Balaicius/STM.)

Lieutenant-Colonel Gordon "Jack" Mohr (AUS, Ret.), entered the Army as an enlisted man during the early days of WWII and was the first American soldier wounded and decorated in the Korean War. He was captured in a failed Communist coup in October 1948 while working with the U.S. Army as an adviser to South Korean forces in pre-war Korea. He was tried by a "People's Court," tortured, and sentenced to death by firing squad. With the help of a South Korean sergeant, he escaped the night before his set execution date and made his way back to friendly forces on the 38th Parallel when the war began on June 25, 1950. He was wounded 4 times, never severe enough to be hospitalized—though once hit with 97 pieces of shrapnel after the back end of his jeep had been blown off by a 122 mm shell! A few days later another jeep he was driving was strafed from behind (by 4 of *our own* planes) being riddled with 27 fifty-caliber bullets: all 4 tires were blown out and shells coming in from over both of his shoulders clipped off the steering wheel just above his hands—without receiving a scratch! He received the Silver Star from

Major-General William Dean for action during the opening hours of fighting and became one of the most highly decorated soldiers of that conflict. In all, he received 12 combat decorations and 4 Army Commendations. He then became one of the most ardent opponents of Communism, fighting tirelessly in a "no-win" war against an unending campaign of propaganda fomented by the secret personages behind Communism. Many years later, when Seoul, Korea was celebrating the anniversary of the war's end, Col. Mohr was invited to return to Korea to partake in the ceremonies. He was scheduled to leave for Seoul, but at the last moment, for some reason, decided not to take the flight. That flight turned out to be the fated 007 flight that was shot down by the Soviets. As it turned out, Congressman Larry MacDonald (another outspoken Christian opponent of Communism) *was* on that flight and died along with everyone else on board. Is it just a coincidence, as it is reported, that ex-president Richard Nixon was on that same flight but was *ushered off* by the Secret Service on its stop in Anchorage, Alaska? An evangelist and seminar speaker, Col. Mohr has authored nearly 100 books, booklets, and pamphlets. His main books are: America's Destiny, Behold: The International Jew, Blueprint For Antichrist, The Effects of the Talmud on Judeo-Christianity, The Hidden Power Behind Freemasonry, Know Your Enemy, The Mystery of True Israel, and The Satanic Counterfeit. For many years he published a newsletter, *The Christian Patriot Crusader*; currently he publishes a quarterly *Intelligence Report*.

(Col. Mohr highly endorses the books written by Balaicius/STM.)

Dr. George Moore, M.D., M.R.C.P. (London), wrote Ancient Pillar Stones of Scotland (1865), History of Ireland, The Lost Tribes or the Saxons of the East and of the West (1861), and The Ten Tribes (1861).

G.(eorge) **Campbell Morgan** (1863-1945), was a famous Congregationalist minister and evangelist who was called "a prince among evangelists," and was considered to be "the Prince of Expositors." He worked with D. L. Moody and Ira Sankey in an evangelistic tour in 1883. He was the Master at the Jewish Collegiate School in Birmingham, England (1883-1886). In 1904 he took over the pastorate of the "white elephant of Congregationalism," the Westminister Congregational Chapel, a dying church at Buckingham Gate, London. Twelve and one half years later he left the church as one of England's most active and best known churches. He pastored 3 other churches in England. He served on the faculty of the Bible Institute of Los Angeles (1927-1928) and was a Bible lecturer at Gordon College of Theology and Missions, in Boston, MA (1930-1931). He was also the pastor of Tabernacle Presbyterian Church in Philadelphia, PA (1929-1932).

Eustace Mullins is a popular seminar speaker and is considered the foremost researcher and writer exposing political conspiracy. He is the personal protege of 3 of America's great men: Ezra Pound, George Stimpson, and H. L. Hunt.

(***Ezra Pound*** was the famous poet/critic who edited works of William Butler Yeats and T. S. Eliot, and helped them get started as writers. Pound commissioned Mullins to write History of the Federal Reserve, taught him how to research at the Library of Congress and edited the book. It was translated into German; 10,000 copies were printed, but were then confiscated by the Zionist-controlled German government and burned in Oberimmergau. It is thus the only book that has been publicly burned by a government in Europe since WWII. Mullins is also Pound's official biographer. ***George Stimpson*** founded the National Press Club in Washington, D.C., and was the most quoted journalist in Washington in his day. ***H. L. Hunt*** was an oil man in Dallas, Texas.)

Mullins was an employee of the Library of Congress in Washington, D.C.; after faithful service he was fired because of his other journalistic activities. He is the only employee ever fired by the Library of Congress for political reasons. Mullins was also a consultant on road financing to the American Petroleum Institute in Rockefeller Center, New York, and he was an editor and involved in public relations for Chicago Motor Corporation. He has authored The Biological Jew, Ezra Pound: This Difficult Individual, Great Betrayal: Story of The Constitution, Murder By Injection: Exposing America's Medical Monopoly, Rape of Justice, The Secret Holocaust, Secrets of The Federal Reserve, The World Order: Our Secret Rulers, A Writ For Martyrs, and over 100 shorter works.

(Eustace Mullins highly endorses the books written by Balaicius/STM.)

Rev. H. Newton, B.A., was Vicar of St. Michael's, Borough, Southwark. He wrote Israel Identified in the Anglo-Saxon and Kindred Protestant Nations (1874).

James Bernard Nicklin (born 1881), was an inventor, technical school teacher, industrialist, and metallurgist. When he was 33 years old the Chief Inspector of Aircraft Steel in England approached him just after the War had begun in 1914. He wanted Nicklin to produce 20 tons of Vanadium Steel (in accordance with a paper Nicklin had written in 1906), putting at his disposal any steel works he needed. A popular and tireless speaker and writer, Nicklin authored: The Great Shaking (1918), Divine Time Measures (1933), The Great Tribulation (1941), Their Days Are Numbered (1942), The Approaching Climax (1946), Signposts of History (1956), and Testimony in Stone (1961), over 200 booklets and pamphlets, and numerous articles for the *National Message* magazine (British-Israel World Federation, London) and *Destiny Magazine* (Destiny Publishers: Merrimac, MA). (See A Life With God and the Great Pyramid: J. B. Nicklin (1971), compiled by Willem and Helene (van Woelderen) Koppejan.)

John Norden (1548-1625?), the famous Elizabethan topographer, dedicated his classic geographical survey of England, *Speculum Britanniae*, to Queen Elizabeth:

> To the High and Mighty Empress Ellizabeth...Powerful protector of the undoubted faith of the Messiah, The Most Comfortable Nursing Mother of **the Israel of God in the British Isles**....

Professor Edward F. Odlum, M.A., B.A. B.Sc., F.R.G.S., F.A.S., F.R.C.I., Inst., was a Fellow of the American Geographical Society, scientist, educator, and lecturer. He authored The Bible Basis of A Perpetual Israel Kingdom Governed by the Royal Line of David (1929), God's Covenant Man: British-Israel (1927); Great Britain Great (1926), and an unpublished manuscript: *A Dictionary of Classical Antiquity*.

Born in Ontario, he received his degrees from Victoria University. Judge Howay, a noted British Columbia historian, recorded that under the direction of Dr. Haanel, Odlum built the first electric light (a big arc light) used in Canada; and in collaboration, they built the first telephones used in Canada for public purposes. Odlum and Haanel also founded the Science Association at Victoria University and chartered the establishment and building of a science hall, which Odlum was instrumental in having named *Farraday Hall*. Odlum taught in the public schools of Ontario and the Collegiate Institute at Coburg (which he once attended). He also served as the principal of Pembroke High School. Later, he accepted the principalship (conducted by the Methodist Church of Canada) of a college (*Tokyo-Eiwa-Gako*) in Azubu, Tokyo, Japan (where he supervised 600 students and 14 tutors). This excursion also allowed him to continue his scientific work and to study the ethnology and history of the Japanese people. Odlum took some of the phones he had made in Canada to be used in Japan.

After having lived in Tokyo for three years, he returned to Canada in 1889, stopping in Vancouver (which he eventually made his home). While visiting relatives he met a lady who knew of his great interest in history. She asked him if he had ever considered the possibility that the Anglo-Saxon-Celtic peoples were the descendents of the ancient Israelites. He immediately replied that the notion was "pure nonsense." However, he could not get the idea out of his mind. He began studying the Bible and decided to write a paper refuting the idea. After only a few days' study, he realized the subject was far greater and more involved than he had imagined. It was not long before he realized it could not be refuted because it is true.

Odlum met regularly with a small group in Vancouver to study the matter; they came to call themselves the *British Israel Association* (1909). The group grew, and many chapters were formed throughout Vancouver, to the point that the name was changed to the *British Israel Associations of Greater Vancouver*. In 1939 they published the first issue of their periodical, *The Anglo-Saxon World*, and increased their publishing of books. (In 1974 the periodical's name was changed to *Identity*.) As the association grew and dealings with America and European countries increased they decided to change their name to *The Association of the Covenant People* (1968)

(A sister group, the *British Israel Federation of Canada*, was formed in 1919 as interest and groups appeared in other parts of Canada, Britain, and the United States. Its official periodical, *The National Message*, appeared in 1922 with Rev. Goard and Commander Roberts as editors. The *Covenant Publishing Company* was also established at that time. In 1926 the *Banner of Israel*, the publication of another association, merged with the *National Message*. In 1934 the *British Israel Federation of Canada*'s name was changed to the *British Israel World Federation (Canada)*, as it now had offices in Britain, Australia, New Zealand, and elsewhere. Another sister group was also eventually formed, the *Canadian British Israel Association* in Toronto.)

Odlum's studies, rather than culminating in a dissertation of refutation, ushered him to a firm conviction of the truth that the Anglo-Saxon peoples were indeed the descendents of the Israelites of the Bible. He became one of the greatest proponents of this truth, being a popular author and lecturer. He was once granted permission to examine Britain's Coronation Stone (Stone of Scone). He examined the Stone, as well as natural rock formations throughout Britain. His examination concluded that in agreement with tradition, the stone did not originate in the Isles. He travelled to Israel and found similar rock formations in Luz.

He also wrote a daily article for the *Vancouver Daily Star* newspaper published by his son Victor. When the *Star* discontinued publication, the *Vancouver Sun* assumed the publication of Odlum's column. He also made weekly radio broadcasts during the 1920's and 30's. In collaboration with others, he also helped form a Bible school (c. 1925) and classes were held in the Grandview Congregational Church (pastored by Rev. Goard). Odlum was active in the promotion of the Anglo-Israel truth for close to half a century. (His son Edward F. Odlum, was also actively involved in the Federation's conferences and periodicals.) The last 6 years of his life, he pastored the Sunday evening services in the Bethany Mission in Vancouver. He went on to his reward in 1935. (Material gleaned from 70 Years Old: An Outline History of Our Work Since 1909, M. Alma Hetherington, Association of the Covenant People.)

Brigadier-General Victor W. Odlum, C.B., C.M.G., D.S.O. (1880-1971) was the son of Professor E. Odlum. He served with distinction in the South African War and World War II, commanding the 2nd Canadian Division as a Major-General. He was Minister to China, and Canada's first Ambassador to China (1943-46), Ambassador to Turkey (1947-1952), and Canadian High Commissioner to Australia. He served as a member of the Provincial Legislature (1924-1928), the Board of Governors of the Canadian Broadcasting Corporation, of Union College, and of the University of British Columbia, Vancouver. He also served as a wise counsellor, experienced director, and tireless worker in a host of organizations devoted to public benefit, such as, the Little Theatre, the Association of Canadian Authors, the Vancouver Welfare Association, the Canadian Red Cross, the Boy Scouts, and the Institute of International Affairs. He worked as a reporter and then editor-in-chief of the Vancouver *Daily World*, and editor-in-chief of the *Vancouver Star* (1924-1932). He was a frequent speaker at British-Israel conferences. He was awarded an Honorary Doctor of Laws degree (1950) from the University of British Columbia, Vancouver. The University noted that "through all his many activities, responsibilities, and experiences he remained modest and approachable, genial and humorous."

A Pamphlet written in Nether (Northern) Dutch (1671) declared the English-speaking peoples (*European* peoples) were the Israelites. (English translation, 1672.)

Colonel Pearse, R.E. Brig.-Gen. George Wilson, in his Coincidences?: Pointers To Our Heritage (Linking Britain with Ancient Israel), writes concerning Pearse,

> The route from ancient Assyria to Ar-Sereth where there was a major staging area on the migrations, crosses the Caucasus mountains by a long and winding pass. This pass is known—to this day—by the locals, as the "pass of Israel." An interesting (true) story of this is that after World War I, a British army officer Colonel Pearse R.E. and his companion were making this journey. When they entered the pass they were surprised when their guide told them that the Children of Israel passed this very same way and that it was called the "Pass of Israel." As a joke the Colonel asked the guide if he was an Israelite? To which he emphatically replied—"No, BUT YOU ARE"!
>
> Although Col. Pearse was a practising Christian he was completely ignorant of any connection between the British people and *ancient* Israelites. Subsequently he became chairman of the Streatham branch of BIWF (British-Israel World Federation) and a well-known lecturer on the subject! (p. 10)

Rev. Mark Guy Pearse (Wellington, New Zealand), a Methodist minister:

> If Britain is Ephraim, i.e., the Ten Tribes of Israel—then I can see the prophecies of Scripture being fulfilled in our midst. If...not...then there is no such people answerable to the prophets' description, nor as yet, has there been such a people, nor is

there any promise of such a people appearing.

Sir William Matthew Flinders Petrie, D.C.L., LL.D., F.R.S., F.B.A. (1853-1942), was a British archaeologist and foremost student of Egyptian prehistory; grandson of famous Australian explorer Captain Matthew Flinders. Although Petrie was educated privately and never attended a university, he had numerous honorary doctorates, was a Fellow of the Royal Society, and Professor of Egyptology at University College, London (eventually Professor Emeritus). He was the first to set down scientific standards for excavating; he excavated ancient remains in Britain, Egypt, and Palestine; founded the *Egyptian Research Account* (which became the *British School of Archaeology in Egypt*); he discovered the Greek settlements at Naucratis (1885) and Daphnae (1886), and he discovered the stele of Merneptah at Thebes (1896), which was inscribed with the earliest known Egyptian reference to Israel. Even into his 80's, he was still at work with the *American School of Research* in Jerusalem. He authored: Ancient Gaza: 5 vol. (1931-38); Arts and Crafts in Egypt (1909); Book Of History: History of All Nations; Decorative Patterns in the Ancient World (1930); Descriptive Sociology of Ancient Egypt (1926); Eastern Exploration (1919); Egypt and Israel (1911); Egyptian Science (1939); Egyptians Tales: 2 vol. (1895); Formation of the Alphabet (1912); Growth of the Gospels (1910); Historical Studies (1910); A History of Egypt: 4 vol. (1894-1927); Hyksos and Israelite Cities (1906); Inductive Metrology or the Recovery of Ancient Measurements from the Monuments (1875); The Making of Egypt (1939); Methods and Aims in Archaeology (1904); Palestine and Israel: Historical Notes (1934); Prehistoric Egypt (1920); The Pyramids and Temples of Gizeh (1888); Religion and Conscience in Ancient Egypt (1898); Religion of Ancient Egypt (1906); Religious Life in Ancient Egypt (1924); Revolutions of Civilization (1911); Roman Portraits (1912); A Season in Egypt (1888); Seventy Years in Archaeology (1931); Social Life in Ancient Egypt (1923); Some Sources of Human History (1919); Stonehenge (1880); Syria and Egypt (1898); Ten Years' Diggings in Egypt (1893); and others.

Pilgrim and Puritan Testimony. Many Pilgrims (1620) and Puritans (1630), when they came to America, called themselves "The Seed of Abraham," "God's Servants," "His Chosen," and "A Vine out of Egypt into the Wilderness." They also called America "New Canaan Land," "The New Promised Land," and "The Wilderness" (See **Appendix G**).

Rev. F. E. Pitts (Nashville, TN), was requested by members of Congress to deliver two sermons to Congress on George Washington's birthday. These sermons were entered according to an Act of Congress (in the office of the Clerk of the District Court for the Middle District of Tennessee): *The United States of America Foretold in the Holy Scriptures* (on February 22, 1857) and *The Battle of Armageddon* (on February 23, 1857). These messages revealed that the Anglo-Saxon peoples were the Israelites of the Bible and were printed in booklet form called The U.S.A. in Bible Prophecy (1862). He later wrote, A Defense of Armageddon (1859).

Rev. William H. Poole, LL.D., was a Canadian minister and authored Anglo-Israel or the Saxon Race?: Proved to be the Lost Tribes of Israel (1884; 686pp.) which was presented first as a series of 9 lectures. He gave other lectures and wrote other books, including: Anglo-Israel or The Anglo-Saxon Nation Identified with the Lost Tribes of Israel (1880), Fifty Reasons Why The Anglo-Saxons Are Israelites of the Lost Tribes of the House of Israel, History

The True Key to Prophecy: In Which the Saxon Race is Shown To Be the Lost Tribes of Israel (1880), and The Second Coming of Christ As Taught by Premilleniums, Not Taught in the Bible. His lectures and books were reviewed very favorably by the mainstream media and Christians (and ministers) of all denominations.

Rev. Arthur Pritchard, M.A., authored The Bible and the British Race and The Master Key of the Bible (c. 1927).

Captain Rupert W. B. Protheroe (Canada) after he retired from the Navy, helped the British Israel Association in their many conferences in Canada and the United States (1950-1960). He also took over the operation of their offset printing press. He continued working for the ministry even in the hours before his death in 1970.

Howard Benjamin Rand, LL.B. (1889-1991), graduated from University of Maine; was a member of the Maine National Guard; passed the Maine Bar in 1912, and the Massachusetts Bar in 1913. He practiced law in Haverhill, MA, from 1913 to 1928; owned and managed Haverhill Construction Company from 1914 to 1928. He was the Prohibition Party candidate for Attorney General of Massachusetts in 1944, '46, '50, and '52. Truly a genius, he invented and patented an electric incandescent lamp in 1916 and the lamp socket guides for automobile headlamps in 1918 with the U.S. Patent Office in Washington, D.C. He also patented the automobile headlights and reflectors in 1915 with the Patent Office in Great Britain and Australia and with the Patent Office in France in 1916. He was also the co-inventor, with the late R. Nason Hoyt of Haverhill, MA, of an apparatus for removing carbonized material from textile fabrics, which was patented with the U.S. Patent Office in 1953. He also nearly completed a perpetual motion machine before his death, and had invented and built his own camera of immense size. He was an incredible man who kept busy and in good health even up until his death at the age of 102. He credited his having followed God's dietary laws his whole life, as the key to his long and healthy life.

A prolific author, his main works are: Behold He Cometh! (1955); Day of Decision (1951); Digest of Divine Law (1942); Documentary Studies (3 vols.) (1947-1954); Gems of Truth (1968); The Hour Cometh! (1966); In the Image of God (1967); Joel's Prophetic Message and Warning (1935); Marvels of Prophecy (1959); Primogenesis (1953); Study in Daniel (1948); Study in Hosea (1955); Study in Isaiah (published posthumously in 1996); Study in Jeremiah (1947); Study in Revelation (1941); and many more. He was the founder and treasurer of *Destiny Publishers*, Merrimac, MA (an offshoot from *The Anglo-Saxon Federation* of which he was National Commissioner in 1928), and the editor of *Destiny Magazine* (1937-1968). He also spoke at conferences in the U.S., Canada, and Great Britain. He confessed,

> Very early in life I learned that, when my beliefs did not conform with the truth, I was headed for trouble.... My beliefs were worthless unless they were in line with the facts.
>
> During my early years I was brought up in a knowledge and understanding of the Scriptures and I could repeat from memory all the interesting stories of the Bible from Genesis to Revelation. As I grew older, I pondered over the inconsistency of the attitude so many [Christians] assumed that the Divine laws governing the uni-

verse could not be violated with impunity, though they acted as though God's moral laws had no actual bearing or personal conduct beyond that which they were willing to concede—and they gave no thought at all to God's national statutes. This was a challenge to me and, by my acceptance of all the Divine laws...in the Bible, there was established for me a relationship with God and to my fellowmen that enabled me to place a proper evaluation on all of life's varied aspects....

The early lesson that taught me to make my beliefs conform with the facts...a thorough training in the Scriptures, led me...to apply the logic and reasoning acquired through legal training to an analysis...the Story the Bible tells. An inward urge drove me on to...research in the Bible, covering many years, the results of which firmly established my belief that there is a Divine plan being worked out in the world, not only in the personal lives of man, but in the affairs of nations as well. I discovered that events are following a timetable, keeping a schedule as accurately synchronized as the movements of the earth, sun, moon and stars—and this further strengthened my belief.

...many are fearful today as they contemplate the possibility of atomic destruction. However, the knowledge that there is an overruling God who has set bounds, beyond which evil men and nations will never be able to pass, has given me peace of mind in spite of the present confusion, turmoil and strife. I believe that it is being made quite clear by events that God is even now moving in judgment to compel men to bring their beliefs into conformity with the facts.

I have found that education...itself does not necessarily impart truth...only when we maintain the balance so essential between spiritual understanding—based upon a knowledge of the Scriptures...our standard—and physical and mental growth that we can hope to acquire a discerning spirit.... I have learned that it is the maintenance of such a balance between things spiritual and things material that has brought my beliefs into focus with the truth, with its reward of assurance amid uncertainty (from *This I Believe*, Rand).

George Rawlinson (1812-1902), was the Camden professor of ancient history at Oxford; canon of Canterbury; rector of All Hallows', London. He translated *Herodotus* The History of Herodotus (1858-60) with his brother Henry. He also authored: Historical Evidences of the Truth of the Scriptural Records (1859); Five Great Monarchies of the Ancient Eastern World (1862-67); Manual of Ancient History (1869); The Sixth and Seventh Great Oriental Monarchies (1873-87); History of Ancient Egypt (1881); History of Phoenicia (1889); Parthia (1893); and Memoirs of Maj.-Gen. Sir H.C. Rawlinson (1898).

Major-General, Sir Henry Creswicke Rawlinson (1810-1895) a Military Officer, Diplomat and Assyriologist; he helped reorganize the Persian army with the East India Company (1833-39); was Political Agent at Kandahar and Consul at Baghdad; Director of the East India Company (1856); British Minister in Persia (1859-60); Member of Parliament (1858, 1865-68), and Member of the Council of India (1858-59, 1868-95). He and his brother George translated *Herodotus*. He nearly single-handedly deciphered the Old Persian inscriptions which opened the way to the understanding of cuneiform and other eastern languages. He authored several books on cuneiform inscriptions, the Russian question, and History of Assyria (1852).

Rev. Hollis Read, A.M. (1802-1887), a missionary of the American Board, in his

The Hand of God In History: or Divine Providence Illustrated In The Extension and Establishment of Christianity Throughout The World (1855), wrote,

> All past history is but the unraveling of God's eternal plan respecting our race. The whole course of human events is made finally to subserve this one great purpose (p. 13)....
>
> *The Hand of God is discernible in the discovery and first settlement of America*.... The time had arrived when God would give enlargement to Zion. For this purpose he had reserved a large and noble continent—a land fitted, by its mighty rivers and lofty mountains, its vast prairies and inexhaustible mineral productions, to be a theatre for more extensive and grand developments of the scheme of redemption than had ever yet transpired (p. 34)....
>
> It was at such a time that the "woman, clothed with the sun, and the moon upon her feet, and upon her head a crown of twelve stars," having long, and in various ways, been persecuted by the great red dragon, of "seven heads and ten horns, and seven crowns on his heads," had given to her the two wings of a great eagle, that she might fly into the *wilderness*, where she had a place prepared of God, that they should feed her there a thousand, two hundred and three score days. And here, free, strong, lofty as the eagle, (our national banner,) she lives and breathes, and moves, stable as our everlasting hills, extensively diffused as our far-reaching rivers, and free as our mountain air (pp. 36,37).... (See Revelation 12.)
>
> ...This was the land of promise...God would give to the people of his own choice. Hither he would transplant the "vine" which he had brought out of Egypt. Here it should take root and send out its boughs unto the sea, and its branches unto the river (p. 38).... [See Genesis 49:22 and Ezekiel 17.]
>
> ...when I speak of stern principles which originated at the first settlement of this country...of the admirable institutions of our forefathers...of our high pretensions to freedom, intelligence and piety, I bear in mind that we have proved ourselves unworthy of our noble inheritance, and recreant to our good professions. But I would look beyond these clouds, which ever and anon intercept our vision, to those better things reserved for the second Israel (p. 50)....
>
> We might here trace the agency of a series of wars which subdued many a barbarous nation and gave nationality to Germany; which kept at bay the overwhelming power of Rome, and which opened the way for the establishment of the chosen race in the British Isles (p. 583)....
>
> The Anglo-Saxons are at the present epoch of the world the chosen race through whom the great work of human progress is carried forward. They are the modern Israel, the chosen arm of the Lord for the elevating and blessing the nations of the earth. They are, as directed and used by the Almighty arm, controlling the destinies of the world (p. 682)....
>
> ...should the idea recently broached by a reverend lecturer in England (Rev. J. Wilson) prove to possess as much truth as...interest, viz.... these...Anglo-Saxons are none other than the...descendents of Abraham ...the "Ten Lost Tribes," this will cast a new charm over the history of this extraordinary race, and confirm our already sanguine hopes that this people, whom we have called the modern Israel, shall bless the earth far more abundantly than their renowned progenitors ever did (p. 683).

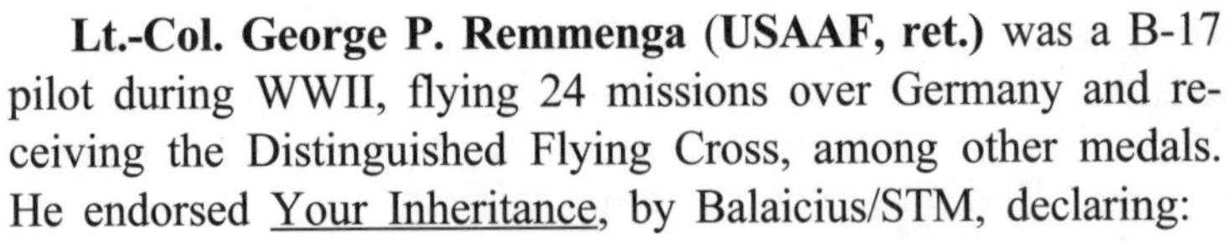

Lt.-Col. George P. Remmenga (USAAF, ret.) was a B-17 pilot during WWII, flying 24 missions over Germany and receiving the Distinguished Flying Cross, among other medals. He endorsed Your Inheritance, by Balaicius/STM, declaring:

At the age of 17, I read through the family Bible, cover to cover. When I completed the reading, I had many questions about the Bible. Those questions have now been answered in Your Inheritance, in a straightforward, scholarly manner. No longer do we have to wonder. Further, a person gains a bright, new view on life, and is inspired with new purposes. Your Inheritance should have a very preeminent place in the library of each patriot, each patriotic organization & true church in this once proud land of ours. Further, every true American family should have a copy of Your Inheritance to properly teach their children of their heritage and the only true purpose in life. I sincerely believe that had my family and I had this book, I might have lived my life differently in many regards.

Commander (and Rev.) L. G. A. Roberts, R.N, was a Commander of the Royal Navy, Rector of Ardley, Bicester, and Oxfordshire; he authored British History Traced From Egypt To Palestine (1927), Commentary on the Book of Isaiah (1931), Druidism in Britain: A Preparation For the Gospel, The Early British Church: Originally Hebrew, Not Papal, Israel in the Book of Revelation, Palestine to Britain, Studies in Jeremiah, Studies in Ezekiel, and others, including a *Map of Israel's Migrations into Britain.*

Professor Roger Rusk (1906-1994), the son of a Presbyterian minister, and brother of Dean Rusk (who was the Secretary of State under President Kennedy, and President Johnson until 1969), was a public school teacher for 13 years. He was also a professor for 28 years at the University of Tennessee, where he held the position of Emeritus Professor of Physics. He was a member of the American Physical Society and the Tennessee Academy of Science. He was a well-known speaker and Bible teacher; he appeared on a TV documentary as the science consultant for a team in search of Noah's Ark, and wrote, The Other End of The World (1988).

Adam Rutherford, F.R.A.S., F.R.G.S., was born in Scotland in 1894. He founded the Institute For Pyramidology and was a popular lecturer and writer. He authored: Armageddon: The Battle of the Great Day of God Almighty (1950), Behold The Bridegroom: Come Ye Out To Meet Him, Coordination of the Great Pyramid's Chronograph, Bible Chronology and Archaeology, The Coronation Chair and The Stone of Destiny (1937), Elements of Pyramidology Revealing The Divine Plan For Our Planet, The Glory of Christ As Revealed By The Great Pyramid, The Great Pyramid, The Great Pyramid: Its Christian Message To All Nations And Its Divine Call To The British Empire and USA (1942), The Great Pyramid: The Divine Blueprint and The Bible in Stone (1952), Hebrew Chronology Scientifically Established (1939), The History of the Great Pyramid: From The Glimmer of Pyramidographia To The Glories of Pyramidology, Iceland's Great Inheritance (1937), Israel-Britain or Anglo-Saxon Israel? (1934), The Midnight Cry: Behold The Bridegroom (1925), A New Revelation In The Great Pyramid: The Controversy of The Cubit Settled (1953), Pyramidology (1941), The Revelation of Science In The Great Pyramid, The Saviour of The World As Revealed By The Great Pyramid (1953), and Treatise on Biblical Chronology (1957).

Rutherford recorded in a footnote on page 108 of his book Israel-Britain or Anglo-Israel that the esteemed Professor L. A. Waddell, in his researches in the religious literature of all ancient civilizations, *found references to a race that was exclusively selected to prepare for the return to the earth of the Messiah, and the name of this chosen people would be* "Brits."

Dr. J.(ohn) **C.**(harles) **Ryle** (1816-1900), the Bishop of Liverpool, was considered one of the greatest scholars of his day. He authored numerous books, the most notable being: Christian Leaders of the 18th Century (1885) (Canon A. M. W. Christopher of St. Aldate's, Oxford confessed that he had read this book during every summer vacation for 30 years.); Coming Events and Present Duties; Expository Thoughts on the Gospels (1856-73; 7 vols.); Five English Reformers (1890); Practical Religion; and Warnings to the Churches. Ryle stated:

> I think we have made great mistakes...it is high time to confess it. What I protest against is the habit of allegorizing plain words of God concerning the future history of the nation of Israel, and explaining away the fulness of their contents, in order to accommodate them during the next half century as has prevailed during the last fifty years, it will not only be foremost, as it is already in power and influence, but it will be absolutely the largest in respect to actual numbers.... the reason why God has given to this race [British] its rapid increase, its dominance in both hemispheres, and its vast influence, is because God has appointed it [Britain] to be His instrument for the setting up throughout the world of that universal monarchy which shall never be destroyed, and of which the rule shall not be left to another people. Already England and America are foremost in missionary effort, and in the printing and the circulation of the Word of God. But as yet, it is but a feeble effort, and when the whole English speaking population awakens to a sense of its greatness, and the high purpose for which God has bestowed upon it so large an extension and so high a place, the Kingdom of earth will rapidly be made the Kingdom of our God, and upon the ground, now being with so great toil prepared upon it, will rise the *great mountain** which shall fill all the earth (from Coming Events and Present Duties). (Brackets and emphasis mine.)

(*Referring to the Great Mountain of Israel; the Stone Kingdom; Ezekiel 17:22; Daniel 2:35,45; 9:16. Interestingly enough, the communist revolutionary Karl Marx similarly confessed, "England seems to be the rock against which all revolutionary waves are broken.")

Dr. Ryle further stated,

> I warn you, that unless you interpret the prophetic portion of the Old Testament in the simple, literal meaning of its words...Will you dare tell Him that

Zion, Jerusalem, Jacob, Judah, Ephraim, Israel did not mean what they seem to mean, but mean the Church of Christ? I believe it is high time for the Church...to awaken out of its sleep about Old Testament prophecy...For centuries there has prevailed in the Church...an unwarrantable mode of dealing with the word "Israel." It has been interpreted in many passages in the Psalms and Prophets as if it meant nothing more than Christian believers. Have promises been held out to Israel?...Have glorious things been described as laid up in store for Israel?...In reading the Words God addressed to His ancient people, never lose sight of the primary sense of the Text (Facets of The Great Story, Tourtel, p. 136).

Dr. John Sadler, M.A., M.P. (1615-1674), was a Member of Parliament and wrote Rights To The Kingdom or Customs of Our Ancestors (1649, reprinted in 1682). Dr. Sadler seems to have been one of the earliest persons to modernly identify, in written form, the Europeans with the Israelites and to point out the similarities between the English and Hebrew languages. In confusing the modern "jews" with Judah, sadly, Sadler was reported by some to have advised Cromwell to re-admit the "jews" to England. Sadler also wrote The King's Cabinet Opened (1645), in conjuntion with Charles I and others.

The Bishop of Saint David's (c. 1377) declared:

And so you may embrace your noble King...for there is through him that peace over Israel which the Scriptures name—Israel being the heritage of God, and that heritage being also England.... I believe that God would never have honoured this country by victories such as He had given to Israel, had He not intended it for His heritage also (from a speech to parliament; Book of the Princes of Wales: Heirs To The Crown of England (1860), Dr. John Doran, LL.D.).

Colonel T. Myles Sandys, M.P.

Major-General Harry N. Sargent, C.B., C.B.E., D.S.O., authored The Changing World (1935), The Marvels of Bible Prophecy (1938), The Modern World and Its Delusions (1944), The Servant Nation (1932), and This Blind World (1933). The portrait at right was done in watercolour by his wife Olive.

Professor Archibald Henry Sayce, D.D., LL.D. (1845-1933), was an eminent English philologist, archaeologist, and scholar (who was the son of Rev. H. S. Sayce, vicar of Caldicot). Sayce was educated at Queen's College and was ordered a deacon (1870) and ordained a priest (1871). He was professor of Assyriology and deputy professor of comparative philology at Oxford. He was a Member of the Old Testament Revision Company, and he was Hibbert Lecturer (1887), Gifford Lecturer (1900-1902), and Rhind lecturer (1906) at Oxford. He was also an honorary member of the Asiatic Society of Bengal, the Royal Academy of Spain, the Anthropological Society of Washington, and a member of many other learned societies. Hardly any *respectable* book on ancient history or archaeology can be picked up without finding his name in it. The Encyclopedia Britannica (11th Edition; 1910-1911) stated, "it is impossible to overestimate his service to Oriental scholarship." (Note: "Oriental" in the classical sense, refers to the ancient East: Israel, Assyria, Babylon, Persia, India, etc.) Sayce contributed many important articles to the 9th, 10th, and 11th editions of the Encyclopedia Britannica, and he edited many other important works; such as: G. Smith's History of Babylonia (1877), Sennacherib (1878), and Records of the Past (5 vols.; 1888-1892); the English translation of G. Maspero's *Histoire ancienne des peuples de l'orient classique* [as The Dawn of Civilization; 3 vols. (1894-1900)]; Murray's Handbook of Upper Egypt (1896); and The Aramaic Papyri Discovered at Assouan (1906).

He wrote the first grammar of the Assyrian language in English. Early in life he mastered Assyrian, Arabic, Persian, and Sanskrit, and over his long life he wrote in 20 different languages. Before accepting his professorship in Assyriology at Oxford, while in Egypt (1890) he helped obtain important archaeological relics for the British museum, one of which was the manuscript in ancient Greek, *the Constitution of Athens*, by Aristotle, which had been presumed lost to the world.

Sayce authored: The Ancient Empires of the East (1884), Archaeology of the Cuneiform Inscriptions (1907), Assyria: Its Princes, Priests and People (1882), An Assyrian Grammar For Comparative Purposes (1872), The Astronomy and Astrology of the Babylonians (1874), Babylonian Literature (1877), Babylonians and Assyrians (1900), The Early History of The Hebrews (1897), Egyptian and Babylonian Religion (*Gifford Lectures*) (1903), The Egypt of the Hebrews and Herodotus (1895), Elementary Assyrian Grammar (1874), Fresh Light From the Monuments (1883), Genesis in the Temple Bible (1902), Herodotus (1883), "Higher Criticism" and the Verdict of the Monuments (1894), The Hittites (1889), Introduction to Ezra, Nehemiah, and Esther (1883), Introduction to the Science of Language (1880), Israel and the Surrounding Nations (1898), Lectures on the Assyrian Language and Syllabary (1877), Lectures on Babylonian Literature (1877), Life and Times of Isaiah (1889), Monuments, Facts, and Higher Critical Fancies (1904), The Monuments of the Hittites (1881), The Origin and Growth of Religion as Illustrated by the Religion of the Ancient Babylonians (*Hibbert Lectures*) (1887), Patriarchal Palestine (1895), A Primer of Assyriology (1894), The Principles of Comparative Philology (1874), The Races of The Old Testament (1891), Reminiscences (1923), Social Life Among the Assyrians (1900), Social Life Among the Assyrians and Babylonians (1893), Tobit and the Babylonian Apocryphal Writings in the Temple Bible (1903), and The Vannic Inscription Deciphered and Translated (1882).

Sir Walter Scott (1771-1832), the renown English novelist, in his novel Woodstock, has Oliver Cromwell repeatedly refer to Britain as "Israel." Examples of this can be found in chapter 30: "Now, as my soul liveth, and as He liveth who hath made me a ruler in Israel...;" and chapter 34: "For surely He who hath been to our British Israel as a shield of help and a sword of excellecy, making her enemies to be found liars unto her...."

Sir and Lady Mark McTaggart Sewart.

Rev. Aumarez Smith, Archbishop of Sidney; Primate of Australia.

Captain and Rev. Merton Smith was born in Glasgow, Scotland and he studied in Glasgow, St. Andrews, and Liege and Leipzig, Germany. He served with the Red Cross in the Franco-German war of 1870. In Germany, he came into contact with the movement of the time, which crystallized in theology as "jewish" *Higher Criticism*, and in society as Marxism. As a student he met Karl Marx and spent 10 years as an agnostic. The sound logic of his firm Scottish background, however, kept him from straying too far. After he completed his studies, he ended up in Chicago, Illinois. He came into contact with D. L. Moody's revival and was converted to Christ. He then began working for Moody's organization in downtown Chicago and soon became Moody's organizing secretary for his campaigns in America and Great Britain. Smith also helped Moody establish the Moody Bible Institute* (which continues to this day in Chicago as a respected Bible institute, mission board, and printing house). He was the pastor of Knox Congregational Church (renamed Grandview Congregational Church after moving to a different district) in Vancouver. When World War I broke out, Smith volunteered to go as a chaplain and was among the first to go overseas, serving in the Canadian camp in England, then later in France and Flanders. When he returned to Vancouver, he relieved Rev. Goard as pastor for a while, after which he undertook several missionary journies throughout Canada, the United States, and Great Britain, preaching the true Israel message. He married in 1921, moved to the Channel Islands, and became commissioner for the Israel message in that area. In 1934 Rev. Smith passed away in his home at Bouley Bay, near St. Heliers, Jersey, at the age of 81. He authored Israel: Her Racial Divisions and Geographical Wanderings (1926), and The Jewish Question and Israel.

(*It is also interesting that, according to Dr. Gary North, "James M. Gray of the Moody Bible Institute in 1927 wrote an editorial favorable to Henry Ford's *Dearborn Independent* series on the Jews. Gray's editorial appeared in the *Moody Bible Institute Monthly*.")

Dr. Protheroe Smith, M.D., authored The Identity of Israel With The English and Kindred Races (1873; Britain).

Professor Charles Piazzi Smyth F.R.S.E., F.R.A.S., F.R.SS.A., F.R.SS.L.&E., C.M.S. Sp. It., Hon. M. Inst. Engin. Sc., P.S., Ed., R.A.A.S, (Munich and Palermo) (1819-1900), was born into a remarkable family and earned notariety himself in several fields. He was the Professor of Practical Astronomy at the University of Edinburgh, and Astronomer Royal for Scotland. He was an eminent pioneer in astronomy, spectroscopy, meteorology, metrology, geodesy, and photography. He was also an engineer and an artist. He authored: The Antiquity of Intellectual Man (1868), The Great Pyramid and The Royal Society (1874), Life and Work At The Great Pyramid (1865; 3 vols.), Our Inheritance in The Great Pyramid, (1867; Smyth received a gold medal from the Royal Society of Antiquarians for this work), Lost Israel Discovered By Still Retaining The Old Standard of Weights and Measures, New Measures of the Great Pyramid (1884), the Edinburgh Star Catalogue, and Ephemeris. He eventually resigned from his appointment (by Queen Victoria) as Astronomer Royal because they refused to publish his later works on the Great Pyramid. Smyth declared,

> The effect of the identity of the Anglo-Saxons as Israel is twofold. First, it causes us to behold and acknowledge therein the accomplishment of a true miracle, and of the mightiest kind, through the ages consummated in our own days. Second, it causes the Bible to become for us, as it was for the Ten Tribes of Israel of old, an infallible book for national guidance in politics, as well as a collection of inspired instruction for each individual soul in religion (Facets of The Great Story, Tourtel, p. 140).

The **Sonnini Manuscript**, also called **The Lost Chapter of The Acts of The Apostles**. This ancient document is reputed by some to be the last part of the book of Acts in the New Testament. It was translated from an ancient Greek Manuscript found in Constantinople. Just a few verses shall be listed:

(The entire translated manuscript, along with historical information on it, proofs of authenticity, and parallel proofs attesting to the veracity of the material contained therein, are contained in a booklet titled, The Lost Chapter of The Acts of the Apostles, With Commentary, by E. Raymond Capt.)

> Verse 1. "...Paul, full of the blessings of Christ...abounding in the spirit, departed out of Rome, determining to go into Spain...and was minded also to go from thence into Britain.
>
> Verse 2. ...he had heard in Phoenicia...certain of the children of Israel...at the time of the Assyrian captivity...escaped by sea to "The Isles Afar Off," as spoken by the Prophet (Esdra)...called by the Romans—Britain.
>
> Verse 7. And they departed out of Spain...sailing unto Britain...
>
> Verse 8. Now when it was voiced abroad that the Apostle had landed on their coast, great multitudes...met him, and they treated Paul courteously and he entered in at the east gate of their city, and lodged in the house of an Hebrew and one of his own nation.
>
> Verse 9. And on the morrow he came and stood upon Mount Lud* and the people thronged the gate, and assembled in the Broadway, and he preached Christ unto them, and they believed the Word and the testimony of Jesus.

(* Ludgate Hill and Broadway is where St. Paul's Cathedral stands in London, England; coincidence?)

> Verse 13. And it came to pass that certain of the Druids came to Paul privately, and showed by their rits and ceremonies they were descended from the Jews* which escaped bondage in the land of Egypt, and the Apostle believed these things, and gave them the kiss of peace."

(* Judahites (more likely Levites).)

Charles Haddon Spurgeon (1834-1892), the famous English-born, American Baptist evangelist, considered one of the greatest Bible scholars ever, in The Treasury of the Old Testament (Vol. 2, p. 154) declared:

> English history, from the first day until now, is as full of instruction as the history of Israel from Egypt to Babylon. Our nation has been as much under the special, and peculiar providence of God as were the descendents of Jacob themselves; therefore, God deals with us as He does not with any other nation.

Spurgeon once addressed the students of his college, stating,

> Do not violently strain a text by illegitimate spiritualizing. Never spiritualize for the sake of showing what an uncommonly good fellow you are: and in no case

allow your audience to forget that the narratives which you spiritualize are facts, and not mere myths and parables.

Further, Spurgeon preached to his congregation,

> The indwelling of the Holy Ghost is a subject so profound, and so having to do with the inner man, that no soul will be able to truly and really to comprehend what I am about to say, unless it has been taught of God.... If you cannot comprehend me, I am much afraid it is because you are not of Israelitish extraction; you are not a child of God, nor an inheritor of the kingdom of heaven (<u>Spurgeon's Sermons</u> vol. I, p. 58).

H. R. H. Prince Michael Stewart, authored <u>The Forgotten Monarchy of Scotland: The True Story of the Royal House of Stewart and the Hidden Lineage of the Kings and Queens of Scots</u> (1999). In his book Stewart traces his own ancestry back to King David and reveals that the Scots are descended from Israel. He also claims his family has been in exile for over 280 years, being the rightful heirs to the British Throne.

Hon. Henry Herbert Stevens (1878-1973, Canada), **M.P. for Vancouver**.

Dr. Ezra Stiles (1727-1795)**,** was considered one of the most learned men in New England of his day. He was widely educated, was a lawyer, a clergyman, had an exceptional knowledge of the ancient languages of the east, and corresponded with learned men in nearly every part of the world. He was a professor of divinity and ecclesiastical history and President of Yale University (1778 to 1795). He founded Rhode Island College (now Brown University). Using an apparatus sent to him by Benjamin Franklin, Stiles performed the first electrical experiments in New England. In 1783 he stated,

> Congress put at the head of this spirited army the only man [Washington] on whom the eyes of all Israel were placed. Posterity, I apprehend, and the world itself, inconsiderate and incredulous as they may be of the Dominion of Heaven, will yet do so much justice to the divine moral government as to acknowledge that this American Joshua [Washington] was raised up by God, and divinely formed, by a peculiar influence of the Sovereign of the universe, for the great work of leading the armies of this American Joseph [Manasseh] now separated from his brethren, and conducting its people through the severe, the arduous conflict, to liberty and independence.

Dr. Henry W. Stough (?-1939) preached the gospel in the United States for nearly 5 decades, preaching in most all 50 states, as well as the United Kingdom. Early in his ministry he was associated with D. L. Moody, and later with J. Wilbur Chapman (who led Billy Sunday to Christ), who called him, "one of America's Greatest Preachers." He went on to be an outstanding evangelist who in size and scope of his campaigns, was second only to Billy Sunday. After World War I, he also preached the identity of the Anglo-Saxon-Celtic-Scandinavian and related peoples as being the very Israel people of the Bible and history. He was associated with the Anglo-

Saxon Federation of America, and the British-Israel World Federation of the United Kingdom, and later with the American-Israel Movement headquartered in Knoxville, Tennessee. Dr. Stough and his wife had 4 sons: Paul, Philip, Harold, and Henry W. Paul was a missionary for nearly 50 years. Philip preached in Washington D.C., Philadelphia, Pennsylvania, and Miami, Florida.

Harold E. Stough moved to London, England to work with the British Israel World Federation and Covenant Publishing, where he has served in its leadership for several decades. He now pastors the famous chapel that was once pastored by the hymnist and Anglican priest Augustus Toplady (1740-1778, who penned the famous hymn, "Rock of Ages," and the book Absolute Predestination). **Henry W. Stough** was ordained a Baptist minister in Knoxville, Tennessee the same year his father, Henry, died. For 60 years Henry W. was active as an evangelist, a pastor, a teacher, and the Director of the Anson Baptist Association and the Chowan Baptist Association. Henry W. compiled and printed nearly two dozen messages that he and his father delivered on the Anglo-Israel truth (many of them are still available in 8½x11, comb-bound format). Henry also wrote the well researched book, Dedicated Disciples (1987).

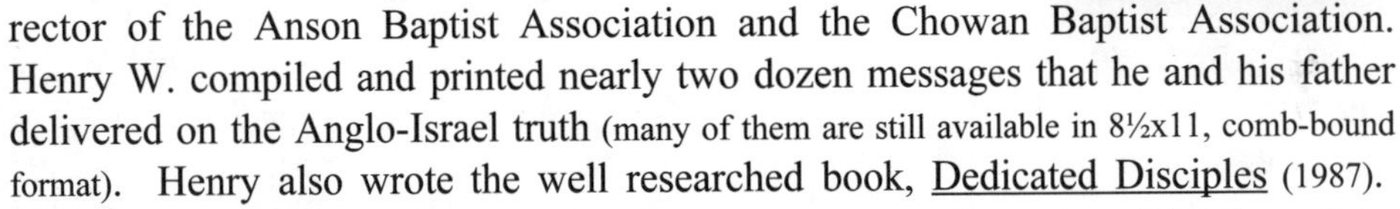

Lieutenant-General George E. Stratemeyer, was Operations Division of the War Department General Staff (Pentagon).

Patience Strong, in her lifetime was considered the most popular and most widely read poet of the century; her lovely and inspiring verses have been published in books, newspapers, magazines, wall calendars, greeting cards, and even printed on place mats and porcelain ornaments. For over 40 years her verses have been published in the national press and various periodicals without a break. The fact that she was a firm believer and unabashed proponent of the Christian Anglo-Israel message, is probably the only thing that prevented her from being officially declared England's Poet Laureate. She was also a reporter for Britain's national newspaper, the *Mirror*. She authored: Beyond the Rainbow (1950), Blessings of The Years (1963), The Broad Horizon (1943), Doctor Anonymous (1967), Echoes From The Quiet Corner (1944), Gates of Memory, Gift of The Spirit, The Glory of the Garden (1947), God's In His Heaven (1964), Golden Hours (1952), Golden Rain (1943), Gospel of Happiness, Happy Are They (1974), Happy Hours, Healing Years, House of Dreams (1938), Inspiration, A Joy For Ever (1973), The Kingdom Within (1957), Life Is For Living (1971), Light Ahead, Magic Casements, The Magic of Memories, Morning Glory (1958), The Other Side of the Coin: Thoughts and Afterthoughts on a Visit to South Africa (1976), Over The Ridge (1939), Paths of Peace (1940), Paths of Promise (1951), Patience Strong's Book of Homes and Gardens (1953), Poems From the Fighting Forties (1982), The Quiet Hour (1939), Quiet Moments (1939), Quiet Thoughts (1938), Quiet Waters (1956), The Round of the Year (1945), Silver Linings (1955), Someone Had To Say It

(1986), Strength of the Hills, Sunlit Byways (1951), The Sunny Side (1947), Sunshine and Shadow (1954), Tapestry of Time, Trees of Life (1960), Wings of the Morning (1955), With A Poem in My Pocket (autobiography) (1981), and Yesterdays and Tomorrows.

Rt. Rev. Samuel Thornton, D.D., was the First Anglican Bishop of Ballarat (Australia), and afterwards the Assistant Bishop of Manchester (England). He declared, "British-Israel truth is most wonderful. I wish I had known it twenty-five years earlier. It makes clear so many things that had been obscure" (Facets of the Great Story, Tourtel, p. 138).

Rev. Canon Bishop Jonathan Holt Titcomb, D.D. (died 1887), was Vicar of St. Stephen's, South Lambath, England; the first Anglican Bishop of Rangoon, Burma; deputy for the Bishop of London, superintendant of the stations of the Established Church on the Continent of Europe; Vicar of St. Peter's Brockley (1886), and President of the Metropolitan Anglo-Israel Association. He was courageous and fearless in his proclamation of the Israel truth. He authored The Anglo-Israel Post-bag (or how Arthur Came To See It) (1876), British-Israel: How I Came To Believe It (1929), Is It Reasonable? (A Dialogue on the Anglo-Israel Controversy) (1877), Joseph's Birthright, England's Possession (1880), Message To The Church From The Nineteenth Century (1889), and Revelation in Progress from Adam to Malachi (1871); and he was a frequent contributor to the *Banner of Israel* Journal.

Professor Charles Adiel Lewis Totten, M.A., (1851-1908); First Lieutenant, Fourth Artillery, AUS (Ret.); Professor of Military Science and Tactics, at Yale University. The Encyclopedia Americana (1950) says of him:

> American inventor and military instructor...he... graduated ...West Point...1873 and was...instructor in military science and tactics at...Amhurst Agricultural College, at the Cathedral School, Saint Paul, N.Y., and at Yale University. He patented improvements in high explosives, in collimating sights and in signal shells; besides a system of weights and measures and improvements in linear and other scales. He patented a war game which he described in a publication entitled Strategos, The American War Game (1880).

Totten authored many other books (most on Israel-Identity): (most in the Our Race... series) Answer of History (1893), Bethel: Stone of History (1902), Book of the Prophet Daniel (1895), Canon of History (1896), Chronological Vindication of the Scriptures (1892), Coming Crusade, Facts, Fancies, Legends and Lore of Nativity, Compendium of History (1898), Confirmation of History (1896), Eastern Question (1896), Fall of Jerusalem (1892), Fact of History, Focus of History (1894), Gospel of History (1900), Great Seal of Manasseh (1897), Heart of History (1894), Hope of History (1892), Important Questions in Metrology (1883), Irish Genealogies, Joshua's Long Day and the Dial of Ahaz (1891), Key of History (1894), Lost and Found (1900), Lost Israel Found In the Anglo-Saxons (1890), Man of History (1895), Measure of History (1893), The Millennium (1892), Our Race: Its Origin and Destiny (1898), Outcome of History (1897), Philosophy of History (1891), Renewal of History (1892), Riddle of History (1892), Romance of History (1890), Seal of History (1897), Secret of History (1891), Skeleton of History (1895), Story of Ireland (1905), Truth and History (1894), Voice of History (1890), and Ye Compact (1896), (all between 226 and 400 pages) among others.

Totten once declared,

> I cannot state too strongly that the man who has not yet seen that the Israel of the Scripture is totally different from the Jewish people, is yet in the very infancy, the mere alphabet of Biblical study, and that to this day the meaning of seven-eighths of the Bible is shut to his understanding.

After Totten's death, the *Totten Memorial Association* donated to the *Anglo-Saxon Federation of America* Totten's remaining unsold books with cuts and plates—weighing between five and six tons!

Jonathan Trumbull (1710-1785), the Colonial Governor of Connecticut, in a letter to General George Washington (then Commander of the Continental Army) dated July 13, 1775, wrote, "Now therefore be strong and very courageous, May the God of the Armies of Israel shower down the blessings of His Divine Providence upon you" (Christian History of the American Revolution (1976), Verna M. Hall; p. 511).

In August 1776, responding to Washington's plea for more troops, he wrote, "Play the man for God, and for the cities of our God. May the Lord of Hosts, the God of the armies of Israel, be your Captain, your Leader, your Conductor, and Saviour" (The Light and the Glory (1977), Marshall & Manuel; p. 312).

Later that year he wrote another letter on October 14, 1775 in reference to Thanksgiving, expressing his prayers that God would "...guide our affairs in this dark and difficult Day; and make them known what Israel ought to do...that He would confirm and increase Union and Harmony in the Colonies, and throughout America" (Thanksgiving Proclamation, November 16, 1775).

The United States Supreme Court in 1840 said, in reference to the neglect of the Constitution for seven years: "We may well ask, with some feelings of surprise, where during these seven years, were slumbering the watchmen of our American Israel?" (12 Fed. Cas. p. 993, case # 6914).

General Pedro A. del Valle, USMC, was Commander of U.S. Marines in the Pacific theater in World War II.

Major Knil van der Vecht, C.F., Ph.D. (1885-1960), after a career in the Royal Dutch East Indian Army, returned to Holland and devoted the rest of his 30 years to studying and writing on the pyramids, and translating and promoting David Davidson's works. He founded two Anglo-Israel societies in Holland: "Bond Nederlands Israel" and "Nederlandsche Israel-Kring" for which he served as president. He then became a well-known radio speaker and lecturer throughout Holland. He suffered injustice from the Nazi's during the occupation, and his works and those of Davidson's which he translated were banned as dangerous and officially ridiculed. However, after the war, he gave lectures on the pyramids to an audience of 1000, since the interest of many Protestant Dutch was aroused. He authored De Stenen Spreken (1935) (*The Stones Speak*), based on Davidson's work; an abridgement of this work was still in print in 1971, titled Teeken in Egypteland. He also wrote Israel, Daniel's Laatste Wereldrijk (*Israel, Daniel's Last World Empire*). He also published a magazine *Het Stenen Koninkrijk* (*The Stone King-*

dom) for 17 years (1938-1940 and 1946-1960).

H.M. Queen Victoria (ruled 1837-1901), stated, "The Bible is the secret to Great Britain's greatness." She also had her own ancestry traced back to King David, which was displayed in a chart once housed in the British Museum.

Rev. N. J. D. Waddilove, M.A., Prebendary of Ripon, England, and Domestic Chaplain to the Duke of Roxburgh; he wrote The Lamp in the Wilderness (1840).

Major-General Edwin A. Walker, AUS, Commander of 24th Infantry Division in Germany.

General Sir Walter Walker, K.C.B., C.B.E., D.S.O., (Britain) former NATO Commander-in-Chief, General Walker spent 19 of his 40 years of service in active operations, fighting terrorists, and 4 years fighting Japan. He served with distinction in the Malayan Emergency (1953-1959), in the Burma Campaign (1945), was Director of Borneo Operations and Commander of all British and Commonwealth forces in the 4-year campaign against Indonesian Confrontation. After leaving the Tropics and arriving in Europe to deal with a new environment of warfare (nuclear), he was 3 years Deputy Chief of Staff in charge of Plans, Operations, and Intelligence of Allied Forces in Central Europe. After this he became Army Commander of Northern Command in England for two years. He was then promoted to full General and was Commander-in-Chief of Allied Forces in Northern Europe from 1969 to 1972. He was responsible for the defense of Europe on land, at sea, and in the air from the border of the Soviet Union in the Arctic to the city of Hamburg on the Elbe River. He wrote, Bear At The Back Door (1978), Defense of the Western World (1977), and The Next Domino (1980).

On the dust cover of the book Fighting General, written by Tom Pocock and published by Collins in London, it was written of General Walker:

> For almost the whole of his time in the Army, ever since he joined the Gurkhas [in India] as a subaltern in the thirties, General Walker has been in command of troops actively engaged in operations. Few officers, and no Generals, come near the variety and extent of his frontline experience. When not employed in exchanging fire with the enemy, there has been more than a whiff of grapeshot left over for colleagues and superiors in Whitehall...

Major B. de W. Weldon wrote The British Nation Proved to be the Remnant of Israel, The Evolution of Israel: The Story of the English Race from 721 B.C. to the Present Day (1928), and The Origin of the English (1934).

Colonel Finch White (c. 1896; England).

Rev. Joseph Wild, D.D., pastor of the Union Congregationalist Church, Brooklyn, New York; he authored The Bond Street Pulpit, The Future of Israel and Judah (1880), How and When the World Will End (1879), The Latter Days: The Prophetic Discoveries (1921), Lost Ten Tribes (1879), Manasseh and the United States (1879), and Talks for the Times (1886).

Dan and **Jones Williams** were the founders of the Apostolic Church in Britain.

The Hon. Henry Williams, M.L.C.

General Musspratt Williams.

Brigadier-General George S. Wilson, attended Woolwich Military College and was commissioned into the Royal Artillery in 1929; served in India and led the last cavalry charge made by the British army; and served in Palestine until British forces were forced to evacuate in 1948. He authored Coincidences?: Pointers To Our Heritage (Linking Britain with Ancient Israel).

Lieutenant-Colonel H. Speed Wilson (USMC, Ret.), courageously served our nation in three wars. For his service as a combat pilot in World War II and Korea he was awarded 3 Distinguished Flying Crosses and 19 Air Medals. During combat in Vietnam, he served as Chief of Staff of the 9th Marine Amphibious Brigade (an air-ground team of 20,000 Marines); he was awarded the Legion of Merit with a Combat "V" and the Republic of Vietnam's Distinguished Service Cross (one of the highest decorations awarded to a foreigner). During his eight years of duty in Washington, D.C., he served on many planning and policy boards; he retired in 1973 after 31 years in the Marines; he authored Rapture: Prophecy or Heresy? and is a popular speaker at Anglo-Israel Bible conferences.

(Colonel Wilson highly endorses Your Inheritance, by Balaicius/STM.)

Rev. John A. Wilson, M.A. (1779-1870), was born in Kilmarnock, Scotland and was a Presbyterian minister. He authored Our Israelitish Origins: Lectures on Ancient Israel and The Israelitish Origin of The Modern Nations of Europe (first published in 1870 by Nisbet & Co., London; it was first given as a series of lectures in 1840—attracting the attention of notable men such as Sharon Turner and Piazzi Smyth—and were soon printed due to their popularity; it went through several printings in both London and American editions), as well as: The Book of Inheritance and Witness of the Prophets Respecting Ephraim and the Raising Up of Israel (1874), Sixty Anglo-Israel Difficulties Answered (1878), Sketches of Some of the Scriptural Evidences Respecting the So Called Lost House of Israel (1843), The Title Deeds of the Holy Land, The Millennium or the World To Come (1842), and The Mission of Elijah (1881).

General Robert E. Wood was a former chairman Sears, Roebuck & Company.

Lieutenant-Colonel J. G. Wright, after retiring from the military and from Pharmacology, became the Secretary General of the British Israel Association in Vancouver, and eventually their 6th president. He expanded the printing and publications of the Association and started a successful book club, which had to be discontinued at the beginning of the war in 1939 due to paper shortages. Col. Wright was also an instructor at a British Israel Seminary in Dayton, Ohio. The Seminary was founded in 1947 under the leadership of Rev. Millard J. Flenner. Col. Wright died in 1950. (Photo above from 1947.)

Rev. J. Stafford Wright, was Principal of Tyndale Hall, Bristol, England.

Dr. Holt Yates, F.R.A.S.

Captain A. H. F. Young, R.N.R.

Rev. Dinsdale T. Young (1861-1938), a popular English Methodist (Wesleyan) Minister, he began preaching at the age of 15. He pastored numerous churches, including Wesley's Chapel, City Road (1906-1914), London, as well as Westminster Central Hall where he attracted capacity crowds. He was also the president of the Wesleyan Conference (1914). He travelled extensively as he preached across the country, travelling 10,000 miles a year. He is said to have preached 30,000 sermons. He died with the words on his lips, "I triumph." He declared,

> "I increasingly believe that the weight of argument is with the British Israel position...I am more and more drawn to the great truths which the Federation represents. My heart warms to it, because of its splendid adherence to the Bible...The British Israel Federation has lighted a lamp, the golden beauty of which will never be obscured. In the great truth which this Federation holds, you have the explanation of the wonderful British Empire" (Facets of the Great Story, Tourtel, pp. 138-139).

He authored: The Crimson Book, The Enthusiasm of God, Messages For Home and Life, Neglected People of The Bible, Silver Charms, and Stars of Retrospect (autobiography).

* * * * * * * * * * * * *

Is it just a coincidence that so many of these men were high-ranking military officers? These were certainly not simpleminded, easily deceived "weirdos." When face-to-face with a multiplicity of conspiracies contrived by evil people, such men do their homework, locating the *source*. They do not foolishly dismiss logical conclusions achieved as a result of analyzing obvious patterns simply because the answer is *unpopular*. They faced the enemy head on, staring him straight in the eye, unaffected by the pressures of politics. As in any area, when one does deep study, it is inevitable that one will learn *more* than one expected.

(That is, when these men got to the *root* of all conspiracies and wars and learned that one group of evil people was responsible, these military men realized that these subversive people were *not* who they claimed to be (i.e., "God's Chosen People"). It is only natural then that these military leaders did a little more study to find out who the *real* Israelites of the Bible actually are—the Anglo-Saxon and related peoples.)

It should again be mentioned that the above constitute only a *thimbleful* of all the names I have gathered. I could list scores of other military officers and hundreds of other people (many of them leaders in their field)—medical doctors, psychologists, theologians, lawyers, politicians, policemen, businessmen, pastors, ministers, priests and bishops of every denomination, engineers, scientists, etc., who were/are firm believers in this truth. And the numbers are growing daily as YaHWeH, in accordance with His own schedule, is slowly removing the blindness from the eyes of His people.

In the late 1800's and early 1900's, various associations in Canada held meetings to which the public flocked. Denominationalism was not an issue. Ministers of every denomination embraced this truth. Radio stations and secular daily newspapers, as well as mainstream Christian periodicals, gave *fair* reviews, most often *very favorable*. Today, however, we are misrepresented, smeared, demonized, and persecuted by the "government," its media, *and its churches*. We are discriminated against and vilified. We have been labeled a "dangerous cult," and ungodly, un-American legislation threatens to outlaw our faith.

What has precipitated this 180-degree change? We have been dispossessed. European immigration has been severely curtailed while the flood gates have been opened widely to all third-world peoples. The goal is to outbreed and mongrelize us in our own land, thus assuring our being easily outvoted so our nation's policies can be turned against us. Propaganda has brainwashed European-descended Americans into severely curtailing their own birth rate, while third-worlders get extra welfare for each child. Foreigners have gained the ascendancy in the government, in the media, and in our churches. They have changed our law, our faith, and our way of life. It is our own fault. It has happened because we became complacent with the blessings God gave us, and we slowly forsook God's Ways. Yet He will deliver us *still* if we *but repent*.

Why?

Why is it that so many of our European ancestors knew that we were the true Israelites of the Bible, yet we are *again* in *national blindness*? George Santayana said, "Those who do not learn from history are doomed to repeat it." How true. Israel, as a nation, continually broke God's laws, and further, the Israelites continued to sin and intermarry with non-Israel peoples—even after God had powerfully and miraculously delivered them from 400 years of bondage in Egypt; even after they had been punished for this very sin. Because of Israel's rebellion, idolatry, and adultery, God allowed Israel to be conquered and enslaved.

History has repeated itself among the true Israel people of today, the white race. The European and European-descended nations were once the greatest, most powerful, most prosperous, safest, wealthiest, and most moral nations in the world. As we have turned from God's laws and degenerated as a people (racially, morally, and spiritually), however, God has allowed prophecy to take its course. We are now oppressed in our own land by our enemies (See Leviticus 26 and Deuteronomy 28). Each day we lose more freedoms and we inch closer to a police state, and many people are not even safe *in their own homes*. Politicians live in luxury and spend money frivolously as if there was a limitless supply. Political corruption is the *norm*. The "government" takes from the hard-working people, giving their substance to those who refuse to work and to every other nation on earth—even to our enemies.

This is <u>not</u> how our nation was established. We were once *really **free***. Yet the average American is ignorant of European and American origins and struggles for freedom. Many of our forefathers died to secure freedom and prosperity. But we have forfeited nearly everything they died to give us. No doubt, they would not have given *their fortunes and very lives* if they had known we would squander our inheritance in riotous living like a whoring, drunken sailor on shore leave.

Most people are blind to the facts. "This is still the greatest nation on earth," they chime. That is like boasting that *a coma patient in a vegetative state* is healthier than the corpses in a graveyard! Ignorant people draw comparisons between America and *other* nations, rather than drawing the *proper parallel* between America *as it is now*, and America ***as it once was and should be***! Most people do not even know what freedom is. They are content to be "upper-class beggars," not realizing that they could live like kings. Like Esau, we have sold our birthright for a bowl of pottage (temporal convenient satisfaction), and we are now paying the price. Benjamin Franklin said, "Those who would give up essential liberty to purchase a little temporary safety, deserve neither liberty or safety." Again, the ancient cry of the Prophet Hosea echoes mournfully in the wind:

> My people are destroyed for lack of knowledge: because thou hast rejected knowledge, I will also reject thee...seeing thou hast forgotten the Law of thy God, I will also forget thy children. As they were increased, so they sinned against Me: therefore will I change their glory into shame.... they set their heart on their iniquity.... I will punish them for their ways, and reward...their doings. For they shall eat, and not have enough: they shall commit whoredom, and...not increase: because they have left off to take heed to YaHWeH (Hosea 4:6-10).

But there is hope—***if*** we recognize *who we are* and *how* we fit into God's plan, and ***if*** we learn that *through obedience* we can secure for ourselves and our families those things that God has promised to us by Covenant. It is up to each person to make the choice: temporal pleasure and convenience, or standing up for *what is right*, which in the end will alone prevail. Christ YeHoWSHuWaH said,

> "He that is not with Me is against Me; and he that gathereth not with Me scattereth abroad" (Matthew 12:30).

Claim Your Inheritance

Please don't be like Esau. Don't despise your birthright and inheritance, only to regret it later and find *no place* of acceptance. Scripture records the integrity of Moses, who forsook the ill-gotten, temporal riches and sonship of Egypt (the world) to join himself with his *rightful* family. Though he knew he would be persecuted for a time, he realized the greater inheritance (and *responsibility*) that was rightfully his (Exodus 2; Hebrews 11:23-31). Don't reject the truth because it is not held by the majority. (The majority is usually *wrong*.) The majority cannot overrule *God*—and all those who follow the *majority*, rather than what is right, will one day answer for their offenses against God and His people. Christ YeHoWSHuWaH declared,

> But whoso shall offend one of these little ones which believe in Me, it were better for him that a millstone were hanged about his neck, and that he were drowned in the depth of the sea (Matthew 18:6; Mark 9:24; Luke 17:2).

There is no safety in the consensus of the majority. There is safety only in *complete* obedience to God Almighty:

> He who dwells in the secret place of the Most High, shall abide under the shadow of the Almighty...[nothing shall harm you]...Because thou hast made YaHWeH (which is my refuge, even the Most High God) thy habitation...Because he hath set his love upon Me, therefore will I deliver him: I will set him on high, because he hath known My Name. He shall call upon Me, and I will answer him: I will be with him in trouble; I will deliver him, and honour him. With long life will I satisfy him, and shew him My salvation (Psalm 91:1,9,15,16). (Brackets mine.)

We have all been in blindness at times in the past. The great thinker and patriot Thomas Paine rejected the Bible as a *fable*, because, although he had seriously studied the Bible, he saw that none of the prophecies were fulfilled in the "jews." The sad thing is that *he himself* was in spiritual blindness concerning *his own* identity—as most people are today (even as I once was). There is no shame in being wrong. Everyone is wrong at times. That is the nature of being human. What *is* shameful, however, is when people *refuse to forsake falsehood and embrace the truth once it is clearly presented.* Paine did not see the *whole* of prophecy, which shows that true Israel would have a *new name* and a *new land.* He did not see that *he himself* was one of the very Israelites in whom all the great prophecies had been fulfilled. How many other people have been turned away from the Bible and Christ YeHoWSHuWaH (the Truth) because they have believed *lies* they have been taught?

An intelligent person does not *blindly* accept the claims of others—especially when it involves something of great importance. Before he buys a car, he will have a mechanic inspect it. Before he hires someone, rents anything to, or loans anyone money, he will do a background check. He will call references and check credit. Why then do people not take the *same precaution* and *invest the same time and energy* into ***verifying*** what their *preachers and teachers* tell them *about the Bible and history*? The answer: Because most people are lazy and spiritually "cheap"! They don't want to spend the little bit of energy or time it takes (though Scripture study is the best-paying investment one could ever make).

Scripture says to *lay up treasures in Heaven* (Matthew 6:20) and *we reap what we sow* (Galatians 6:7). This can be done only by *knowing what the Bible actually says* and by investing in the *Kingdom* through obedience *now* (Matthew 5:19). Sadly, few people today truly know what God requires, because the Bible has been so misrepresented. Those who have been a part of this conspiracy will one day fearfully answer to God. For those who *now* know the truth, it is time to *put away* false ideas and all that which is not based upon *reality.* God commands us to *know* His will, and God says, to him that knoweth to do good and doeth it not—it is sin (James 4:17).

Satan has fooled God's people into thinking we do not need to live as God requires. What a clever scheme! For when we are in rebellion to God, He does not hear our prayers and will not deliver us or bless us (Psalm 66:18; Proverbs 28:9). Only those who follow God's ways are under His protection and have His mark upon them (Revelation 9:4). Further, Christ will not return to deliver us until we repent and seek God on *His* terms. Christ will not return for a rebellious bride unwilling to place herself under His authority (II Chronicles 7:14).

(If this book has intrigued you, please order So, You Call Yourself A Christian... and Are We Keeping God's Law Yet? by Balaicius/STM, which clearly present the *simple* things God requires of us, so that He can bless us as obedient children.)

Fearful, ignorant, or evil people will call this Anglo-Israel or Christian-Israel message "racist" or "white supremacist." But God demands the purity of His people—regardless of what *man* might say. We must seek to please and obey *God*, not man (Acts 5:29; Ephesians 6:6; Colossians 3:22). The world's greatest scientists attest to the fact that the importance of *genetics* cannot be *underestimated.* Yet the establishment downplays genetics entirely when it relates to *mankind*, and does not even allow the simple, bare facts to be presented in an *open forum.* Thus, individuals are unable to make an *informed decision* on the matter. Freedom itself hinges upon this basic tenet: the informed, consensual choice of each individual.

We shall all stand before God in judgment; and we shall reap in this life that which we sow, whether righteousness or disobedience, honesty and integrity or dishonesty and fear. Certainly there are some misguided or evil people who will twist the biblical truth of racial purity to suit their fallen hearts and minds. There are always tares sown in among the wheat. *However, the truth is not* ***invalidated*** *because of the wrong motives of some sinful men.* God's people are to be holy. The preaching and practicing of racial purity and separation are matters of obedience to God. The preaching and practicing of racial purity in obedience to God do not constitute hatred of other races. When other races force themselves on those who wish to be pure and obedient to God, *they* are the haters. Let sinful men think what they will. God will reward each his due. William Penn, nearly 300 years ago, declared, "Men are generally more careful of the breed of their horses and dogs than of their own children" (Fruits of Solitude, 1693). Is the heritage God gave us to be despised simply because others are jealous of it themselves and hate God's order? *All* races should practice purity and self-respect. God commands it, and man can devise no excuse for not obeying. Many people claim that race mixing is so bad now that it is *too hard* to obey God. God cannot change His law or standards of holiness. The *road back* might not be easy—but it is the *only* way. "Draw nigh to God, and He will draw nigh to you. Cleanse your hands, ye sinners; and purify your hearts, ye double minded" (James 4:8). God requires us to make the first move. We must start obeying *before* He will bless or help us. This will separate the *remnant who overcome* from those who will not be delivered from the wrath to come.

Think about it. There are days, weeks, even *whole months* set aside to *nationally* celebrate Black, Eastern Indian, Hispanic, Oriental, or "jewish" history, culture, and pride—but no national celebration is allowed for the white race that founded our great country. (In fact, on July 4th of 1999—on America's anniversary of freedom—the "government" in Washington D.C. celebrated a "festival of the world" rather than our own Independence Day. The enemy is in control.)

There are Black, Eastern Indian, Oriental, and "jewish" groups that preach racial purity, separation, and the supremacy of *their* race—even in a country that is *not theirs*. What is unreasonable or "immoral" about white people wishing *the same for themselves in their own country*? It is what the founders of our nation *expected* and it is a matter of *obedience* to God; but the very opposite is now legislated. There are two sets of rules: One set favors the foreigners in our land; the other keeps *us* down. (The roles have actually been reversed, but the media never mentions this fact.)

In most libraries or bookstores, one can find thousands of volumes on Black, "jewish," Hispanic, Eastern and American Indian, and Oriental history and civilization. But one is hard pressed to find any books on the white race. What is the cause of this historical, cultural, and racial *blackout* (or, rather, *whiteout*)? It is to keep you from finding out the truth about your inheritance. Once you have learned this truth—once you have understood who you are and how God has ordained that you should live—you will be set free from not only spiritual bondage but from *all* bondage: intellectual, economic, religious, political, medical, and societal.

Because our inheritance has been hidden from us and the Bible has been poorly taught (and merchandised!), many people have been turned off to God's Word, and many others have been left with nagging thoughts that drain their enthusiasm. We have been taught the *lie* that the Bible was not written to *us* but to the "jews;" and that although we cannot *eat from the table*, we can *lick the plate* when the "jews" are done. Most modern churches praise the "jews," holding them high in a *special place of importance*; yet when one speaks the truth, showing that God's Israel people are actually the *Nordic peoples* and that those special Covenants and Promises apply to the Nordic peoples, he is castigated for being a "racist"—and he is then told that *all* people are *equal* in God's eyes (a deceitful double standard!).

If people ***really*** *want to believe* the truth, however, they will accept *wherever* it leads. Otherwise, they are untrue. All deceit, lies, and error will one day be exposed. Many who are trapped within the web of evil are blind, but many are also knowingly involved in the promotion of these lies. Though they may prosper now, they will have their day with God. Though we may suffer walking on this hard and narrow road, against the tide, with the majority against us, in the end we will receive a crown of righteousness and our eternal reward. Until that time: STAND! (See Ephesians 6:13 and II Timothy 2:3.)

Let me encourage you, my brother (or sister)—the Bible was written to *you* and *your* family. Each book is a personal letter and a family record. The Bible contains every law we need to be moral, healthy, happy, pure, and blessed; the only way of salvation through Christ YeHoWSHuWaH's sacrifice on the cross for His people; words of tremendous comfort; immense hope; enormous blessings; good counsel and direction; and warnings of things to come. Accept your place in the Covenant! Return to your God (even if it is to seek Him *for the first time*). He is full of love for His children. He is patient and longsuffering and desirous to deliver, forgive, restore, and bless. Seek Him while He may be found. Today is the day for your deliverance, salvation, and reinstatement to a position of honor in your inheritance.

How To Claim Your Inheritance

Please understand: it is *not* enough to merely be descended from Abraham, Isaac, and Jacob—that is, to be an Israelite. You must also have recognized and received Christ YeHoWSHuWaH as your Saviour and accepted His sacrificial death in your place. For those unfamiliar with the Bible's teaching on man's fallen state and need for salvation, the following brief overview is offered:

God created the world and all that exists. He set Adamkind at the head of this creation on earth, to govern it. God gave all intelligent life (angels, Adamkind, other races) a "free" will—the ability to choose. God knows what is best, but He allows us to make our own choices, and therefore we suffer when we make the *wrong* choices, reaping what we ourselves have sown.

Satan (formerly God's highest-ranking angel) turned from God, being blinded by his own pride, beauty, power, and wisdom. Satan foolishly attempted to overthrow God. God cast him out of heaven to earth, along with a third of the angels (who had been fooled into following him in his rebellion). Satan then deceived Adamkind into rebelling against God. Man chose to sin, and because of God's law ("the soul that sinneth shall surely die"—not just physical death, but eternal separation from God) man was doomed. God loved His people so much, however, that He prepared a way to save them. God Himself, in the person of Christ YeHoWSHuWaH ("Jesus") took upon Himself the form of a man (Adamkind) to save those (Adam/Israel) who were under the law (Galatians 4:4-5). He sought out His people who would listen and urged them to repent and return to God and His ways. The enemy sought to silence Him, not understanding His mission. He was crucified and put to death as a common thief after having been tortured. He bore the punishment in our place, thus appeasing the requirements of a righteous and holy God. He rose again from the dead and ascended into heaven and is seated at the right hand of God the Father, where He prays for His own—even interceding for us as our Advocate before God. If we repent and turn from our sin, accepting His payment for our sins, we are made clean in God's sight, and promised eternal life in God's coming kingdom (the future life here on earth after all evil has been purged.)

(For a greater explanation of how Christ was able to take our place, a moving description of what Christ actually suffered for us, what God requires for us to live a life that is holy in His sight, and for in-depth explanations of many mysteries of Scripture, see The Mystery of the Law and Grace Solved! by Balaicius/STM.)

Some might ask, "What do I need to do?" Scripture tells us:

"Believe on Christ YeHoWSHuWaH and thou shall be saved" (Acts 16:31).

> ...if thou shalt confess with thy mouth the Lord YeHoWSHuWaH, and shalt believe in thine heart that God hath raised Him from the dead [for your justification], thou shalt be saved...with the heart man believeth unto righteousness; and with the mouth, confession is made unto salvation (Romans 10:9-10).
>
> For God so loved the world, that He gave His only begotten Son [Christ YeHoWSHuWaH], that whosoever believeth on Him, should not perish but have everlasting life.... He that hath the Son, hath Life; but he that hath not the Son shall not see life; but the wrath of God abideth on him (John 3:16, 36).

"...as many as received Him [Christ YeHoWSHuWaH], to them gave He the power to become the sons of God...to those who believe on His Name" (John 1:12).

"Not by works of righteousness that we have done, but by His mercy He saved us" (Titus 3:5).

"...all have sinned and [*fallen short of God's Divine expectations*].... by grace are ye saved through faith...[*not of your own ability*]; it is the gift of God, not of works, lest any man should boast" (Romans 3:23; 6:23).

If you have never sought Christ YeHoWSHuWaH to confess Him as your Saviour, submitted yourself to, and been received by Him, if you have never accepted His death as the payment for your sin, then enter the Covenant now! All you need to do is pray to Him, right now—even if you have never prayed before. Below is a prayer you can use as a *template* or *model* for your own prayer. You can speak to God in your own words or in words similar to those provided, but please understand that prayer is not a *magic formula*. It is not an *incantation*. It is simply talking to God. If prayer seems odd or mysterious to us, it is only because we rarely speak to God, and thus we feel awkward, uneasy, and unfamiliar—*even guilty*—for not speaking to Him frequently as we should. Just repeating the words listed below will do *nothing*. It is not the *words*. It is the ***sincerity of your heart***; your communicating with God.

However, we must approach God on *His* terms. Sincerity alone is worthless, if one is in *error*. If a mother sincerely wants her sick child to get well but mistakenly gives him poison instead of the proper medicine, her sincerity is *in vain*. We are the sinners. God is the Creator, the Lawgiver, the Judge, and the Forgiver. The only way to obtain forgiveness from the one we have wronged (God), is through Christ YeHoWSHuWaH, our representative before God. If we wish to be received by God, we must come on *His* terms. Sadly, some people are so proud they refuse to humble themselves, admit they are wrong, and ask for forgiveness.

If forgiveness is never sought, *there is no true repentance*. In addition to asking for forgiveness, according to God, *restitution* has to be made. Christ has provided this restitution for us, but to share in the forgiveness and restitution He provided, we must enter into this pardon and reinstatement on *God's* terms. We cannot *hire someone else* to represent us before God. Each individual must, in a sense, *personally* appear before God in prayer, in the name of Christ YeHoWSHuWaH, in order to enter into this Covenant God made with us through our forefathers, from which we have been estranged. For this reason, I have listed the prayer below as a guide:

Dear Heavenly Father, I come before You now, realizing my sin, being ashamed of it, and realizing how little I truly know. Thank You for Your love in choosing me as Your own. Thank You for sending Your Son, Christ YeHoWSHuWaH, to die in my place for my sins and the sins I inherited from my ancestors. Please forgive me of my sins and accept the sacrifice of Your Son for my complete atonement. Wash me and cleanse me so that I may be acceptable to You. Fill me now with Your Holy Spirit, so that I may be indwelled with Your ever-abiding Presence, to guide, direct, and empower me, and fill me with all wisdom and understanding of Your Word. Please reveal Your will to me, and teach me the truth that has been hidden from me, as I seek to learn it. Fill me with the desire to please You and follow Your ways, and teach me how to obey You as I seek my place in the Covenant and in Your kingdom. Please open the eyes of all Your children, as You have opened my eyes. I ask this all in the name of Your Son, Christ YeHoWSHuWaH. Amen.

(If you have just received Christ YeHoWSHuWaH as your Saviour and Lord and entered the Covenant, please write to Sacred Truth Ministries and let us know. One final note in this matter: the laws God gave us to follow are simple and truly liberating; in fact, many of these laws are matters of *common sense* that you already follow. Please understand that keeping God's Law does not *save us*; however, it is proof that we are really His. Christ commanded His disciples to water baptize all those Israelites who were converted, as an outward sign or witness of the inward reality that had transpired (being baptized by God's Holy Spirit). Water baptism is not anything magical; it a simple matter of obedience. For more information about these matters and essential information you will need to grow and mature in faith, please contact us, sending a SASE.)

In Closing

Do you *now* have any desire to do some study to learn more about your relatives who left you such a priceless inheritance? Do you *now* have any desire to learn more about the terms of the Covenantal Inheritance of which you are a part? Have you ever thanked your ancestors for the legacy and freedom they left you? The way true thanks is shown is by *living a life of which the ancestors would be proud* and *continuing the legacy* they left you, *building upon* it *to pass on* to future generations.

Scripture records that whenever God's people departed from the true faith, God sent prophets to them,

...to bring them again unto YaHWeH...then Zechariah arose and declared, "Why transgress ye the Commandments of YaHWeH, that ye cannot prosper? because ye have forsaken YaHWeH, He hath also forsaken you" (II Chronicles 24:19-20).

I speak to you now as one of these prophets. As Joshua declared, "Choose you this day whom you will serve" (Joshua 24:15), so also declare I to you the very same challenge. Will you despise the Covenant and your inheritance as Esau did? Or will you, as Moses, embrace your true and glorious inheritance, and despise the evil, sinful inheritance of this world, which is guilty of the blood of Christ? Christ said, If you are not for Me you are against Me; if you do not work with Me, you seek to undo the very work I do (Matthew 12:30). Scripture also tells us that whoever is a friend of the world is an enemy of God (Romans 8:7; James 4:4). *It's time to choose sides*. Society is getting *worse*, not better. When Christ returns, whose side will you be on? When Christ returns, everyone will be forced to follow His ways (Luke 19:27). By following His ways *now*, we show we are His and that we desire His return.

I realize that what I have presented in this book will not be popular with many people. I ask you the question the Apostle Paul asked: "Am I become your enemy because I tell you the truth?" (Galatians 4:16) If you believe that I have not told the truth, then *please* prove me wrong.

(If you choose to believe that what I have presented is not true, then please do not hate me: pray for me, as I pray for you. It is not that I am fearful of your hatred: I am not, for Christ told me to expect some people to hate me (John 15:18-19; I John 3:13). However, I do not want you to soil your conscience, thinking we need to be enemies if we can't agree on this topic. I love and pray for all my family members (no matter how distant or how antagonistic)—unconditionally. If a family member is in sin, it should not cause hatred but a burdened heart that reaches out in love through prayer.)

We must each follow what we believe to be true, until Christ returns to teach us all things. Not everyone will be able to accept what I have presented in this book. This does not mean that we should become enemies, but that each of us should hold true to that of which God has truly convicted our hearts. But our beliefs must be based upon the *facts of God's Word*—not our own opinions, feelings, prejudices, wishes, or family/religious traditions. Our way must yield to *His*.

If this book alone has not convinced you, please look into the matter further. Consider other books STM has to offer. I don't claim to know all truth. I am searching, however, and thousands are having their eyes opened by the Father, as they become dissatisfied with the cares of this life, which have choked the seeds of truth and life from their hearts. God's ways are not our ways. That is for certain. Why, then, follow the *ways of the world*, which are in direct opposition to God? This truth is *not* a matter of superiority. It is a matter of *truth*, and it is a matter of obeying God and following *His* ways as our only hope.

If anyone thinks the information presented in this book is all merely *coincidence*, I challenge him to find *even half* as many "coincidences" in the prophecies of Scripture that are fulfilled in history, archaeology, philology, anthropology, law, morality, exploration, technology, benevolence, evangelization, etc., concerning *any other people*: "jew," Black, Indian, Arab, African, Hispanic, Oriental, etc.

Some people, after reading this book might reply, "Well that all sounds good, and I believe it is true—but you are not going to change the world. Things are too messed up." My answer is, "I agree. Things are too messed up, and I am not going to change the world. But I don't *want* to change the world. I just want to wake up enough people like you so that *you can save yourselves and your families*." Society is *not* getting better. It is getting *worse*—and *very quickly*! Those who know the truth and *do nothing* about it will have *no excuse* before God and will be held *doubly accountable*.

I feel that I have presented *more than enough* evidence to prove that the true Israel people are in fact the Anglo-Saxon peoples—although I could *easily* have presented *10 times* more information. If any still will not believe, however, I interject what Abraham himself declared to the rich man, who in Hell, begged for God to raise someone from the dead to go witness to his unbelieving brethren: "If they will not believe Moses and the prophets, neither will they be persuaded though one rose from the dead" (Luke 16:31).

May YaHWeH, the Great God of Israel, the God of our fathers Abraham, Isaac, and Jacob, grant His people the spirit of repentance and remove the blindness from their eyes, and may all Israel truly *desire* to repent and have their eyes opened.

Postscript

Please note: This book has <u>not</u> been written to offend anyone or to promote hatred; it <u>cannot</u> possibly be misconstrued as "hate literature." Rather, it has been a presentation of truth that the *real hate criminals* have tried to keep hidden. Volume II of <u>Your Inheritance: The Best-Kept Secret In The World: The Impostors Exposed</u> will be an exposé of the *real* hate crimes and criminals, and their offenses against God's true Israel people. Proclaiming the truth cannot be a "hate crime." If it can be (in the subversive agendas and evil minds of certain people), then it is clear that the real "hate criminals" are those who oppose the truth. If the truth itself is a hate crime, then all that can exist is immorality, injustice, and tyranny. Truth is the *only* anchor of righteousness.

<u>The Impostors Exposed</u> will contain eye-opening quotations from many famous people, including: Johann Sebastian Bach, Ludwig van Beethoven, Fyodor Dostoyevsky, T. S. Eliot, Henry Ford, Sr., Benjamin Franklin, President Ulysses S. Grant, the Brothers Grimm, Martin Heidegger, Victor Hugo, Carl Jung, Immanuel Kant, Rudyard Kipling, Charles Lindbergh, Franz Liszt, Martin Luther, H. L.

Menchen, Friedrich Nietzche, Alexander Pope, Ezra Pound, the Romonov Tsars of Russia, Johann Schiller, William Shakespeare, General William T. Sherman, Arthur Shopenhauer, Peter Stuyvesant, Mark Twain, Voltaire, Richard Wagner, George Washington, and many more of the greatest minds this world has ever known (scientists, world rulers, popes, historians, military leaders, etc.). Many of these people did not realize that the Anglo-Saxon peoples are the literal descendents of the Israelites and that the "jews" are the Canaanites. But they *did* know that the "jews" were subversive and evil, and that the Christian Anglo-Saxon peoples of the world were fulfilling the role of God's people. The purpose of this future book will not be to attack the "jews." The purpose will be to expose numerous conspiracies which happen to be "jewish" (by the "jews'" own confession).

Some people will, in ignorance, claim that this book is "anti-Semitic." This could not be further from the truth and is completely *illogical*. The evidence proves that the *Nordic* peoples are the *true* Semites, and that the "jews" are *Semite imposters*. Further, the Arabs are as much *Semites* as the "jews" are. History has shown in the past 50 years how much the "jews" hate the Arabs, discriminate against them, and even perpetrate crimes against them—yet the "jews" are not called "Anti-Semites." Why not?

Some, then, will claim the book to be *anti-"jewish."* However, though the book will expose conspiracies and evil, it will not *have made* the "jews" do what they themselves have chosen to do. The book will rely greatly upon the "jews'" own testimony. It will record *facts*. People who make such violent, smoke-screen accusations are ignorant. They *hate the truth and all that is holy*—and they will rewrite (*falsify*) all of history, obliterating the truth entirely, if given the chance.

(If *anyone* is "anti-jewish" it is many "jews" *themselves*: for they behave in such a manner that *brands them all* as insurrectionists, parasites, and criminals—thus giving a bad name to the entire "race." See Jewish Fundamentalism in Israel, by Israel Shahak.)

Is it "anti-German" to publicize Germany's guilt in the war? Only if what is presented is *false*. (—and *most* of what *has been presented* **is** *false* and *hateful*: yet it is *not* considered "racist," "anti-Germanic," "hate literature," etc. Why the double standard?) The facts should speak for themselves. *Both sides* of every case should be allowed to be presented *openly* on any matter. But this is not allowed. Only the "jews'" (concocted) side is permitted. Why is open, *professional* debate refused? Should this fact alone not cause people to search the matter out?

If I had the supernatural power to do so, I would *gladly* undo all the injustice the world has suffered. But because I cannot undo what has been done, is no reason to erase the historical record which merely records the facts—which by their very nature portray certain people in an "unflattering," *but accurate*, light. As the enemy has taken over, history is now being re-written, making Lenin, Stalin, etc., appear as "good guys." This is an abomination! God will not erase the record—until Judgment Day. Why then should we?

> Woe unto them that call evil good, and good evil; that put darkness for light and light for darkness; that put bitter for sweet, and sweet for bitter! Woe unto them that are wise in their own eyes, and prudent in their own sight! Which justify the wicked for reward [bribe], and take away the righteousness of the righteous from him!.... they have cast away the Law of YaHWeH of hosts, and despised the

Word of the Holy One of Israel. Therefore is the anger of YaHWeH kindled... (Isaiah 5:20,21,23-25).

The reason the enemy hates and fears those who teach this truth is not simply because it touches the modern *taboo* of "race," but because this truth undermines the plans of evil men by laying bare the conspiracy at its very roots; and because minds liberated by the truth are not easily controlled.

Black Muslims and "jews" teach the superiority of *their* race; yet *they* are not NUMBER ONE on the "government" and media's *hit list*. While the true Israel message teaches the importance of preserving the purity of one's bloodlines and pride in one's heritage, it also teaches other matters of equal importance: *holiness of life*, *truth* and *justice in **all** areas*, complete obedience to the Will of God, and to simply *do what is right*. (This used to be known as the PURITAN WORK ETHIC: now an obsolete idea.)

The "government" (and its controlled media, "learning" institutions, and many churches) in its campaign of "smear terrorism" against our faith, maliciously and dishonestly equates the Christian Israel faith with Nazism, National Socialism, the KKK, skinheads, rabid militia groups, Aryanist bank robbers, and such. Nothing could be *further from the truth*; but this clever **lie** is *effective*. Resultantly, 99% of the public, out of ignorance, fear, and revulsion, *slam the door* on the Anglo-Israel message—without knowing a thing about it. Dishonest and hypocritical as usual, the "government" that preaches "tolerance," "understanding," "peaceful coexistence," and "not judging or discriminating against a whole group of people because of a few unsavory individuals"—does the very things it condemns: it is rabidly intolerant, antagonistic, prejudiced, and has waged a hate campaign and *all-out war*, to stamp out our faith and the truth it reveals. Yes, there *are* extremist groups (that are ***extremely*** *few in number*; see The War Between the Children of Light and the Powers of Darkness, by Balaicius/STM). This is irrelevant and a *red herring*. Hitler and Mussolini were Catholic. Does this mean all Catholics are Nazis or Fascists? Ted Bundy and Paul Hill were Baptist. Does this mean all Baptists are murderers?

Any intelligent person can see that 99% of all politics is a greedy grab for power and wealth by evil men pretending to care about the welfare of the people. The politicians are the criminals. Consider their overall plan of world domination and you will understand why they hate this truth so vehemently. It is one of the only bastions of true Christianity that is left. The majority of Christian churches have been corrupted, and have seriously departed from what Scripture clearly teaches. Most churches will soon crumble to oblivion as they are nearly spiritually dead and unrevivable. The church, as society as a whole, has been adulterated—and most Christians cannot even recognize it. This modern day church is called the GREAT WHORE in the Book of Revelation, because she is *in bed with* the BEAST (the Anti-christ in the implementation of his plan to destroy the Remnant of God).

Turn off the TV and educate yourself! Order a few books that will shed light on some important topics, and you will soon clearly see how the truth has been kept from you, while you have been lied to, used, entertained, and lulled into sleepful uselessness. Learn the truth and stand up for what is right! The enemy, like a cowardly bully, will only continue to run *rough shod* over peace-loving people until they can take it no more and stand up and say, "No!" It has gone far beyond the point of being able to ignore. Will you stand up for Christ and His ways? If you do not, He will not stand up for you. You reap what you sow. Therefore, figure out what it is you want to reap, and plant accordingly. "Love not the world, if any man love the world the love of the Father is not in him" (I John 2:15).

Finally, understand that many people (some well-meaning, some not) will try to pressure you to turn you from this truth. Base your *alliance with the truth* on the *facts*—and **hold firm** to your conscience. Ignore what others think or say, *if* what they think or say is devoid of God and His Truth. Be concerned solely with pleasing and obeying *God*. (See Matthew 5:10-12; Luke 6:22; John 15:18,19.)

I Peter 2:15 - Titus 1:9; 2:8 - Isaiah 5:20-21

There are three stages in the revelation of any truth: In the first it is ridiculed; in the second, resisted; And in the third it is considered self-evident. (Arthur Schopenhauer)

....

Shallow ideas can be assimilated. Ideas that require people to reorganize their picture of the world provoke hostility. I know that most men, including those at ease with problems of the greatest complexity, can seldom accept even the simplest and most obvious truth if it be such as would oblige them to admit the falsity of conclusion which they have delighted in explaining to colleagues, which they proudly taught to others, and which they have woven, thread by thread, into the fabric of their lives. (Leo Tolstoy)

....

Our eyes are beholden that we cannot see things that stare us in the face until the hour arrives when the mind is ripened. Then we behold them, and the time when we saw them not is like a dream. (Ralph Waldo Emerson)

....

"God give me strength to face a fact though it slay me!" (Thomas H. Huxley)

....

"A beautiful theory, killed by a nasty, ugly little fact." (Thomas H. Huxley, as quoted by Sir Francis Galton, Memories of My Life.)

....

"Veracity is the heart of morality." (Thomas H. Huxley)

....

Now we see and know in part...as through a glass darkly...one day we shall know, even as we are known...when He shall appear; we shall be like Him; for we shall see Him as He is. (I Corinthians 13:9,12 and I John 3:2)

Your *support* and prayers enable us to continue to spread the light of truth and freedom in this final age of darkness. We care about you, our brethren. Please send SASE (self-addressed stamped envelope) with any inquiry or letter desiring a response. Thank you! May God bless you as you seek Him. Please let us hear from you and join us by helping us reach the rest of our brethren who are still in blindness.

Appendices

Appendix A

Variations in spelling in these ancient languages have often occurred over a period of *a hundred years or more*. Such variations are common *even in English*, over a span of time. Alexander Hislop, in The Two Babylons (1916), states, "The Hebrew *z*, as is well known, frequently, in the later Chaldee, becomes *d*." Languages that are similar, within the same subclass of the larger language family, have aberrations that usually follow precise patterns. Those who know several languages easily see these patterns. As any student of language will recognize, *sound approximations* often are spelled differently in various languages. For example, in Spanish, the *ny* sound is spelled, "ñ", while in Portuguese it is spelled "nh," and in French it is spelled "gn." In German, a "w" is pronounced like a *v*, and a "v" like an *f*, an "s" often like a *z* or an *sh*, and a "z" like a *tz*. In Spanish, a "v" is pronounced like a *b*, a "z" like an *s*, and a "d" like a *th*. In Portuguese, a "d" is often pronounced like a *j* (as in English, in the words *modular* or *education*) and a "t" like a *ch* (as in English, in the words *temperature* and *mature*). These latter examples of a "d" as a *j* and a "t" as a *ch*, are simply a result of sloppy or lazy speech, which eventually becomes colloquially accepted. In Welsh, a "dd" is pronounced like a *soft th* and an "ll" is pronounced like a *hard th*. In Lithuanian, a *ch* sound is spelled "č," an *sh* sound is spelled "š," and a *zh* sound (as in the *second* "g" in "garage") is spelled "ž." Many more examples could be listed.

Before Samuel Johnson published his landmark *Dictionary of the English Language* in 1755, there was *no standardized spelling for any word* in the English language. Any given word was subject to any number of different spellings, depending upon how any individual (literate or illiterate) thought the word sounded. Sometimes the spellings were unintelligible. Most ancient cultures did not have dictionaries, and therefore there was no standardized spelling either. It is *no wonder* that words have such wide divergence of spelling in *ancient* records.

All this is mentioned because, to the person unfamiliar with the linguistic rules of philology and unfamiliar with philographic history, the variations of names we list in these numerous languages might *seem* to be stretching words a bit far to draw a parallel. To the person learned in the history and science of comparative philology, however, the parallels are as clear as any archaeological record could ever be.

In ancient Hebrew and other *pure* Semitic languages, vowels were often not written. Only consonants were written. Vowels were inserted by the reader, according to dialect. This explains why there are often such wide variations in vowel appearance in the spelling of words. Further, Hebrew and other Semitic languages had *hard vowel accents* that would change a vowel such as the letter *a* to "kha" (with the same guttural *ch* sound found in German and Gaelic, and in the Argentine (Castilian) Spanish "j," etc.). Also, in Hebrew, the accent falls on the ***last*** syllable, and thus a word *beginning* with a vowel (like *Isaaca*) could easily lose the first syllable altogether, since vowels were not written. In English, accents tend to fall ***earlier*** in the word, and the *end* is often lost, as is evident in Southern speech, slang, or lazy speech in which the "g" is often dropped off of words ending in "-ing," so that *running* is "runnin'" *and wrestling* is "wrestlin'," etc. Thus, in Hebrew, *Isaaca* could easily become "Saka;" and it is easily seen how *Isaaca-suni* (son of Isaac), which would be written "scsn," could become "Saxon."

It should also be noted that *ancient* Hebrew was an *entirely different* language from modern Hebrew (even as the true Israelites are an *entirely different* people from those who now live in the land of Israel who spuriously claim to be Semites, Hebrews, Israelites, and Judeans). Ancient Hebrew was nearly identical to Phoenician, and the alphabets of both were nearly identical to the ancient Greek and Roman (Latin; early Italian) alphabets. (This can be seen on the chart on page 31 of Tracing Our Ancestors, on page 44 of Missing Links Discovered in Assyrian Tablets, and in many other books.)

It should be pointed out that many philologists have noted the similarities between ancient Hebrew[x1] and Germanic languages (including English), Goidelic languages (Irish, Scots Gaelic, Manx), and Brythonic (or Cymric) languages (Welsh, Cornish, and Breton); and many experts have claimed that these languages are *nearly identical* with ancient Hebrew (as we shall see).

Appendix B

Consider the following confessions of "jewish" testimony:

➾ "Strictly speaking, it is incorrect to call a contemporary Jew an 'Israelite' or a 'Hebrew'" (*The Jewish Almanac*, 1980, p. 3).

➾ "The ten tribes are certainly in existence. All that has to be done is to discover which people represent them" (*The Jewish Chronicle*, May 2, 1879).

(If the 10 Lost tribes are not comprised of the "jews" but are represented by some other people, who could this other people be? Would it not be the very people who fulfil all of the hundreds of Bible prophecies detailing the characteristics of God's Israel people? Would it not be the very people who have been serving God in their blindness for the past 2,000 years as the nations of Christendom—the white race?)

➾ "...the ten tribes have disappeared, they must exist under a different name" (Jewish Encyclopedia (1905), Vol. 21, p. 249).

➾ The Jewish Encyclopedia (1925), in Volume 5, page 41, clearly states that the "jews" of today are *Edomites*. (The Edomites are Canaanites: the enemy of Israel.)

➾ "...that from the standpoint of literal prophecy, Moses and the prophets are fulfilled in Great Britain, and the other great Anglo-Saxon people, the United States, the Jews, and in no other" (*The Jewish Yearbook*, 1903).

➾ "...The Isles afar off mentioned in the 31st chapter of Jeremiah were supposed by the ancients to be Britannia [England], Scotia [Scotland], and Hibernia [Ireland]" (Dr. Moses Margoliouth, c. 1800). (Brackets mine.)

➾ "Some time ago, after the Hungarian uprising, numbers of people came into Britain. There was amongst them a converted Jew, a protestant minister, and he arrived at Southampton, and as he walked across the gangway, he immediately looked up into heaven and said, 'Thank God that at last I am in the land of Joseph. Joseph was lost, but Joseph has been found'" (*Brith*, 1964, Rev. G. H. Thomas).

➾ "We believe that the ten tribes of Israel exist within the Anglo-Saxon/Celtic Scandinavian/American people and that they in fact constitute them and that they are Hebrews" (*The United Israel Bulletin* [a "jewish" and strongly anti-Christian paper], 1951).

X-1 —not to be confused with *modern* Hebrew or Yiddish.

➾ In These Are Ancient Things (Association of the Covenant People in Canada), a prayer is recorded from the *Jewish Prayer Book* of 1844, as quoted by Rev. F. C. Ewald (missionary of the ***London Society for promoting Christianity amongst the Jews***), in his Missionary Labours in Jerusalem. This prayer reads:

> May He that dispenseth salvation unto kings, and dominion unto princes, whose Kingdom is an everlasting kingdom, who delivered His servant David from the destructive sword, who maketh a way in the sea, and a path through the mighty waters bless, preserve, guard, assist, exalt, and highly aggrandise our Most Gracious Sovereign Lady Queen Victoria; Adelaide, the Queen of Dowager; the Prince Albert; Albert, Prince of Wales, and all the Royal Family. May the Supreme King of kings, through His infinite mercy grant them life, preserve them and deliver them from all manner of trouble, sorrow and danger; subdue the nations under her feet; cause her enemies to fall before her; and grant her to reign prosperously. May the Supreme King of kings, through His infinite mercy, inspire in her heart and in the heart of all her councillors and nobles, to have compassion and benevolence towards us and towards all Israel. In their days and in ours may Judah be saved and Israel dwell in safety, and the Redeemer come unto Zion, which God in His infinite mercy grant and say, Amen.

➾ The Jewish Encyclopedia also states under the heading of *Flags*, that the symbols of the tribes of Ephraim and Manasseh (Joseph) are the unicorn and/or bull. Scripture declared these would be their symbols (Deuteronomy 33:17). (—and these have been the very symbols of the United Kingdom since recorded history.)

➾ Modernly, the (Australian-born) "jewish" author Yair Davidy has written 3 books (printed in the state of *Israeli*) and authors a newsletter (The *Tribesman*) proving the Anglo-Saxon peoples are the Israelites of the Bible: The Tribes (1993, 480 pp.; it begins with an endorsement by Rabbi Avraham Feld, who lives in Jerusalem); Ephraim (1995, 290 pp.); and Lost Israelite Identity (1996, 448 pp.). Although a Germanophobe/anti-Germanite, who thinks the Germans are *Assyrians* and the "jews" are *Judah*, Davidy does believe the other Anglo-Saxon peopes are, in fact, the lost tribes of Israel. In my opinion, his documentation concerning the Khazars[x2] and "jews" is in err.

➾ Rev. Eliezer Bassin C.M., Ph.B., (born in Russia) wrote British and Hebrew Fraternity, The Lost Ten Tribes: Anglo-Israel by a Jew (1884), and The Modern Hebrew and the Hebrew Christian (1882). (Some of his works were in English, Hebrew, and German.)

Bassin, a *converted* "jew," born of wealthy Russian parents, stated (1926):

> Before I became a Christian, I believed as most of my Jewish brethren still believe, that the Ten Tribes of Israel exist, somewhere, as a powerful nation, having a king of their own and that they are hidden from the sight of men until the coming of the expected Messiah. It is my conviction that Britain is the nation with whom God has identified Himself from first to last. I as an Israelite of the House of Judah, claim you as Israelites of the House of Ephraim. As believers in the faithfulness of our covenant-keeping God, I call you awake from your sleep.

➾ Edward Hine (1826-1891), was another "jew" who believed the Anglo-Saxons were descended from Israel. He wrote extensively on the topic, authoring: The Anglo-Saxon Riddle (1872), The British Nation Identified With Lost Israel (1874), Cui

---

x2 —a Turko-Mongoloid people of southern Russia who converted to Judaism in 9th century. See The Thirteenth Tribe by the renowned "jewish" author Arthur Koestler, who proved that 99 percent of all "jews" in Israel don't have a drop of Abraham's blood in their veins. Koestler was mysteriously assassinated shortly after revealing this bombshell.

Bono? Or The Political, Social, and Religious Uses of the Identifications of Anglo-Saxons with Israel (1880), England's Coming Glories and Flashes of Light (1876), Forty-Seven Identifications of the Anglo-Saxons with the Lost Ten Tribes of Israel (1874), Memoirs and a Selection of Letters from the Correspondence of Edward Hine (1825-1891) (1901), The Nation's Glory Leader (1878-1879; 6 volumes), and Oxford Wrong.

Other similar testimonies can be found in Our Descent From Israel Proved By Cumulative Evidence (1931), by Hew D. Colquhoun, as well as many other books.

Appendix C-1:
The Phoenicians Were A Branch of the White Race

The Phoenicians were undoubtedly Hebrews themselves, and most likely even Israelites. The Hebrew and Phoenician languages were identical, except that Hebrew was written *right to left* and Phoenician was written *left to right.* The Phoenicians had racial characteristics identical to the Israelites and Greeks. In his scholarly Missing Links Discovered in Assyrian Tablets (1985), E. Raymond Capt, M.A., A.I.A, F.S.A., Scot., records:

> The Phoenicians, generally, were tall men with red hair and blue eyes.... According to Manetho, an Egyptian priest, the Hyksos Dynasties in the later period of their rule in Egypt were of Phoenician origin. Phoenician was not the name they called themselves. Rather, it was a nickname [others placed upon them]...the word "Phoenician" means "redheaded men" (p. 43).

The Phoenicians are credited with inventing our alphabet around 1200 B.C. Capt reveals that, "Simultaneous with the spread of the alphabet, the name 'Hebrew' came into existence" (p. 45). Is this just a coincidence? God told Abraham that all the world would be blessed through his legitimate descendents. The technology with which the entire world has been blessed would not have been possible were it not for a *coherent language*, and history tells us that it is the white race that invented the alphabet and the vast majority of all the technology through which the world has been blessed. Interestingly, Cornwall and Smith, in their An Exhaustive Dictionary of Bible Names (1998), indicate that the name *Abram* (the birth name of Abraham) means not only "father of height" but it can also mean "high and lofty thinker." Truly, the Israelites (the Nordic peoples) have fulfilled the command of YaHWeH to "look unto Abraham their father" (Isaiah 51:1-2) and have shown themselves to have been created in the image of God Himself (Genesis 1:26) by demonstrating His creative, ingenious character.

The Golden Age of the Phoenicians is considered to have been c. 1400-1000 B.C. The date of the Israelites' exodus from Egypt was c. 1450 B.C. After they left Egypt, they wandered for 40 years due to their sin of not trusting and obeying God. Thus, they began their conquest of the Promised Land c. 1410 B.C. The nation of Israel reached its Golden Age during King David's rule, c. 1011-971 B.C. Is it merely *another* coincidence that the Israelites and the Phoenicians experienced their Golden Ages at the same time? Hardly. Have any other great nations (especially those who lived side-by-side) ever experienced the height of their culture and power at the same time—without ever fighting each other? Nowhere in Scripture is it recorded that Israel ever waged war with the Phoenicians; yet they fought against *every other people* in the area at the time.

The Phoenicians were excellent architects and craftsmen, with a penchant for the sea. In fact, they dominated the seas. The Phoenicians became prominent at the very time the Israelites left Egypt. Later on in naval history, they sailed to Portugal and Spain and colonized the region—and, *oddly enough*, the area was named *Iberia.* As we saw, the Phoenicians *did not call themselves* "Phoenicians." This was a nickname given to them by others. So it is quite natural that the lands to which they migrated were named after *the name by which they **did** call themselves*: ***Hebrews***. The Phoenicians later sailed farther north to Scotland and Ireland, where they also settled and left their name: *Hibernia.* Haberman also contends that Hebrew-Phoenician colonists settled in Italy and came to be known as *Umbri* (meaning "Hebrew") and *Etrusci*[x3] (p. 74). No doubt the Parthians also were of Hebrew-Israel-Phoenician stock. (Secular histories of the Phoenician settlement of Spain can be found in most good libraries.) It was the *(Israelite) Phoenician-descended* Spanish Armada that ruled the seas for a time. It was the *(Israelite) Phoenician-descended* Vikings who dominate the seas and sailed around the world. Scripture prophesied the future great naval power the Israelites would constitute. Is it a coincidence that the Phoenicians also resisted and were subjugated by the Babylonians and Persians, *at the same time* the Israelites were, in the 6th century B.C.? Is it also a coincidence that the Phoenicians disappeared from history around the *same time* the Israelites did? It is quite clear the Phoenicians were *Hebrews*, and more specifically *Israelites of the Tribe of Dan.* Even their physical characteristics and nature were identical with the historical descriptions of the Classical Greeks (Danites) and Israelites of antiquity, as well as their later Viking descendents. Are the "jews" known as great ship builders, navigators, or sailors?

The terms "British," "Briton," "Britannia" and others are of *Phoenician origin*, as is shown by Professor L. A. Waddell in his excellent book Phoenician Origin of Britons, Scots, and Anglo-Saxons (1924). Herodotus tells us the Phoenicians occupied the sea coast of Syria, which was known as *Palestine* (vii. 89). It would appear that much of the so-called Phoenician civilization was really *Israelitish.* Any one of these facts *in itself* is not proof that the Phoenicians were Israelites. When considered as a whole body of evidence, however, it is indisputable.

Alexander von Humboldt believed that the Greeks themselves were Israelites, and he stated that the Greeks, when they used the word "Phoenicians," included the Israelites as the same with these people. W. G. De Burgh, in his Legacy of The Ancient World, says that the Phoenicians were Shemites. (Shem constituted the chosen line from Adam to Eber.) Martin A. S. Hume, in his The Spanish People, states the Phoenicians were of "the indominable race of Shem." (See The Encyclopedia Britannica, under the heading "Phoenicians," and Rawlinson's History of Phoenicia (1889).)

Appendix C-2:
The Ancient Egyptians Were A Branch of the White Race

The ancient Egyptians were (and even up until Joseph's time the pharaohs were) a white, Adamic, Shemitic (and even Hebrew) people. (See Alfred P. Schultz's Race or Mongrel (1908), John D. Baldwin's Pre-Historic Nations (1869), Professor L. A. Waddell's Makers of Civilization in Race and History (1929) and Egyptian Civilization

[3] —the Umbrians and Etruscans. Umbrian is an extinct dialect of Old Italian.

(1930), Professor George Rawlinsons's Origins of Nations (1885), Professor Archibald H. Sayce's Races of the Old Testament (1891), The Egypt of the Hebrews and Herodotus (1895) and Israel and the Surrounding Nations (1898), G. Elliot Smith's Ancient Egyptians and the Origin of Civilization (1923), and Myron Fagan's How The Greatest White Nations Were First Mongrelized, Then Negroized (1965). See also Charles Marston's The Bible Is True (1938), The New Knowledge About The Old Testament (1933), The Bible Comes Alive (1937).)

Professor G. Elliot Smith (University of Manchester, England), one of the leading authorities in his day on the Egyptian people, wrote in his The Ancient Egyptians and Their Influence Upon European Civilization (1911),

> The hot, dry sands of Egypt have preserved through a span of more than 60 centuries the remains of countless multitudes of the earliest peoples known to have dwelt in the Nile Valley; and not the mere bones only, but also their skin and hair and the muscles and organs of the body; and even such delicate tissues as the nerves and the brain, and most marvelous of all, the lens of the eye, are available for examination today. We are able to form a very precise idea of the structure of the body of the Proto-Egyptian...no resemblance whatever to the so-called "wooly" appearance and peppercorn-like arrangement of the Negro's hair.

Appendix C-3: Mythology and Folklore

Mythologies (Greek, Roman, Druid, and Norse): Israel ancestry is clearly evident in Aryan mythologies, for those who have eyes to see. Of course, since the Israelites were in national blindness, and since the Israelites were prone to sin by practicing the pagan religions of other peoples with whom they came into contact, we cannot expect the Hebrew reminiscences to be pure, but *confounded* and *adulterated.* (See Romans 1:18-23.) However, it is quite astounding, that *all* the white nations are *Christian* (Why is that?), and began converting to Christianity at a very early date. Some of the nations of dispersed Israel had preserved their ancient Hebrew religion much better (such as the Welsh/British Druids); thus it was easier for some to convert (or rather return) to the pure Hebrew religion (albeit, perfected in Christ, the long awaited Messiah). Although time does not permit any lengthy digression, a few examples will be presented.

In *Greek* Mythology, Hercules was a son of God who did mighty deeds; these deeds are nothing less than accounts of Samson, Christ, and other mighty Israelites combined into one person.

In *Roman* mythology, the Supreme God was called Jove (or *Jupiter*) (from which the common English expression "by Jove" comes). What most people do not realize is that the proper pronunciation of Jove is *Yo-vey*, which is nothing less than a variation of the Hebrew Covenant Name for God—YaHWeH (many experts agree that the "w" in YaHWeH should be pronounced like a "v": a w actually being "vv").

Druidism is nothing less than Hebrewism. Druidism is replete with the concept of the Trinity. (See The British Edda (1929), by Professor Waddell and *The Welsh Triads*.)

Norse mythology has a record of the Genesis flood, indicating that the flood was caused by the blood of a slain giant. This is quite accurate, *symbolically*: God destroyed the earth by a flood for several reasons; one of which was to destroy the race of giants sired by fallen angels with some of the daughters of Adam whom they abducted (Genesis 6:1-4). According to mythology, one family escaped the flood on a skiff, and thus were those who formed the new race after the flood. While on the skiff, they had 2 ravens which reported to them what was going on. In Scripture, Noah sent out a raven *first*, later a dove. The enemy of the mortal gods and all men was Loki, who was from the south and of a swarthy complexion. No doubt this is reference to Satan (you can't get further south than *hell*) and his children, the Canaanites.

The Norse god Odin, is the head *mortal* god. Norse Mythology also records an All-powerful *Immortal* God known as Alfadur (All-Father), who was uncreated and eternal. The fact there were many "mortal" gods is no surprise, for Christ Himself said it was written, "ye are gods" (John 10:34). Odin himself was a *man*, who led the Scandinavians with his 12 pontiffs to their new home. He was their Lawgiver; when he died, they immortalized him by imputing unto him, all the attributes of the All-Father. This itself is an Israel reminiscent, for upon the death of Moses (the Law-giver, who ruled the 12 tribes of Israel), God removed his body from access by the Israelites, lest they immortalize him and worship him as a god (combining his qualities with the very attributes of YaHWeH Himself). **Odin** was the name *adopted* by this Scan**din**avian ruler. His original name was Sigge Fridulfson. Why would he adopt the name Odin? Some of the houses of Scandinavia are descended from the tribe of **Dan**. The name Dan means "judge" (or ruler). No doubt, he took this name to distinguish himself as the ruler, or as having descended from Dan. (In Irish, it would be understood that the name O'Dan would signify descent from Dan. It seems possible the Norse language had similar qualities.) Variations of Odin are Wo**den** or Wo**tan** (Teutonic counterparts). In Old German, *Wo* means "to inspire or spiritually arouse." Coupled with the name "Dan," it is easy to see how one who was to be the judge and proclaim God's Law, would also be the one to *inspire or spiritually arouse* his people in regard to their *heritage and religion.* The mortal god Odin, no doubt, is in reference to Christ who came in the flesh to be born and redeem His people. Odin was said to eat no food, but was sustained solely through drinking wine by which he was nourished forever. Luke 7:34 says Christ came eating and *drinking*; at the Last Supper, Christ offered *wine* saying, "here is My blood [symbolically] drink ye of it." It is the blood of Christ by which we are saved; since Scripture says, "the life is in the blood," it seems quite natural that this would be the dominant element in the religion. Christ was sacrificed on a cross, referred to in Scripture as a "tree;" His side was pierced and He gave His life for His people Israel, promising to go before them and prepare a place for them, where He would one day receive them again unto Himself. Odin himself endured quite similar sufferings for similar reasons. The Norse record states, "I know that I hung on a wind-rocked tree; *nine* whole nights, with a spear wounded and to Odin offered Myself to Myself." (In *Scripture*, the number 9 represents *Judgment* or *Finality*.) Odin is said to have allowed himself to be wounded with a spear and hung on a tree, so that he would then claim the souls of all his men slain in battle; he would go to the Godheim (with the All-Father) and then welcome his men there (See John 14:2 and Ephesians 4:8).

Also, Thor, a son of Odin, is said to have destroyed a serpent while dying in the process; Christ was said to come to crush the head of the Serpent (Satan) and die in the process (then to be resurrected); Christ referred to the Canaanite pharisees as the Serpent's Children. Thor was the *god of thunder and lightning*, the *god of the sky and the storm*; he is also called Perun (in Lithuanian mythology, Perkūnas). This mortal god *Thor* is also Christ Himself, who became a man and who is associated with thunder and lightning (Zechariah 9:14; Matthew 24:27; Luke 17:24; and Revelation 4:5.) and who had power over the wind and the storm (Matthew 8:27, 14:32,33; Mark 4:41).

The Norse also practised the baptism of their infant children at the time they were named. Circumcision of the male Hebrew/Israel children was the sign of the Old Covenant; the infant was circumcised on the 8th day on which he was also named. Baptism is the sign of the New Covenant in Christ.

(Note: the New Covenant did not "do away" with the Old: it corrected its faults (Matthew 5:17, Galatians 3:17). When a car is *recalled* by the manufacturer because of defects, the car is not *thrown away* and a new car manufactured to replace it—the *defective parts alone* are replaced. See The Mystery of the Law and Grace Solved!, by Balaicius/Sacred Truth Ministries.)

(For more information on differing Mythologies, consult some of the books already listed herein, as well as an Encyclopedia or any books on specific Mythologies such as: Gods and Myths of Northern Europe, by Davidson.)

Folklore: Folklore is replete with Israel truth. (A fine book on this topic, Stories of Lost Israel in Folklore, by James B. Haggart, contains the meaning behind the stories of such notables as *Snow White, Sleeping Beauty, Cinderella, Hansel & Gretel, Jack and the Beanstalk, Little Red Riding Hood* and others.)

One story that it does not recount is *Jack and Jill*. The Israel message in this folktale is quite clear. "Jack and Jill went up a Hill to fetch a pail of water. Jack fell down and broke his crown and Jill came tumbling after." *Jack* is a nickname for Jacob. Jacob was the former name of Israel; and all Israel is understood within her Federal Parents of Adam and Eve. In this story Jack is *Adam* and Jill is *Eve*. We are told in Scripture "who shall ascend the *Hill* of the Lord?" "I will look to the *hills* from whence cometh my help;" and "the Lord is in His Holy *Hill*."

"Jack and Jill went up the Hill to fetch a pail of *water*..." Water in Scripture is symbolic of the Holy Spirit. Going up the hill *to fetch* water represents the temptation of the Serpent in the garden, to which Adam and Eve succumbed: "Ye shall become like God." Jack fell down and broke his crown and Jill came tumbling after." Jack *fell down* (Adam's Fall) *first*, representing his responsibility in sin, being the family head; *and broke his crown*, representing falling from former glory; and Jill *came tumbling* after. Eve is called the "mother of all living," thus representing the whole human race falling in Adam.

A contemporary Christian singer Wayne Watson on his album *Man in The Middle* (1983) sings a song entitled "Jack and Jill." Though the writer of the song may not have realized the full meaning of the folktale, he did make the connection, and went even further to paint a beautiful picture in a simple song. After the first verse, which is the folktale itself, the song continues: "Well Adam and Eve they were deceived, by Satan's cunning laughter; they bought his lies, they compromised, and man came tumbling after;" a bridge then follows: "child, you lost your crown, you're beaten down, you cannot find your way back to Him; the road is rough, but don't you give up, just look to the hill." The third verse continues more movingly, "Jesus Christ, was sacrificed, and He walked up that hill; was lifted up, He drank the cup, for fallen Jack and Jill." The fourth and final verse is a repeat of the first, the tale itself with a new and glorious twist: "Jack and Jill went up the hill, and found the living water; who once were cursed, now never thirst, and live forever after."

Appendix C-4:

Most Every Great Civilization Was Founded by Members of White Race

It should be noted that the white, Adamic, Hebrew, Israel peoples were the builders of the great civilizations of the world: Egypt, Greece, Rome, India, Spain, Portugal, (and even the Inca, Aztec, and Mayan Empires), etc. When the early race builders began to intermarry with the aboriginal or imported nonwhite peoples, this marked the beginning of the decline of these civilizations. (See Why Civilizations Self-Destruct by Professor Elmer Pendell, The Passing of The Great Race by Madison Grant, Race or Mongrel by Schultz, and other titles already mentioned above.) This is not "white supremacy;" this is not *fanciful imagination*; this is a **fact of history**.

Scripture tells us that King Solomon built a rather large navy. So extensive were its travels that it returned to Palestine only once every three years, laden with treasures and exotic goods and animals (I Kings 9:26-28; 10:11; II Chronicles 9:21). Some of these journeys were launched in conjunction with the Phoenician king, Hiram. Since the Phoenicians were Hebrews themselves, such a joint venture does not seem strange (rather like the Irish teaming up with the Scots: cousins). It is also well known that the Phoenicians were the most capable sailors of their day, sailing all over the world. The extent of Solomon's navy's travels has recently come to light with amazing evidence, which furnishes more incontrovertible proof.

Over the past 16 years, Chinese archeologists in western China have unearthed some very interesting discoveries. (See *Discover* magazine, April 1994, "The Mummies of Xinjiang" by Evan Hadingham or The Mummies of Ürümchi (2000), Barber.) They discovered 3,000- to 4,000-year-old (dated at c. 300 B.C. to 2000 B.C.) mummified bodies of *Caucasian* men, women, and children—113 in all—at various burial sites ranging from the central Asian region of Xinjiang to northwest China. Unlike other prehistoric mummies, which are painstakingly preserved by a detailed process, being solely done to rulers or nobles, these bodies were of the *common people* and were quickly preserved by nature itself, by the hot, dry climate. One site was a hill or mound called by the Chinese, the "Red Hillock."

The Chinese had kept the find a secret. However, Dr. Victor Mair, a professor of Chinese at the University of Pennsylvania, while leading a tour group through a museum in the city of Ürümqi, in China's central Asian province of Xinjiang, serendipitously wandered into a newly opened room and stumbled upon a glass case containing the bodies of an entire family. Mair recollects, "The Chinese said they were 3,000 years old, yet the bodies looked as if they'd been buried the day before." Mair became even more dumbfounded when he realized that they had obvious *Caucasian* or *European* features: blond, wavy hair (that of the women being long and braided), thin lips, long noses, deep-set eyes, and long skulls. Each was clad in long, dark purple woolen garments and felt boots. Mair recalls,

> I was thunderstruck. Even though I was supposed to be leading a tour group, I just couldn't leave that room. The questions kept nagging at me: Who were these people? How did they get out here at such an early date?

Of keen interest, one of the corpses that was discovered showed traces of a surgical operation having been performed on his neck and sewn up with horsehair sutures. It is well known that traditional Chinese medicine was vehemently opposed to surgery. Hadingham then noted that a Chinese text of the third century A.D. mentioned the life of a doctor named Huatuo whose exceptional skills included surgery. Hadingham also noted that the name Huatuo was *uncommon* in China. The name also struck him as bearing close resemblance to the Sanskrit word for medicine. (Sanskrit[x4] was one of the first languages of the Aryan peoples.)

But this was not all. Because of the dry climate, the clothes and other items buried with the corpses were beautifully preserved. Their clothing is described as being rich and of the finest quality, felt leather-soled boots, leather coats, and brightly colored garments made of fabrics that had been produced on sophisticated looms. In a pattern characteristic of European techniques, the fabrics had been carefully dyed green, blue, and brown and woven into a diagonal, twill pattern forming a plaid. The expert who examined samples of these garments indicates these are characteristically European and that similar types of garments were found in Austria, Germany, and Scandinavia during the same period. Further, one man had been buried wearing a two-foot-tall conical hat (like that depicted in the drawing found in the Behistun Rock) studded with magnificent gold-leaf decorations. Interestingly, Evan Hadingham himself mentioned that King Darius made mention of the "Sakas of the pointed hats." At least one of the men was wearing a bracelet made of red yarn. (This is possible evidence that the mummy was an Israelite of the *Zarah line* of the Tribe of Judah (Genesis 38:27-30) whence the European heraldries that depict a red hand (or a hand encircled by a red thread) are derived.)

Also found were fragments of a wagon wheel—nearly identical with those found on the grassy plains of the Ukraine as far back as 3000 B.C. One of the graves also contained a bovine horn. The graves also entombed pottery, wooden bowls (containing fragments of mutton), spoons, combs, loaves of bread, portions of lamb, needles made from bone, hooks, bells, and spinning whorls for spinning thread. Further, many horse-riding items were found (some of exquisite workmanship): bits, reigns, whips, cheekpieces, straps, and a saddle. Symbols of the sun were found in these graves. Clearly, these are *Scythian/Israelite* artifacts, not "Chinese."

Evidence of a long-extinct Indo-European language, Tocharian, has been found in this region of central Asia. Further, in caves of the very foothills of the mountains west of Ürümqi there have been found Tocharian inscriptions, along with paintings of "Swashbuckling knights wielding long swords...with full red beards and European faces." Hadingham also states that the people of the Xinjian province have a very distinct appearance and culture and that the Uygur (the major ethnic group in the area today) display unusually fair hair and complexions, strongly suggesting that they absorbed the racial stock of these early Caucasians.

It seems the Chinese desired to keep this a secret, since they claim their civilization was a "homegrown affair." Some scientists, however, now suggest these Caucasian peoples introduced the wheel and the first metal objects to China.

[x4] Modern Lithuanian is nearly identical to ancient Sanskrit, yet the Lithuanian language, although a living language, is so ancient it makes the Vedic Sanskrit look modern by comparison. The Lithuanians are direct descendents of the Scythians. Their ancient legend recounts that they were originally from the east, and their God told them to travel west until they again reached the sea. This and much more will be expounded in great detail in Sacred Truth Ministries' future book The Lithuanians: The Overlooked Nordic Tribe.

The Chinese archeologist who discovered these graves set out looking for remnants of ancient civilizations, determining if he looked along the rivers, he would find them. The Phoenicians were known to sail along rivers through uncharted territories, as were the Israelites and Vikings. Whether these Caucasians were deposited here by King Solomon's navies is immaterial. Greater evidence exists that this region was the cradle of Aryan civilization: the Tarim Basin.[x5] These corpses are most likely the remnants of ancient Hebrews—even possibly the earliest Shemite (Semite) descendents of Adam.

(The same subterfuge has recently occurred in the U. S. with the discovery of *Kennewick Man*. The reportedly 9,000-year-old *Caucasian* skeleton was found in Kennewick, Washington. News reports began to leak out in the summer of 1997. When the local Indian tribes heard that he was *white*, they quickly claimed him as an "Indian." They said that science was wrong (maintaining he had to be an Indian since they claim to have been here first—even though history records otherwise). The skeleton was locked in an Army vault while a trial ensued, and the skeleton was eventually given to the Indians, who buried him in a *secret* place. The site where he was found has recently been covered with hundreds of tons of soil to "prevent erosion," thus forever concealing further evidence. The site was expected to contain many more skeletons due to its location along a river bank.)

Appendix C-5:

The Israelites Were A Branch of the White Race

C. F. Parker, in Israel's Migrations or An Attack Answered (1947), states,

> The most concrete evidence as to the ethnological characteristics of the true Israelites is to be found in the period c. 1400-900 B.C., and when they had been in occupation of the Promised Land for over 500 years. This evidence shows *conclusively* that the Israelites *were of the Nordic type*,[x6] a fact that has taken the scholarly world completely by surprise.... It is evident that to the element of surprise, not a little confusion has been added, in that the predominating and almost sole type to be found in the lands of Israel's settlement was Nordic, **but has wrongly been called "Amorite"** by even the highest authorities on the subject (p. 9).

(Boldface, brackets, and quotation marks for emphasis are mine ***in all*** quotations from Israel's Migrations or An Attack Answered by C. F. Parker.)

Parker then supports this claim, calling to remembrance the fact that the Israelites were the predominant people in the land of Israel; yet for some unknown reason they have falsely been referred to as "Amorites." The books of Exodus, Numbers, Joshua, Judges, Samuel, Kings, and Chronicles record the subjugation of the Amorites by the Israelites. Parker further says,

> **Nowhere** do we find that the Amorites **predominated in all the land occupied by Israel** in the time of...[Israel's] settlement. They [Amorites] were annihilated on the east of the Jordan [River] by Moses (Deut. ii.24-37) (p. 9).

Parker continues,

[x5] See Tracing Our Ancestors by Haberman for many interesting details which also shed light on these archeological findings.

[x6] In a footnote, Parker indicates the term "Nordic," although a modern designation, is used to refer to the white race, regardless of the period being addressed (although it would not be a valid designation in a *strict* manner of speaking). (More precise designations would be Proto-Nordic, Proto-Caucasian, etc.)

> The census figures of the Bible testify to the great strength and numerical superiority of...Israel...As Israel was at her greatest power under David and Solomon, and her internal enemies were subdued *and in the minority*, it is clear...the predominating type throughout the land of Israel was *Israelitish*, not **Amorite** as has [erroneously] been supposed. According to [Professor] Sayce and others, the predominating type in the land of Israel at the time of her greatest supremacy was Nordic; therefore, the Israelites were Nordic [and hence, the "Amorites" were not Nordic] (p. 10).

Parker adds, "Foreign testimony in this respect is most valuable, in that it is *impartial*." He relates that during the time of Rehoboam (c. 927 B.C.) the ruler of Egypt (Shishak) invaded Israel and took captives, recording these campaigns by inscribing them on the walls of the Egyptian temple at Karnak. These records reveal Israelites were taken captive from the cities of Gaza, Megiddo, Rabbati, Taanach, Shunem, Haphraim (of Issachar), Mahanaim (east of Jordan), Gibbeon (of Benjamin), Ajalon (Judah), Jehud (border of Dan), and other places (I Kings 11:40; 14:25; II Chronicles 12:1).

The time these Israelites were taken captive to Egypt was 200 years before the majority of Israel was taken captive to Assyria, and about 325 years before the remaining residue of the people of the land of Judah was taken to Babylon. It is probable that many of these Israelite captives then escaped Egyptian captivity and migrated, mainly by the Mediterranean Sea, northward into Europe. This would have been most possible at the time that King So (Sib'e) of Egypt confederated with King Hanun of Gaza to aid King Hoshea of Israel from the attacks of Assyria (II Kings 17:4), which ended in defeat (c. 720 B.C.). As Egypt's power was severely weakened, it would have been easy for the captive Israelites to make an escape. Since all efforts to repel the Assyrian attack were unsuccessful, it is reasonable to assume the Israelites travelled elsewhere.

Not only did the Egyptians meticulously record the details of their conquests in *writing*, but they also impressively recorded their campaigns by *engraving in stone* the *profiles* of the people they captured, thus identifying their racial type. Quoting Professor Sayce (from Higher Criticism and the Monuments, 1894; pp. 353-354), Parker records,

> From the time of Thotmes III it was [the] usual [practice of nations] to crown [engrave] the oval cartouche [a smooth portion prepared for engraving pictures] in which the name of the conquered locality was written with the head and shoulders of a typical representative of its population. The prisoners brought back to Egypt served as models, and the Egyptian artists drew their outlines **with almost photographic fidelity**. Now it is remarkable that the heads which surmount the names of Shishak's...[**captives *from the land of Israel***] are [*called*] "Amorites".... They [the Egyptian artists] reproduced the features of...[a] fair-skinned, light haired, blue-eyed and long-headed...race.... It must have been the prevailing type. In no other way can we account for its having been selected by the sculptors of Shishak to typify the population of the Kingdom of Judah to the entire exclusion of any other type.

(The terming of this blond-haired people as "Amorite" is dumbfounding. It was the **Israelites** who were taken captive. Why then would "Amorites" be depicted as the captives? The problem is, the experts had trouble overcoming years of programming which caused them to think the Israelites as a darker, Mediterranean people; though the Bible itself describes them otherwise.)

Parker again quotes Sayce from Races of The Old Testament (p. 116):

> [Evidently] The [modern] Jewish type [what we now know to be the impos-

tor "jews," the Edomite-Canaanites] was so scantily represented [among the Israelite captives]...the Egyptian artist passed it over [entirely] when depicting the prisoners who had been brought from Judah (p. 11).

Parker also quotes Sayce from page 16 of The Hittites (1925):

The "Amorites" [sic, Israelites], on the contrary, were a tall and handsome people. They are depicted with white skins, blue eyes, and reddish hair, all the characteristics, in fact, of the white race. Prof. Petrie points out their resemblance to the Dardanians of Asia Minor, who form an intermediate link between the white-skinned tribes of the Greek seas... (p. 12).

Quoting Sayce again (from Higher Criticism..., p. 355), Parker relates, "The blond "Amorite" [sic, Israelite] was widely spread.... In short, the mountainous country of Palestine was largely in the hands of "Amorite" [sic, Israelite] tribes" (p. 12).

Parker then concludes,

These are plain statements, yet the significance of them has been missed: *it is that the latest findings of archaeology demonstrate conclusively that the Israelites (not Amorities) were Nordics.*

The accuracy of this conclusion is put beyond doubt when we discover...the Israelites obtained their Nordic characteristics from their ancestors the Hebrews, who were also Nordics, as is clear from the statements by **Sir Leonard Woolley**...in his excellent book [pp. 291-292] Abraham, Recent Discoveries and Hebrew Origins (1935):

c. 2278. After the conquest of the Guti, Ur-Nammu, governor of Ur, sets himself up as king and establishes the Third Dynasty of Ur. The great imperial age of Ur is continued by Dungi (2260)...[to] Ibi-Sin (2195). During this time, the first appearance of Amorites [sic, Israelites] amongst the population of southern Mesopotamia, *these being probably the* ***Habiru*** *or* ***Hebrew*** *immigrants*... (Parker, pp. 12-13).

(**Sir Charles Leonard Woolley** (1880-1960) directed the joint expedition at Ur in Mesopotamia between the British Museum and the University of Pennsylvania. He also wrote: The Sumerians (1928), Digging Up the Past (1930), Ur of the Chaldees (1938), A Forgotten Kingdom (1953), and Excavations at Ur (1954).)

(Historians erroneously use the term "Amorite" when they refer to Nordic peoples. The important thing to remember is that the *people* to whom they are referring is the issue, not the erroneous label they attach to them. It should be noted that the Amorites, Hittites, and Hurrians were not pure relatives of the Hebrews. Such erroneous statements have been made as a result of confusing the Hebrew people (who were migrating through the lands of other peoples) with the aboriginal Canaanite peoples. Remember, the name *Hebrew* means "colonizer"; thus, they were always colonizing both vacant lands and lands inhabited by Canaanites (who were *illegitimate* inhabitants (squatters), since God had promised the land to His people).[x7])

Parker then asserts,

[x7] Some might struggle with the fact that God gave the *Promised Land* to the Israelites, *when there were already other peoples living there*. The bottom line is the **sovereignty of God**. As we have already seen, Scripture tells us that "the earth is the Lord's and the fullness thereof" and that God gave the earth to the sons of *Adam* (giving them the Dominion Mandate), and later, specific portions to Israel. **Romans 9:13-23** again reminds us that there is no unrighteousness with God, and He does what He has chosen for His own purpose. Scripture also tells us that God's understanding and ways are higher than ours, even as the Heavens are above the earth (**Isaiah 55:9**).

The Nordic people [erroneously called "Amorite"] occupied *exactly* the territory of Israel, even to that [portion of land east of the Jordan River]—**a fact which further confirms their identity as *Israelites*....** Sayce identifies these people as similar to the "fair Kelts of an Irish village"; *but he also traces them into Britain and Ireland!* There is no break in the chain of evidence, and the accuracy of his identification is further established when he remarks: [from his, The Hittites, (1925)]

Now it is curious that wherever this particular branch of the white race has extended it has been accompanied by a particular form of cromlech, or sepulchral chamber built of large uncut stones.... placed upright in the ground and covered over with other large slabs, the whole chamber being subsequently concealed under a tumulus of small stones or earth. Frequently the entrance to the cromlech is approached by a sort of corridor. These cromlechs are found in Britain, in France, in Spain, in Northern Africa, and in Palestine, especially on the eastern side of the Jordan, and the skulls that have been exhumed from them **are skulls of men of the dolichocephalic or long-headed type** (Parker, p. 16ff).

Note—The mound seems to have been constructed by the Israelites by reason of ancestral custom. Jacob and his brethren "took stones, and made an heap: and they did eat there upon the heap." God's command to Ephraim (the holder of the birthright of Israel) [the prominent leader of Israel] was to "Set thee up waymarks, make thee high heaps," during the period of wanderings. See Gen. xxx1.46; Jer. xxxi.21 (Parker, p. 15).

Parker continues to explain these "heaps," saying,

T. W. Rolleston, speaking of these peculiar burial chambers, gives us even more detailed information as to their placing between Britain and Palestine; he says (in Myths and Legends of the Celtic Race (1911), pp. 52-53):

...They were the so-called Megalithic People, the builders of dolmens, cromlechs, and chambered tumuli, of which more than three thousand have been counted in France alone. Dolmens are found in Scandinavia southwards, all down the western lands of Europe to the Straights of Gibraltar, and round by the Mediterranean coast of Spain. They occur in some of the western islands of the Mediterranean, and are found in Greece.... Roughly, if we draw a line from the mouth of the Rhone [River; originally Rho**dan**] northward to Varanger Fiord, one may say that, except for a few Mediterranean examples, all the dolmens in Europe lie...west of that line. To the east none are found until we come into Asia. But they cross the Straits of Gibraltar, and are found all along the North African littoral, and thence eastwards through Arabia, India, and as far as Japan.[x8]

Parker continues,

As we have seen, Moses annihilated the Amorites east of the Jordan [River], and their name in the previous statement by Sayce is therefore an error on his part due probably to his [erroneous] preconceived idea that Israel was of the popular [sic, infamous] "Jewish" type. He states that the bulk of the Jewish (meaning Israelitish) population was Nordic (quotation, p. 12), *and that as true Nordics they have migrated into North Africa, Spain, western France, Britain and Ireland* (Parker, p. 18).

[x8] For more information on these cromlechs and stone heaps and the proof that they were all built by the same people (the white race), see Stonehenge and Druidism, The Great Pyramid Uncoded, and Jacob's Pillar by E. Raymond Capt, Tracing Our Ancestors by Frederick Haberman, Celtic Druids (1829), Godfrey Higgins, and Prehistoric London by E. O. Gordon.

As we have already seen, the Egyptians recorded the facial features of their captives, and the portraits of the Israelite captives clearly designate them as Nordics. However, a bit of confusion has resulted from poor understanding concerning the Assyrian drawings of their Israel captives. Parker explains this, saying,

> The *Assyrian* artists, however, fared badly in the matter of portraiture. As has been pointed out by both Mr. H. A. Marchant and Brig.-Gen. W. H. Fasken, Sayce himself clears up the seeming discrepancy between the representative type portrayed on the ***Egyptian*** monuments and the reliefs of the *Assyrian* sculptors when he says: [from Bypaths of Bible Knowledge, Vol II (Assyria), p. 89]
>
> Up to the last, however, the Assyrian artist succeeded but **badly** in human portraiture. Nothing can surpass some of his pictures of animals[x9]...Unlike the Egyptian, who excelled in the delineation of the human form, he [the Assyrian] did not draw from nude models. The details of...[clothing] were with him [the Assyrian] of more importance than the features of the face or the posture of the limbs. We cannot expect to find [discriminating] portraits in the sculptures of Assyria. Little, if any, attempt is made even to distinguish the natives of different foreign countries from one another, except in the way they dress. All alike have the same features of the Assyrians themselves (Parker, pp. 19-20).

Now we come to some of the most starling and convincing proof, which has been ***right under the noses*** of the "experts" the whole time, yet for some reason ***they all* missed it**. This piece of evidence proves that the Israelites were the blond-haired, blue-eyed white race that has erroneously been called "the Amorite type": **the Amorites were a race of *giants*** (Amos 2:9).

The Israelites themselves were a tall people; yet the Amorites are described as *giants*. When the Israelites went to claim the land of Israel, which God had given to them, they were fearful of the *giants* in the land. The men who were sent to spy out the land came back with the report that these giants, by their enormous size, made them [the Israelites] appear *as grasshoppers* by comparison (Numbers 13:33). The Amorites also lived in this land in the *mountains* (Numbers 13:29).

Now, since the Amorites were of such extreme stature, would not this *obvious and distinctive characteristic* have been portrayed in the drawings made by both the Egyptians and the Assyrians? How could such an *incredible trait* not be depicted *in any* record—if indeed it was really the "Amorites" who had been captured? Further, could this race of giants have been conquered by the Egyptians (who were not accustomed to mountains), who were a plains, desert, and river delta people?

The Israelites were a tall people, averaging 6 feet in height. The *modest height difference* between the Israelites and other peoples might have been overlooked in drawings of *normal* captives; but how can anyone believe that *giants*—who were 8, 9, or maybe even 10 feet tall[x10]—would not have been portrayed as *towering* specimens alongside other people in the Egyptian and Assyrian drawings?

Finally, among the ***Dead Sea Scrolls*** found in Cave 1 is a scroll fragment called the *Genesis Apocryphon* (also called the *Scroll of the Patriarchs*), which records that Sarah (Abraham's wife) had pure white skin and long, lovely hair.

[x9] —that is, their drawings of animals were so poor, it is hilarious to think that these were *serious* drawings intended to represent what they actually caricature.

[x10] Goliath was 9 feet 9 inches tall **(I Samuel 17:4)**; and had many giant relatives **(II Samuel 21)**.

Appendix C-6:

Christ (Jesus) YeHoWSHuWaH (A Pure Israelite) Was White

The following was found in a letter written to the monarch of Rome by Publius Lentrelus (a resident of Judea in the days of Tiberius Caesar). This letter first appeared in the writings of Saint Anselm of Canterbury in the 11th century A.D.:

> There lives at this time in Judea a man of singular virtue...Jesus Christ...his followers love and adore him as the offspring of the Immortal God.
>
> He calls back the dead from the graves and heals all sorts of diseases with a word or a touch. He is a tall man, well-shaped, and of an amiable and reverend aspect; his hair of a color that can barely be matched, falling into graceful curls, waving about and very agreeable.... His forehead high, large, and imposing; his cheeks without spot or wrinkle, beautiful with a lovely red; his nose and mouth formed with exquisite symmetry; his beard and of a color suitable to his hair...his eyes bright and blue, clear and serene. [His] Look innocent, dignified, manly, and mature; his arms and hands delectable to behold (from p. 75, Appendix B of The Resurrection Tomb by E. Raymond Capt).

Appendix D

In most cases down through history, after the "jews" received their *demands for blessings*, they have turned around and bitten the hand that has fed them, **persecuting** their benefactors. When their benefactors, in righteous indignation, defended themselves and responded to such evil attacks, the "jews" then claimed to be the ones who were being persecuted.[x11] Have the "jews" blessed the United States, Britain, and Germany? Or have "jews" dragged us into wars that cost us hundreds of thousands (even *millions*) of lives and billions of dollars—by their own confession? Recently, hundreds of thousands of Soviet "jews" who fought under Stalin have come to the U. S. and are demanding welfare and U. S. soldier's benefits because we were "allies." We never lost one war before we recognized the "jews" and aided them in stealing the land of Palestine from the Arabs. Yet look at our losses in Korea, Vietnam, and elsewhere. We are all over the world fighting wars for third-world peoples, while without lifting a finger, we let the Communists murder hundreds of millions of white Christians in Eastern Europe.

Has morality and righteousness *increased* since the "jews" entered our lands? No, to the contrary (as a result of "jewish" Hollywood,[x12] "educators," politicians, and *terrorist-tactic* special-interest groups), society has degenerated, the family has disintegrated, perversion and immorality have abounded, crime has increased exponentially, faith in God has nearly disappeared, public expression of Christianity has all but been outlawed, laws have been written to cater to criminals and punish the victims, while our sovereignty has been lost and we are *second-class citizens* in ***our own land***. A flood of anti-Christian, nonwhite peoples continues to inundate our

---

[x11] Your Inheritance: Part II: The Impostors Exposed will intricately explain the degradation of society, world wars, Communism, and what the "jews" actually believe—the Talmud and Kaballa. It will explain why the "jews" were expelled from nearly every nation of Europe at least once, and why they were even banned from the early American colonies (and it was not because they were being persecuted as "God's chosen people").

[x12] See An Empire of Their Own: How The Jews Invented Hollywood (1988), Gabler (a "jew").

land (as a result of the "jewish" legislation and propaganda of "civil rights"), making us foreigners in our own country.[x13] We have been told man is progressing and getting better; but one can only believe this *if he closes his eyes* and pretends to envision the lie he has been told.

Now, it is not my intention to put the "jews" down or blame them for everything. If the truth is unpleasant, this is no reason to attack the one who speaks it. Why not agree to an open forum to present, in civilized fashion, the proof each side has to offer? If the "jews" are actually guilty of what they are accused, let them admit it and accept responsibility (and change if possible). Any other race on earth that is suspected of war crimes is put on trial, condemned, punished, and forced to pay restitution—except the "jews." They are considered above reproach. Why? (Because they have taken over the reigns of the media and the "government.")

I certainly do not blame only the "jews." *We ourselves* are **first** and *foremost* to blame, for we disobeyed God's law and allowed God's enemies to enter our land; we acquiesced to liberal "morals." Judgment begins in the *house of God* (I Peter 4:17), that is, with *true Israel.* God will one day root out all those things that offend and will burn them with fire (Matthew 13:25-41). But for now, we must leave to God those things that we are unable to do (cleanse America and the entire earth of all evil) and get our own house in order.[x14]

Each person can investigate these facts and their causes and relationships and draw the only valid conclusions himself. (Sacred Truth Ministries' catalog or the distributor of this book should have ample books to help you in this area of study.) My intention now is to draw a simple comparison, to present a lineup of people for identification as the true Israel of God—based upon the ***facts*** of the case. It is up to you to determine if you will choose the people *to whom the facts and evidence point* or if you will make your decision based upon other irrelevant and intellectually dishonest factors (fear, indifference, conflict of interests, bribery, blackmail, threats, misplaced pity or affections, peer pressure, love of family tradition over love for God, fear of public criticism, emotionalism, refusal to admit the truth, or refusal to accept the sovereignty and testimony of God Almighty). Today, few people care about the truth for the truth's sake. Few people do what is right any more simply because it is right. Why is that? What happened to change this?

Appendix E

In Israel's Migrations or An Attack Answered, Parker states on page 13:

> That the "fair Kelts of an Irish Village" are indeed Israelites is thus clear. Even their [Kelts'] language further confirms such identification, for it (Erse) is akin to both Gaelic and Welsh. The similarity of the last-mentioned [Welsh] to Hebrew is so great that it drew forth considerable research on the part of the noted

---

[x13] Again, there are two sets of rules—one for them and one for everyone else. If no one has civil rights in Palestine but the "jews," why do they demand that our country (and every other white nation) give equal rights to everyone? Are there equal rights in Arab lands? African lands? Why do the white nations then have to give equal rights? Because our enemies, who control immigration and legislation, know that this will cause the downfall of the bulwark of Christianity and will rapidly mongrelize the race that made America great—and there will be no one to stand in their way.

[x14] For more information concerning true Israel's proper relationship to an evil world, see The War Between the Children of Light and the Powers of Darkness: How the Christian-Israelite Can Live in an Evil World System... by Balaicius/STM.

["jewish"] Hebrew Scholar of the last century, Dr. Moses Margoliouth,[x15] and the following comment:

A small remnant of [Solomon's subjects] remained in Cornwall since that time (the time of the building of his Temple). I have traced that remnant by the paths of philology, and the byways of nomenclature. I might adduce an array of whole sentences, exactly alike in the languages of Hebrew and the ancient Cornish. I might adduce some of the proper names which prevailed among the aboriginal Britons long before they knew anything of Christianity, such as Adam, Abraham, Asaph...Daniel, Solomon... (The Hebrews In East Anglia (1870), Margoliouth).

Parker also states that the terms "British," "Briton," and others are of Phoenician origin, as shown by Professor Waddell in his excellent book, Phoenician Origin of Britons, Scots, and Anglo-Saxons (Parker, p. 29).

In Missing Links Discovered in Assyrian Tablets (1985), Capt states,

All etymologists know that the Greek, Latin, German, Icelandic, Norse, Danish, Dutch and several other languages figure in the structure and vocabulary of the present Anglo-Saxon (English) language. While Greek and Latin words have contributed to the English language, more than 75 percent of English words come direct from Hebrew words or their roots. Of course, many of these old British words are used in *modern dress*; their spelling and...the pronunciations, have been varied as time has passed (p. 187).

Capt offers a long list of identical English and Hebrew words (pp. 187-191) from God's Covenant Man (1916) by Professor Edward Odlum.

Rev. John Heslip, in Who And Where Are The Lost Ten Tribes?, records,

Another has written, "scarcely any Hebrew root can be discovered that has not its corresponding derivative in the ancient British language." An eminent Cornish scholar of the last century, who devoted a great deal of time to prove the affinity between the Hebrew and Welsh languages, observes,

It would be difficult to adduce a single article or form of construction in the Hebrew grammar, but...the same is to be found in Welsh, and that there are many whole sentences in both languages exactly the same in the very words.

Canon Lyson finds 5,000 Hebrew roots in the English tongue.... This is quite understandable in...light of the fact...the British Isles were peopled by...descendents of the Ten Tribes. On any other premise it is hardly understandable (pp. 17-18).

William Tyndale (1492?-1536), the English reformer (who was strangled to death and then burned for his translation of the Holy Scriptures into English), announced his remarkable discovery that because of the similarities between Hebrew and English, English was the most suitable language for a translation of the Scriptures. He said,

The properties of the Hebrew tongue agreeth one thousand times more with the English than with the Latin or the Greek. The manner of speaking is in both one, so that, in a thousand places, there needest not be but to translate the Hebrew word for word.

This is no mere coincidence, for God declared (Isaiah 28:11) that He would speak to His people in another language; and truly, no language has so spoken to God's

[x15] The researches of Dr. Margoliouth led him to become a believer in British-Israel Identity, to which his own article in *The Banner of Israel*, Nov. 21, 1877, testifies (pp. 23-24). See Also his The Jews in Great Britain (1846).

people greater than the English language, through hundreds of Bible translations and untold millions of books, pamphlets, sermons, and films. It is important to note that Tyndale is still highly regarded for his remarkable expertise in Hebrew, and also for his command of his own tongue (English), and the Greek, and many other languages.

(Though *modern* English is altogether a different language than ancient Hebrew, the intermediary languages mentioned clearly form a link between the two.)

Conor Mac Dari wrote The Bible: An Irish Book, Irish Wisdom Preserved in the Bible and the Pyramids, and The Bible an Irish Book of Pre-Roman Spiritual Culture. In The Bible: An Irish Book, Mac Dari stated,

> This volume is dedicated to the memory of my father who, in my early boyhood, taught me the letters of the Irish alphabet, the initial step which in later years enabled me, with the aid of historical research, to interpret its character-names and to prove the true Source of the origin of the Bible.

(Although Mac Dari obviously got the cart before the horse, thinking the Bible was Irish (rather than the Irish being descended from the true Hebrew-Israelites), he clearly recognized the two were one and the same.)

L. Maclean, F.O.S., a Gaelic scholar, in The History of The Celtic Language (1840), quoting Webster's Analysis of the English Language, recorded,

> ...The Saxon words constitute our mother tongue, being words which our ancestors brought with them from Asia. The Danish and the Welsh are also primitive tongues and may be considered a part of our vernacular language. They are of equal antiquity with the Chaldeae and Syriac.

Gladys Taylor, in "Our Mother Tongue," (published in Vol. 3, No. 3; June 1994 of *The Covenant Report* (BIWF 242 Dominion Rd., Mount Eden, Aukland, 3, New Zealand), states,

> ...Early 19th-century philologists had arrived at the conclusion, which they firmly maintained, that the early Celtic languages were derived...from a parent tongue of central Asia.... and...came to the conclusion that the roots of the Gaelic tongues were both Semitic and pre-Hebrew.

Taylor continues,

> A close study shows the Gaelic of the ancient bards to be more ancient than that of the Hebrew Old Testament, although obviously derived from the same parent language. The fact that the Welsh is so close to Hebrew as to be understood by a Hebrew scholar...is an indication that the tribes who brought the Welsh language were Hebrew-speaking and were later arrivals than the earliest settlers in Ireland. The Silures of Wales were a dominant and artistic people whose literary style may well have been adopted from earlier settlers in that region.

It is reported that in 1827, the *British & Foreign Bible Society* sent Hebrew (obviously not *modern* "Hebrew") Bibles to Ireland for the Gaelic-speaking peasantry to read. Although they could not read English, they could read Hebrew.

Taylor also draws parallel to the Hebrew names of people prominent throughout the British Isles. In the Irish and Scottish annals, the name of several princes in the genealogies of the royal house of Tara was "Heber" or "Eber"—the very name of the father of the Hebrews. Further, the name is preserved in the very names of the tribes who peopled these islands: the Hibernians (Iberich) and Hebrideans (Ebrideans). Place names of Hebrew origin are also common.

The significance of this becomes more apparent when one realizes that the word *Hebrew* means "one who crosses over," that is, "**a colonizer**." Even as the Hebrew/

Israelites "crossed over" the Jordan River into the Promised Land, so too after the Israelites' captivity, they crossed over into Europe, then across the English Channel into the Isles, and later across the oceans to America, Australia, South Africa, etc. to the new Promised Lands to which God promised to lead them.

Taylor then recounts,

> ...The fact of the existence of the parent language of the Semitic peoples in the widely separated regions of central Asia and the British Isles is given further prominence when we discover that, some two thousand years before Christ, while it [Hebrew] was being used in Britain, another offshoot was in current use in Crete, precisely midway on the trade route to the west. Linguistically, as well as geographically, Crete stands in this halfway position and the recent findings of Dr Cyrus H. Gordon, on the subject of Creten languages, add enormously to our knowledge of migration chronology. In the report of his discoveries (*Daily Telegraph*, April 4, 1962), we were told that..."Minoan Linear "A" inscriptions and also "Eteo-Creten," long taken to be the pre-Greek speech of Crete, are both actually Phoenician. The Eteo-Cretan is written with the Greek alphabet.

Australian-born British archaeologist Vere Gordon Childe (1892-1957), in, Prehistoric Monuments of the British Isles, writing about the finds at Skara Brae, on the Orkney Islands off Scotland's coast, wrote, "The courtyard homes represent an Atlantic-Mediterranean plan, traceable to Minoan Crete by 2000 B.C."

Huddleston, prefacing John Toland's History of the Druids (1740), recorded,

> Of all the phenomena of language, the most remarkable is the affinity of...Celtic and Sanskrit—two languages which cannot possibly have come in contact for more than three thousand years, and must, therefore, owe their similarity to the radical tincture of the primary language of Asia. That the Celtic is a dialect of the primary language of Asia has received sanction of the celebrated philologist, the late Professor Murray,[x16] in his "Prospectus to The Philosophy of Language."

Haberman stated, "...Gaelic, the name of the language of Ireland, and the related [Scots] Gaelic of Scotland, both of them [are] branches of the Phoenician, as is also the Welsh and the Manx" (Tracing Our Ancestors; p. 120). (Brackets mine.)

Colquhoun, in Our Descent From Israel Proved... (1931), states,

> Several other scholars have noted the extraordinary affinity between the Hebrew and the Welsh languages. Dr. Davies, in his Welsh Grammar tells us that almost every page of the Welsh translation of the Bible is replete with Hebraisms, in the time, sense and spirit of the original. Another authority, Dr. Duncan M'Dougall, writing in the *Evangelical Christian*, says "You can take any sentence in Hebrew and change it into Gaelic, word for word, without altering the order of a single word or particle [of speech], and you will have the correct Gaelic idiom in every case...." (Brackets and emphasis mine.)

Capt, in Missing Links... (p. 191), quotes the Vicar of Lampeter in Britain (and Chaplain in the Royal Navy), Rev. Eliezer Williams (1754-1820), a noted researcher and prolific writer on ancient Celtic histories: (See The English Works of the Late Rev. Eliezer Williams..., 1840, or the individual titles: Ancient Celtic Tribes, Druids and Celtic Bards, Historical Anecdotes of the Welsh Language, and History of the Britons.)

> Scarcely a Hebrew root can be discovered that has not its corresponding derivation in the British language.... In Richard's Welsh and English Dictionary

[x16] Presumably, Dr. J. A. H. Murray, the eminent Scottish philologist, lexicographer (1837-1915).

(published in Bristol in 1750) and in several other philological works, the affinity...Welsh bears to the Hebrew language is strenuously maintained. But not only do the words themselves indicate that similarity between the two; their variations and inflections afford a much stronger proof of affinity.

Capt provides a small list of identical Welsh and Hebrew words, taken from British History Traced From Egypt and Palestine (1927) by Major (and Rev.) L. G. A. Roberts, Com. R.N. (Commander of the Royal Navy). Capt then states, "But it is not in single, isolated words only, that this resemblance strikes us; the conformity is equally remarkable in the idiomatic phrases of both languages, and in the formation of entire sentences..." (p. 193).

Roberts on page 34 in his, British History Traced... recounts that Charles Edwards (Oxford), a Welsh writer in his Hanes y Fydd* (1675), confessed when he first undertook the study of the Hebrew language, (* pronounced, "fyth")

...in the exuberance of his devout exaltation at finding the vernacular language of his country [Welsh] approached so near to that of Holy Writ [Hebrew], he declares he...considered it impious on his part not to have withdrawn the veil of silence and concealment from this what he styles miraculous conformity.

Capt (Missing Links..., pp. 196, 197) also quotes Beale Poste:

With respect to the derivation of the Welsh language...there is so much admixture of the Hebrew...that Rowlands, in his Mona Antiqua pp. 316 and 317...might almost be said to regard it [Hebrew] as his mother tongue, and the Welsh to be an immediate deviation from it...A foreign savant pronounced some years ago that it (the English) comprised within its compass six thousand pure Hebrew words (Celtic Inscriptions on Gaulish and British Coins; p. 148).

Other works that contain much proof that Hebrew is identical with Welsh, Irish, and other Celtic languages are:

Comparative Vocabulary of Forty-Eight Languages, Rev. Jacob Tomlin.

English Derived From Hebrew (1869) by R. Govett.

God's Covenant Man: British Israel (1927), Prof. Edward Odlum.

"*Hebrew and English: Some Psychic Likeness*" (a series of articles that appeared in *The National Message* in 1947) by Rev. J. Courtenay James, B.D., M.A., Ph.D.

Our British Ancestors (1865) by Canon Samuel Lysons contains an extensive glossary of English words that are derived from Hebrew roots.

Suggestions on the Ancient Britons (1864), Barber.

Quarterly Magazine and Celtic Repertory, July 2nd, 1832, No. 15, Vol. IV, article "Welsh Hebrewisms," by Gläs. (From British History Traced..., Roberts; p. 32.)

Welsh Grammar, Dr. Davies.

(Further evidence that the Welsh and Hebrew languages are identical and further proof that the Welsh are Israelites can be found in the *Welsh Triads*: the records of the ancient Druid religion (which is identical itself with the pure Hebrew worship of YaHWeH, as is the ancient Celtic religion). For more information along these lines, also consult: Celt, Druid and Culdee (1973) by Isabel Hill Elder, Celtic Fire (1990) by Bishop Robert VandeWeyer, The Dooms of Alfred the Great, The Drama of the Lost Disciples (1961) by George F. Jowett, Prehistoric London (1914) by E. O. Gordon, Stonehenge and Druidism (1979) by E. Raymond Capt, Tracing Our Ancestors (1934) by Haberman, The Traditions of Glastonbury (1983) by E. Raymond Capt, and St. Paul In Britain (1860), by Rev. Richard Williams Morgan.)

Appendix F

Albert Schweitzer[x17] said,

"I have given my life to try to alleviate the sufferings of Africa...something that all white men that have lived there like I must learn and know...these individuals are a sub-race. They have neither the intellectual, mental, or emotional abilities to equate or share equality with the white man in any of the functions of our civilization. I have given my life to try and bring unto them the advantages which our civilization must offer, but I have become well aware that we must retain this status; [we] the superior...they the inferior. For whenever a white man seeks to live among them as their equals, they will either destroy him or devour him. And they will destroy all of his work. Let the white men from anywhere in the world, who would come to help Africa, remember that you must continually retain this status: you the master and they the inferior like children...you would help and teach. Never fraternize with them as equals."

Many people will consider the above statement insulting or "racist." But remember *who* made the statement: Albert Schweitzer. Remember he was in Africa *not* to "subjugate" or "exploit" the Africans but to *help* them. If people object to such a statement, let such peoples *refuse all help* and *save themselves*.

People will behave in another country even as they behave in their own land. This fact was clearly presented by one of the most least-likely individuals, Paul Harvey, the well-known radio news personality: On his radio program on June 26, 1993 he drew parallels between the movie *Jurassic Park* and the current Somalian "crisis."* (Footnotes, brackets, and "*" comments are mine.) Harvey stated,

> Our nation with the best of intentions[x18] is creating a human Jurassic Park, USA. With only the best intentions we have been seeking to rescue the refugees of self-destructing societies and endow them with a new lease on life.[x19] We[x20] invite subjugated Haitians to make their new homes here. Members of sects that practice voodoo[x21] no longer welcomed in Nigeria and Cuba, we[x20] invite to Florida. Somalians who cannot tolerate one another in Somalia, we transplant here.... The result is an inevitable collapse of the past and the present. *Jurassic Park's* mathematician Dr. Ian Malcolm tells the scientists they were so busy seeing if

---

[x17] Dr. Schweitzer (1875-1965) was the brilliant French philosopher, scientist, medical doctor, author (one of foremost authorities on Johann Sebastian Bach), musicologist (an exceptional organist of Bach's work), clergyman, theologian (Principal of St. Thomas Theological College, 1902), missionary, anthropologist, philanthropist, and profound Christian. He won the Nobel Peace Prize (1952).

Liberals always praise Schweitzer as the ultimate humanitarian who gave his life to try and help the poor Africans, but they never share his *full uncensored opinion* of the matter.

[x18] —"with the *best* of intentions"(?): anyone who believes this lives in a fantasy land. Even as in Kuwait/Iran and Kosovo, *oil interests, money, power, and political leverage* were the *only* motives that governed the U.S.'s intervention.

[x19] —all expenses paid in full by the U.S. taxpayer. Did you voluntarily pay for this? Did you vote on it? This is proof that socialism is what is practiced in the U.S.

[x20] We? I did not invite anyone. Did you invite anyone? This is a subtle, psychological, propagandist programming technique of Soviet brainwashing: desensitization and imbedding of thoughts suggesting cooperation. [There is no "we"—only a "them" (the enemy who cloak themselves as "we").]

[x21] —as well as cannibalism, ritual murder, gang violence, "white collar crime" (check kiting, credit card fraud), etc.

they *could*, that they forgot to ask if they *should*.... Today's nations, with a greater depth of experience than ours, overwhelmed by uninvited [peoples] who can't or won't assimilate, are now sending them home....[x22] You cannot housebreak a dinosaur. And that irrefutable jungle law remains singularly unimpressed by any Supreme Court of any era. Should I tell you how the movie ends? The Americans, their good intentions having boomeranged, ended up running for their lives.

*(1) Many shocking reports indicate that there never was any "crisis." There have been numerous reports that soldiers who were there in Somalia saw field after field of lush farm crops and vegetation. Whether this is true is insignificant when one considers, if the average Somalis can afford $5 a day for *chat* (the official Somali past-time: getting high), they certainly could have afforded to buy food; even if they had none in their own country (which seems *not* to be the case), they could have bought it from another country, as everyone else does. Most people do not realize that although $5 may seem like nothing to us, to a third-world person this probably represents a ***month's*** *worth of food.* [And the reports indicate that the Somalis do not merely spend $5 on drugs; they spend *$5 a* ***day*** on drugs. Yet they expect us to send them food and other financial aid.] This is no different than welfare fraud here in the U. S.—except this is on an international scale. It is *illegal* for the U.S. "government" to give away or "spend" *even one penny* of taxpayer money for *any cause* that is not agreed upon by *100 percent* of the taxpayers. If a person, on his own, chooses to donate some of his money to some supposedly humanitarian cause, that is entirely up to him. However, if the "government" gives away *even one penny*, it has perpetrated a *criminal act.* Therefore, the "government" is guilty of High Treason against the people of the United States and the U. S. Constitution: this is *Communism* in practice. (See the famous speech by Congressman Davy Crockett to Congress; included with The Liberty Document, by Balaicius/STM.)

The government-controlled media has long succeeded in fooling people into believing incredible things regarding international "atrocities." So why should they stop creating fantasies when the American public feeds off of such sensationalism? While these incredible atrocities are religiously advertised,[x23] these same world "humanitarians" turn a blind eye to the ***real*** atrocities occurring simulta-

---

[x22] Of course the "government"-controlled media makes such people and nations out to be "Nazis," as if people *did not have the right to choose* to people *their own country* with *their own people*. Germany has been forced to accept 10 to 20 times more refugees than other nations (especially during the orchestrated Bosnian war)—and the German taxpayers must pay for all of the immigrants' housing, medical care, and costs of living. The main purpose for this is to weaken Germany—which was also the purpose of "unification." A nation is merely a large extension of a family. It is a *nation-family's right* to choose not *to bring into their nation-family* nonproducing, inassimilable, anti-Christian, immoral, race-destroying nonfamily members. But this right is denied. Since the white Christian nations are the only thing that stands in the way of the ("jewish") Communists' world domination, they are bent on destroying the white nations. The white nations are forced to accept nonwhite immigrants and pay all their expenses. Only the white nations are attacked by the "United Nations' Peacekeeping Force" if they in any way try to preserve their nations. If blacks rise up *en masse* and murder all the whites (Haiti, Rhodesia, South Africa etc.), nothing is done. If the blacks riot here in America and burn an entire city to the ground, nothing is done. Yet if a white group in South Africa tries to preserve their own nation, *they must be destroyed.* Civil rights are extended only to "people of color" and "jews"—those who have assumed the role of the "persecuted."

[x23] —not unlike the emotionally charged sales pitches common to U.S. television car commercials or the shameful *Feed the Children*-styled, heart-tugging "info-mercials" with which Americans are routinely barraged.

neously elsewhere.[x24]

Because the average white Christian is in rebellion against God and His Word, he *needs* such "atrocities" to distract him from his own guilty conscience. If his emotions are caught in a firestorm of rapture and misplaced anger and empathy, he seems to feel as if he has sacrificed a virgin to appease the angry gods of his soul (which of course only brings temporary relief—until the effects of this wear off and the next *caustic, hollow* **illusion** is created, necessitating the need for renewed "heroic" emotionalism).

Somalia—like most other nonwhite nations, including Haiti, the Philippines, Uganda, Rhodesia, and Palestine—was once ruled by white Christian nations. When thus ruled, these colonies were peaceful and prosperous. When these peoples demanded "freedom,"[x25] they reverted to killing not only every white man, woman, and child (after rape and torture), but hundreds of thousands of *their own people*. They reverted to anarchy, cannibalism, and voodoo. Today they cannot support themselves. The white nations must periodically save them. We are "damned if we do" and "damned if we don't." If we don't help them, we are *cruel, heartless, "white-bred," Capitalist pigs*. If we rule over them to maintain peace, safety, and order, we are *white Imperialist devils*. Like hopeless drug addicts, they want only a *quick fix* (at our expense). Once they get their fix, they demand to be left alone (except for their monthly welfare check)—until they again cry for help. Evil people know how to *play the heart strings* of the benevolent, righteous, good-hearted (although, sadly, often brainless) nations of Christendom.[x26] *Why is it that these virtues and altruistic traits are found only among the white, Christian nations?* Some might claim it is because we are the wealthiest. This is a lie. What can *we* afford? What is our nation's debt? Many Arabs, "jews," East Indians, and African dictators are by far wealthier, yet they are unwilling to even help their own people. Why should they spend their own money, when the gullible white nations will foot the bill? (*Liberation Theology* is communism and incongruent with Scripture.)

This is the fulfillment of prophecy. God created Adam-kind to govern the planet, to subdue and have dominion. He is the only one who cares for the entire planet. It is his by inheritance from Almighty God. As we saw, the name *Hebrew* means "colonizer," while the name *Israel* means "he who rules successfully as a prince with God over man." Therefore, it is perfectly clear that the white, Adamic-Hebrew-Israel peoples are now and have always been fulfilling the role God ordained. Further, God declared that if we forsook His laws, our enemies among us would rise up and become the head and make us the tail, and we would become the oppressed in our own countries (Leviticus 26; Deuteronomy 28). Since part of God's law demanded strict separation from all other peoples, it is

---

[x24] The "atrocities" are ingenious diversions to draw international attention away from reality—such as the 100 million-plus white Christians who were actually massacred in eastern Europe in the early and mid-1900's; such as the Soviet tanks that rolled into Lithuania while news teams were focusing on Kuwait and Iran. Had it been *"jews"* who were being killed in Bosnia or South Africa, and not white Christians or Muslims, the United Nations and the United States would have stepped in *the very **first** day* of killing (or after they allowed the first few *token* "jews" (*sacrificial pawns*) to be killed).

[x25] —something by their very nature, they cannot have on their own—the only "freedom" they on their own can know, is lawlessness: "freedom" without responsibility, safety, or progress of civilization.

[x26] —maybe it should be spelled "Christen-dumb"—for it certainly is no longer "Christ's Domain"!

clear what our downfall has been. No white nations in this millennia have ever been conquered militarily by another people. This is because the white nations are God's Israel people. Although we have not yet been conquered from without, however, we have been subverted from within—and it has been *our own doing.* It too is a fulfillment of prophecy. Whole libraries are needed to contain all the complex laws man makes each year (most of them unjust and solely for those in power to obtain greater power and wealth). But God's laws are simple and relatively few. One of the most important laws commands us to remain separate from other peoples. God's enemies know this, and they use it to their advantage.[x27]

Scripture declares, "Can the Ethiopian (African) change his skin (nature) or the leopard his spots (nature)?" (Jeremiah 13:23). I have known missionaries who lived in Africa, and they have confirmed the reports I have read that even long after many Africans supposedly *accepted Christ as their Savior*, no amount of teaching, counsel, admonition, exhortation, Bible reading, or prayer could change their nature or life-style. They continued in random fornication and adultery, mayhem and murder, and other base behaviors such as theft, trickery, deceit, and betrayal. They consider these traits *normal* and *even admirable*. Further, it is not satisfying to merely commit these acts, but the complete fulfillment is achieved by telling ones *friends*, so they can all *laugh about it together*. One has merely to watch the evening news or read the daily newspaper to see that these people live no differently in our land.

(Please do not misunderstand me. I am <u>not</u> saying other peoples should not be taught about Christ, God, or His ways. How can they know or live by His ways unless we teach them? This is a whole other issue. My point is: *No one* will follow the laws *in any nation* if the laws are *optional*. Other peoples may live

---

[x27] The prophet Balaam tried to curse the Israelites because Israel's enemies offered to pay him handsomely to curse them. However, God would not let Balaam curse Israel. When he would open his mouth to curse them, only blessing would come out (blessings that foretold how Israel's enemies would meet with destruction). As long as Israel obeyed God, God protected her from her enemies. However, Balaam gave Israel's enemies some very evil (although profound) advice: If the Canaanites could get their women to seduce the Israelite men to commit whoredom and intermarry with them, they could bastardize the Israelites' race and seduce the Israelites to worship false gods, and Israel's God would then chastise Israel by removing His protection and blessing from them. (See Josephus, Antiquities, Book IV, Chapter VI, Paragraph 6, 7, 8, etc.; Numbers 22-24; 25:1-3; 31:16.)

This has always been our downfall. When we turn from God's ways (racial purity tops the list), we divorce ourselves from His grace and illegitimize our descendents. This has been the downfall of every great civilization in history. Not only does the white race suffer, but *all races* suffer, for then the other races have no one to protect them from each other, and tyranny and brutality abound.

Early on, even in the late 1800's, evil people began steering America's immigration policy in the wrong direction. Between 1821 and 1880, German immigration was 29.7 percent of all immigration. By 1903, however, it had dropped to 4.5 percent. Likewise, immigration from Ireland during the same periods dropped from 30.2 percent to 4.7 percent, and immigration from England, Scotland, and Wales declined from 16.4 percent to 3.3 percent. Furthermore, of the same periods, Latin- and Magyar-speaking immigrants rose from a combined 3.7 percent to 29 percent. The population of the U.S. around 1908 was about 80,000,000 (statistics from <u>Race or Mongrel</u> (1908), Schultz). Now it is around 275,000,000. Since 1900, white population has been severely curtailed, and white birth rates have dropped about 80 percent (while the death rate due to murder and disease has increased 1,000 percent). For the past 25 years or so, white immigration into the United States has been severely restricted, while nonwhite immigration has no ceiling. Further, when whites emigrated to America, they paid their own way. Most nonwhite immigrants (as well as residents and citizens) live on welfare. We have become a third-world country with pockets of civilization. (See <u>Racial Purity: Absolute or Obsolete</u>? (including *Just How Bad Has the Browning of America Become...?*) by Balaicius/STM, due out 2001.) Our nation is purposely being *run into the ground*!

however they wish in *their own* land (without our periodic aid: "you reap what you sow"); but in ***our land***, the law must be enforced on all!—otherwise most people will ignore the law and live as they please, and *all* will suffer.)

Finally, the highly-esteemed British-America philosopher and psychologist **Raymond B. Cattell** (born 1905) stated,

> "Civil disobedience" was blown up into a saintly cult by Gandhi, and masqueraded as a vague new religion (especially among the *literati*) only because the tradition of the English Christian gentleman made massive executions impossible. When the English withdrew, slaughter on a grand scale, as an inevitable consequence of the inherent insincerity of the mutual impositions and aggressions hidden in "passive resistance," followed almost immediately (A New Morality From Science: Beyondism (1972); chapter 5).

Appendix G

— **Arnold Joseph Toynbee** (1889-1975), the British historian and educator, in volume 1, pages 211 to 212 of his, A Study of History (1934), wrote,

> The Protestant temper...attitude and conduct in regard to Race...[and other areas] is inspired largely by the Old Testament...The "Bible Christian" of European origin and race who...settled among peoples of non-European race overseas...inevitably identified himself with Israel obeying the will of Jehovah... doing the Lord's work...taking possession of the Promised Land...[and] identified the non-Europeans...with the Canaanites whom the Lord...delivered into the hand of his Chosen People to be destroyed or subjugated.

— **William Bradford** (1663-1752), a Pilgrim leader who became the first governor of the Plymouth colony shortly upon their initial arrival recorded,

> Being thus arrived in good harbor, they fell upon their knees and blessed the God of heaven who had brought them over this vast and furious ocean, and delivered them from all the perils and miseries thereof, again to set their feet on the firm and stable earth.
>
> Bradford often encouraged his people, assuring them of God's commitment to them, His covenant, and His promise. They often read aloud to each other passages of Scripture such as God's promise to "the offspring of Abraham," found in Isaiah 41:9-10 (Faith & Freedom (1988), Benjamin Hart, p. 78).

— **John Robinson**, (1576?-1625), an English congregationalist preacher, one of the pastors who left with the Pilgrims for America (having first fled to "immoral Holland"), intimated that he perceived that *God called His people to go to this new land to build a New Jerusalem*. He further stated, "the people of God in old time, were called out of Babylon, the place of their bodily bondage, and were to come to Jerusalem, and there build the Lord's Temple" (Faith & Freedom, pp. 71-72).

— **John Cotton** (1584-1652), a Puritan preacher, in his farewell sermon to his congregation in England, drawing his sermon from the Old Testament, stated that *God had selected them as his new* ***chosen people*** *and that the virgin wilderness of the American continent had been reserved for them over all these years by God.* He stated that *they were the new* **Israelites**, quoting the promise of God to His people, "**I will appoint a place for My people Israel, and will plant them,**

that they may live in their own place" (II Samuel 7:10). (Boldface mine.)

Cotton also stated, **God keeps His promises**, and "**What He hath planted *He will maintain*.**" (Holland's very motto.) Recognizing there would be hardships, Cotton encouraged his flock and told them, "The Lord hath given us hearts to overlook them all, **as if we were carried up on eagles' wings.**" (See **Isaiah 18:1;40:31.**) However, Cotton also warned his flock to not turn from God's ways and "denigrate **as the Israelites did**."

— **John Winthrop** (1588-1649), a Puritan leader, who became the Massachusetts

Bay Colony's first governor, also warned the people that should they forget God's ways, the new Promised Land would cease to be a land of milk and honey; it would be a barren wilderness, merciless and brutal. He declared, "The Lord will surely break out in wrath against us, be revenged of such a perjured people and make us know the price of the breach **of such a covenant**" (see **II Samuel 7:14** and see Faith & Freedom, pp. 90-91). (Boldface mine.) Winthrop further stated,

> Now, the only way to avoid this shipwreck and to provide for our posterity, is to **follow the counsel of Micah**, to do justly, to love mercy, to walk humbly with our God.... We shall find that **the God of Israel is among us**.... He shall **make us a praise and glory**... (The Light And The Glory (1977), Peter Marshall & David Manuel, p. 162). (Boldface mine.)

— **Samuel Elliot Morison**, in his Colonial America (1887), in reference to Cotton's sermon (above) wrote,

> Cotton's sermon was of a nature to inspire these new children of Israel with the belief that they were the Lord's chosen people; destined, if they kept the covenant with Him, to people and fructify this new Canaan in the western wilderness (p. 25).

— **John Cotton Mather** (1663-1728), in his Magnalia Christi Americana (*The Great Works of Christ in America*) (Also known as The Ecclesiastical History of New England) (1702), quoted B. Woodbridge, who spoke of John Cotton in the following words:

> Though Moses [Cotton] be, yet Joshua is not dead; I mean renowned Norton; worthy he, Successor to our Moses, is to be. O happy Israel in America. In such a Moses, such a Joshua (Vol. I, p. 284).

Marshall & Manual further state that the *first settlers of America*,

> *...consciously thought of themselves as a people called into a continuation of the covenant relationship with God and one another which Israel had entered into...they even felt that passages in the Bible...originally addressed to Israel...applied in particular to them*...[for an example, see Deuteronomy 8:7-9]...they saw themselves called into their new **Promised Land** in order to found a new **Israel**, which would be a light to the whole world.... God had put a specific "call" on this country and the people who were to inhabit it. In the virgin wilderness of America, God was...to create a new **Israel of people living in obedience to the laws of God**.... certainly there was no doubt in the minds of the Puritans themselves...**In the Exodus of the Israelites from Egypt, they found a prefiguring of their own circumstances. "Let Israel be...our glass to view our faces**

in," wrote Samuel Fisher in his Testimony of Truth in 1679.... the Puritans understood **New England to be "a type and emblem of a New Jerusalem**...." this call was to be worked out in terms of the settlers covenant with God, and with each other...they saw no delineation between the two Testaments, believing that **an unchanging God had written them both**. They saw themselves as **being called into a direct continuation of the covenant relationship between God and Abraham...**[See] Genesis 12:1-2.... [and] 17:7-8 (The Light And The Glory, pp. 19-24). (Boldface and brackets mine.)

— **William Hubbard**, an early historian of Massachusetts Bay, provides us an appropriate summary of Winthrop's life: He "**has done good in Israel,** having spent not only his whole estate...but his bodily strength and life in the service of the country" (Faith & Freedom, pp. 106-107). (Boldface mine.)

— The **Men of Marlborough**, Connecticut, in 1773 unanimously proclaimed:

Death is more eligible than slavery. A free-born people are not required by the religion of Jesus Christ to submit to tyranny, but make use of such power as God has given them to recover and support their laws and liberties...[we] implore the Ruler above the skies, that He would make bare His arm in defense of His church and people, and let Israel go (History of The United States (1854), George Bancroft, Vol. VI, p. 442).

— The historian **Edward Johnson**, in 1630, in reference to the early Pilgrims and Puritans, stated,

For the Lambe is preparing his Bride, and oh! yee the ancient Beloved of Christ, whom he of old led by the hand from Egypt to Canaan through that great and terrible Wildernesse....And you the Seed of Israel both less and more, the rattling of your dead bones together is at hand, Sinewes, Flesh, and Life: at the Word of Christ it comes.... Then oh! you People of Israel gather together as one Man, and together as one Tree. Ezekiel 37 and 23.... Will you not believe that a Nation can be born in a day? [see Isaiah 66:8].... This year the great troubles in our native country increasing.... [this] wandering race of Jacobites deemed it now high time to implore the Lord for his especial aid in this time of their deepest distress.... As Jacob professes, I came over this Jordan with my staff...a few poor scattered stones newly raked out of the heaps of rubbish, and thou Lord Christ has now so far exalted them, as to lay them sure in thy Sion...the seed of Christ's Church in the posterity of Israel...pleaded the promise of the Lord in the multiplying of his seed; so these people at this very time, pleaded not only the Lord's promise to Israel, but to his only Son Christ Jesus (from Johnson's Wonder-Working Providences of Sion's Savior in New England (1910), pp. 59-61, 237, 238.). (Brackets mine.)

Appendix H

— **Thomas Paine** (1737-1809), the great British-born American Patriot, philosopher, and political leader, was a great intellect who dismissed the validity and veracity of the Bible because the "jews" had not been visited with the fulfillment of the glorious promises made to Abraham and his descendents, the Israelites.

— The American political leader, orator, and scholar **Robert G. Ingersoll** (1833-1899), though the son of a Congregationalist minister, turned into an agnostic, and scoffed at the Bible for this very reason. Ingersoll stated,

God made a great number of promises to Abraham, but few of them were ever kept. He agreed to make him the father of a great nation, but He did not. He solemnly promised to give him a great country, including all the land between the River of Egypt and the Euphrates, but He did not.... God was...dishonest...always promising but never performed (Some Mistakes of Moses; p. 183).

— **John Bunyan** (1628-1688), the great English nonconformist preacher who spent over 12 years in prison for refusing to be "licensed" by the state to preach, who wrote Pilgrim's Progress (1678) (which is considered one of the most influential books to impact western civilization), was moved in his spirit when he wondered if we, the Anglo-Saxon peoples could possibly be the Israelites of the Bible. He asked his father (a tinkerer) if this was possible, but his father plainly said, "No, we're not." Bunyan then states, "Wherefore then I fell in my spirit as to the hope of that, and so remained" (April 1879; see Grace Abounding To The Chief of Sinners; p. 6, paragraph 18).

It is *truly sad*—nay, TRAGIC!—that so many fine people have been dashed in their spirits, led astray spiritually, emotionally, and intellectually, and that many have even lost faith in God and the Bible because they were looking to God's *enemies* (the Canaanites, the modern "jews") for the fulfillment of God's blessings upon His people Israel (the Anglo-Saxon and related peoples). How sad that the average person takes the advice of *some other person*, simply because that person has an *official title* or a *degree* and is thus supposedly knowledgeable. Truly, when the blind lead the blind, both are in danger of falling into a pit (Matthew 15:14). Such a pit has usually been dug *by the wicked*, with the hopes the righteous will fall into it (Psalm 35:7). (May God save His people!)

— **P. W. Thompson, M.A.**, in reference to the overwhelming evidence that the promises of God to Israel have been fulfilled in the British people, at the *exact dates* as prophesied in Scripture, states: (British-Israel: The Plain Argument, 1935)

> As we all must be possessed of some knowledge of Britain's history in that era of terrific expansion, we need not labor the point. It takes the genius of Macaulay to detect the beginning of revival in 1199 the facts of the restoration in 1705 to 1845 are so blatant as to be patent to the greatest dullard who ever wrote history. They are overwhelming.... All these promises were fulfilled to Britain literally and at the same time appointed for their fulfillment to Israel.* Such a series of coincidences ceases to be coincidence. There is design. We move from probability to the nearest approach to certainty. How it is mentally possible honestly to avoid this implication we do not know.
>
> *Some of my clerical and other friends who are not British-Israelites admit that all the promises to Israel have been fulfilled to Britain, and at the exact dates indicated. They suggest, however, that because Israel failed God, Britain has been raised up to take her place. This is...the only way out of the difficulty, but what about the immutability of God's promises? (pp. 9-10).

It seems most Christians today have "a form of godliness, but deny the power thereof" (II Timothy 3:5-4). They *claim* to be Christians—followers and *subjects* of Christ their Lord—yet they do not keep His commandments (Luke 6:46; John 14:15; 15:10). (Most Christians think that His commandments were done away with, in *direct opposition to what Christ actually said.*) (See Matthew 5:17-20 and the boxed section on page 86 of this book.) Such people *claim* to believe God and have faith in His Word, yet they maintain that God does not have to keep His promises. Abraham, faltered in his faith at God's promise to give him a son (Isaac) in his old age. He attempted to "help God keep His promise"—through another woman (Hagar) and another son (Ishmael). God rejected this. Such modern Christians, with similarly failing faith, claim that the plenitude of Covenantal promises God made to Israel and Israel alone—promises God declared He would never break—have failed; and they claim there is no need for God's physical promises to be fulfilled in a **physical Israel**, for they are fulfilled in a "spiritual Israel"—something of which the Bible *never* speaks. *If there is no need for a physical Israel upon whom the promises must be fulfilled, then there was no need for Christ to come to earth, suffer, and die—for all then that was needed was a "spiritual Messiah" to redeem the "spiritual Israel."* **But this is not the case!** God alone will be true, but every carnally minded man will remain untrue (Romans 3:4). How many more people's lives and faith must be destroyed because the average person is too cowardly to embrace and preach the truth because it is not "politically correct"? When we stand before God on Judgment Day, this excuse will not be acceptable! No excuse will be! *Instead of looking for an excuse: Do what is right!*

*Stand now so you can stand **proudly**, without fear or shame on the Day of Judgment.*

"Choose you this day whom ye will serve...
but as for me and my house,
we will serve YaHWeH."
(Joshua 24:15)

"Brethren, my heart's desire and prayer to God for Israel,
is that they might be saved....
God hath not cast away His people whom He foreknew."
(Romans 10:1; 11:2)

"[Wisdom crieth] he that sinneth against Me
wrongeth his own soul: all they that hate Me love death....
I have set before you life and death, blessing and cursing:
therefore choose life, that both thou and thy seed may live..."
(Proverbs 8:36; Deuteronomy 30:19)

(Please help Sacred Truth Ministries spread the truth)

Other Books By Robert Alan Balaicius/Sacred Truth Ministries

Items below are available for the suggested donations. P&H = 5% (3⁰⁰ minimum)

✎ America, Christianity, Liberty & Truth: What Famous Men Had To Say; full of *powerful* quotes on the following and related topics: America was founded as a Christian nation, Liberty, truth, race, genealogy, evolution, "discrimination;" proof the world's greatest minds believed Liberty & Truth inseparable from Jesus Christ & Bible. Volume 1: 54pp., 4^{00}; Volume 2: 80pp., 5^{00}.

✎ Apologetic Expositions: On the Exclusive Promises God Gave Israel Refuting Universalist Interpretations of Isolated Passages of Scripture: Isaiah 56; a very deep study indefatigably proving the Promises God gave to Israel will not be generalized or spiritualized. God's Word is clear. He changes not. Neither does His Will. He is Sovereign. We must accept things as He has declared them to be—not interpret them in the light of modern liberal ideology. Probably the deepest study ever on this passage. The different words for "stranger" and "man" clearly and irrefutably interpreted. It's not "hate" to believe God loves His people in a special way. It's hate, to believe otherwise—for such a mind is at war with God and opposed to the ways He has declared. 88p.p, 5^{00}.

✎ Are We Keeping God's Law Yet?; In-depth discussion of most of the Laws of Scripture; reveals the *spiritual meaning* behind the laws, as well as the *physical reason* why they were given. *Very* detailed, practical, insightful. 96pp. 8½x11, 10^{00}.

✎ Bible Lessons To Nourish Little Minds: Lessons From Nature; shows children how to understand the Bible and apply to their lives through animals and nature; very unique and insightful approach, using clarifying analogies consistent with Balaicius' writing style. Every young child should read this book, it is a building tool of faith and life. 72pp., 8½x11, illustrated, 10^{00}.

✎ Bible Lessons to Nourish Little Minds: Psalm 37; takes whole chapter, verse-by-verse; teaches children how to understand the Bible & apply each verse to their own lives; workbook lesson, can be used in intensive manner for school (homeschool, Christian school, Sunday school), or more relaxed format just for fun; interactive format; very unique/insightful approach, using clarifying analogies consistent with Balaicius' writing style. Deals with some pretty tough topics in a way children can understand, yet not be overwhelmed. Every young child should read this book, it is a building tool of faith and life. 42pp. + answer sheets, answer key, instructions; 8½x11, 10^{00}.

✎ The Christian Israelite and Polygamy: The Frenzy, The Facts, The Foundation & Other Controversial Topics Concerning the God-Ordained Roles of Man and Wife; [Controversial indeed.] Neither promotes nor condemns polygamy; but rather, reveals what *Scripture* saith on the matter, in both law and principle. The minds of modern Christians have been corrupted by liberalism as feminism and paganism have crept into the modern church (which has been carried over unawares even into the Anglo-Israel churches). The carnal mind (masquerading as a converted mind) rebels against the clear teachings of the Word of God which are considered, "old-fashioned," "archaic," "obsolete," "oppressive," "barbaric," etc. God set down the Law. It is up to us to follow it; not dismiss it because it "makes waves" and "rocks the boat" in our families and churches; or because it indicts our hearts of our rebellion against God's Plan. 40pp., 3^{00}.

✎ The Christian Israelite & Salt: The Two-Fold Purpose of Believer: Judgment and Blessing; A very deep study into the parallels between salt and the true Christian—even down to the chemical analysis of salt and its molecular structure. A very deep study, yet nothing too technical that the average person cannot easily understand. Bible Numerics is used to help show the parallel. What role are God's true people to take today in a society infected to the core with evil? 32pp. 2^{25}.

✎ The Liberty Document: The National Debt: Does It Exist & If So Who Owes It? & Some Thoughts On The Hidden Agenda Behind Immigration, Gun Control & The Health sCARE Monopoly; Full of statistics, common law citations, clear thought. Every adult should read this as a purgative for the mind, to cleanse and rebuild thought structures according to reality, not the lies that have supplanted the truth concerning our nation and how it operates, and how our forefathers meant for it to operate. Accompanied by two pamphlets; 49pp. 8½x11; 8^{00}.

✎ Limbaugh, Buchanan, Qauyle & Other Bozos: Pawns in the Enemy's Plan to Destroy Patriotic American People; The enemy's tactics and modus operandi are revealed. How patriotic groups and Anglo-Israel churches are infiltrated. An eye-opening exposé of the entire political circus, freak show which is palmed off on the American people as a free ballot election of good men who want to serve America. They are all traitors and Zionists. 40pp. 3[00].

✍ The Lost Little Princess (A Children's Story Book); beautifully-illustrated, wholesome *moving* story; *non*multi-culturally illustrated; Israel message in a clever parable with *classic* fairy tale flavor; even nonChristians and mainstream Christians love it; if you know the Israel message *it leaps from the page*; truly a classic, epic story. 58pp. 8½x11; 10[00].

✍ The Mystery of The Law and Grace Solved!; Many mysteries of Scripture clearly resolved; moving account of what Christ actually suffered for us; what being "covered in blood of Christ" means; the mystery of "Christ in you" and "you in Christ" revealed; harmony of the Law & Grace easily resolved; proof that the Promises & Covenants God gave to Israel not spiritualized away, nor generalized. 180pp. 8[00] pb; 16[00] Hb.

✍ The Other Side; First writings prepared by RAB/STM (1990). 5 topics: 1) False Prophets of Peace: Is Communism Really Dying?; 2) Who's In Charge? Who's To Blame?: The Crises Facing America and Christendom Today; 3) Public School Education in America Today: Programmed To Fail Through Educational Warfare; 4) Separation or Unity?; 5) On Judging/Is Israel Belief a Cult? Original, Thought-provoking, informative, detailed. 2 booklets: 88pp & 32pp. 7[50] for the set.

✍ *Sound: Body Mind & Soul*, RAB/STMs' irregular news journal, full of important information and deep teaching and spiritual insights; theological studies; trivia, statistics, little-known history, exposés of both old and current conspiracies; spiritual edification; original information as well as news items gleaned from many different sources; survival info for the true believer; material from many different areas of life to help produce a well-rounded believer. You won't be disappointed. As deep, enlightening & interesting as any of RAB/STM's books. Theological questions and answers, dozens of different topics, news unreported elsewhere. Vol. 1 88pp., 8½x11, comb-bound, 12[00]; Vol. 2/3 (double issue), 216pp., 8½x11, comb-bound, 22[00]; Both Vols. 1 & 2/3, 28[00].

✍ So, You Call Yourself A Christian...; Powerful primer proving God's Law could not have been done away with because of God's Very Nature. What makes a Christian a Christian? What makes God God? Proof *Peter's Vision* & other N.T. passages did not abolish Dietary Laws. 76pp. 5[00].

✍ Survival Alert: America The Occupied: Part 1: United Nations Troops in America; Reports abound concerning the imminent foreign military takeover of the United States, the abolishment of all freedoms, and the institution of Martial Law and One-World Government. How close is this to coming to pass? Should we be afraid? Should we prepare? 25pp. 2[00].

✍ Survival Alert: America The Occupied, Part 2: The Largest, Most Powerful & Most Dangerous Cults in America: ATF, FBI, CIA, IRS, etc. and Who Was Behind Oklahoma City Bombing?; very revealing; 27 characteristics which distinguish a group as a cult; decide for yourself whether the American Christian Patriot or the "government" is the *real* cult. 31pp. 8½x11, 5[00].

✍ Void of Offence to God and Man; A much-needed indictment against the attitude and mind-set of many Christian-Israelites and Patriots today. We ought to be able to convince the gainsayers by our true love, sound doctrine & gentle strength--not by our arrogance, haughty attitude, caustic name-calling, or carnal behavior. 20pp., 1[50].

✍ The War Between The Children of Light and the Powers of Darkness: How The Christian-Israelite Can Live In An Evil World System (Including The TRUE Story Of The Phinehas Priest-hood. Deep study exposing extremism, giving the Biblical answer. 506pp., pb 15[00], Hb 25[00].

✍ Which Bible Should the Christian Israelite Use?: Is the KJV the Only Word of God or the Only Inspired English Bible? Is the KJV Even Trustworthy? What About King James Himself? What About Other Versions? How The Bible Is To Be Interpreted? If Error Exists, Why Does God Allow It? & A Look At Many Seeming Mistranslations and Other Confusing Passages; 88pp., 5[00]

✍ Why Did God Create Other Races? and the Theocentric, Scientific Evolution of the Modern Nations and Languages of Israel; God had a purpose for each species of His creation. Some insight into why God may have created races other than Adamkind, and some insight into how our race and language may have "evolved." 28pp., 2[00].